Business Enterprise
in its Social Setting

Business Enterprise in its Social Setting

by ARTHUR H. COLE

HARVARD University Press

Cambridge, Massachusetts

1959

This book has been aided by a grant from the Ford Foundation.

© *1959 by the President and Fellows of Harvard College*

Distributed in Great Britain by Oxford University Press, London

Library of Congress Catalog Card Number 59–7649

Printed in the United States of America

TO EDWIN F. GAY AND JOSEPH H. WILLITS

THEY HELPED BY PUSHING

PREFACE

The ensuing volume has a Janus quality: it looks in two directions. On the one hand, it looks backward, and so in major fashion reveals my indebtedness to the group of rather exceptional individuals who collaborated with me at the Research Center in Entrepreneurial History here at Harvard over appreciable periods until the Center closed its doors at the end of the academic year 1957–58. I have in mind such mature scholars as Thomas C. Cochran, Leland H. Jenks, Fritz L. Redlich, and Joseph A. Schumpeter, who helped me to set up the Center or held my hand in the early days, and the group of adventurous younger folk who threw in their lot with us for longer or shorter periods, some of them venturing to write their doctoral dissertations in the new field: folk such as Hugh G. J. Aitken, Sigmund Diamond, David S. Landes, Harold C. Passer, Henry Rosovsky, and R. Richard Wohl. William Miller and John E. Sawyer were less committed but exceedingly helpful. We all were particularly beholden to Messrs. Aitken, Rosovsky, and Wohl, who launched and maintained our journal of discussion, *Explorations in Entrepreneurial History,* over ten volumes of real "exploratory" writing. My intellectual debt to one or more of these erstwhile associates is evident on nearly every ensuing page, being especially great — and obvious — to the senior quartet of Cochran, Jenks, Redlich, and Schumpeter. In addition, I should state that Aitken, Cochran, and Redlich were good enough to examine the manuscript of the present book at an early stage of its preparation, and to give me the benefit of their criticisms. I fear that they will still find numerous points at which their heads will shake in disapproval.

The ensuing volume has linkage with the past also as a sort of fruit — perhaps a belated fruit and surely an inadequate return — deriving from significant acts of generosity displayed to the Research Center in the decade after 1948, and filtering through to me as a variety of residuary legatee. The Center was launched and sustained by important grants from the Rockefeller Foundation, while we benefited also from a special gift from the Carnegie Corporation of New York. The latter permitted us to undertake an inquiry into entrepreneurship in a foreign country — Brazil — which Stanley J. Stein prosecuted with real valor. Another source of very welcome assistance came from individuals of the Harvard family. Provost Paul H. Buck and subsequently Dean McGeorge Bundy extended protecting hands over our small unit standing unattached to any of the older and larger divisions of the University, while Professors Alexander Gerschenkron and Oscar Handlin bolstered the unit with their prestige and gave me always the advantage of their counsels. When account is also taken of the space and the services supplied by the University, it becomes obvious that the Harvard community contributed much to our welfare. Without such sustenance and security, the Center would have shriveled — and then I would not have had the opportunity to learn from my associates there.

In a broader way, my book looks back on many significant developments outside of Harvard, which have taken place in the past decade or so. The study of entrepreneurial history and of matters closely connected with the latter has spread rather widely in these years, the Center at Harvard serving in considerable measure merely as a vehicle of communication among individuals and institutions dispersed in many regions, from W. T. Easterbrook at Toronto to Noel G. Butlin in Canberra, who, like scores of other scholars, were interested in the subject and enrolled soon as contributors to our efforts at exploration. The Committee on Research in Economic History may well take pride in giving an initial impetus to inquiries in the subject through the outline of the field which it published in 1944; but to a greater degree, it was the importance and intellectual challenge of the topic itself that attracted the attention and provoked the endeavors of such American scholars as G. Heberton Evans, Jr., of Johns Hopkins or Bert F. Hoselitz of Chicago, and such distinguished foreign historians as Ludwig Beutin of Cologne, H. J. Habakkuk of Oxford, and Charles Wilson of Cambridge. The contributions of all such men were incitements to further debates at the Center, and so ultimately grist for my mill.

Last but not least, I would acknowledge certain personal obligations which also look backward. There is my long-standing indebtedness to Edwin F. Gay, my sponsor in the field of economic history, who, as I have stated in my dedication, "pushed" me into responsible activities with both the International Scientific Committee on Price History and later the above-mentioned Committee on Research in Economic History. Following hard on the foregoing, there is my debt to Joseph H. Willits, then attached to the Rockefeller Foundation, who not only acted to create the Research Committee and to sustain both it and the Research Center, but initially "pushed" me into attempting to develop the latter when I was timid of success. I am likewise beholden to the deans of the Harvard Business School under whom I served — Deans Donham, David, and Teele — for allowing me to take time and to expend efforts in the affairs first of the Research Committee and later of the Research Center as well, sometimes, I fear, at an appreciable cost to the Library at the School over which I was supposed to be the chief officer. And quite recently I became indebted to Miss Ruth Crandall and Mrs. Andrew B. Jack, who came to my rescue when my eyes began to fail me, and who both saw the manuscript completed for submission to the printer and subsequently guided the document through the trials of actual publication. In the case of Miss Crandall I was merely adding to a chain of indebtedness that stretches back continuously to work on my first book thirty years ago. Finally, I would extend my thanks to my many friends at the Harvard University Press, both for their kindnesses in connection with the issuance of the Center's several monographs, and now in helping with my own small endeavor.

The present volume, however, looks forward also. In both construction and objectives, I hope it to be new; while I have borrowed heavily from the output and spoken ideas of my erstwhile associates at the Center and from friends elsewhere, I must exonerate them from the uses to which their data and concepts have been put. Stimulated by the example and words of my friends Oswald Knauth and Robert L. Masson, I have ventured to attempt to be creative, especially to attempt to point out uniformities and to formulate generalizations — at least low-order generalizations — in and about historical materials. I was warmly spurred in this direction by the assertion of my ever-provocative colleague in explorations, Thomas Cochran, who complained a couple of years ago that social scientists in general, and economists in particular, took little interest in what we were doing, indeed, had been offered no help in grasping hold of what we believed to be important in entrepreneurial history. I felt it my duty to try to remedy the deficiency.

The book looks forward in the sense that it is related intimately to the problem which has latterly been disturbing economists and which threatens to continue disturbing them for some time to come, economists and indeed many social scientists and governmental administrators — the problem of economic growth. Economic historians have long been studying economic growth, including that of "underdeveloped countries" such as England or the United States in times past, but they have not put their findings into forms which attracted the attention of theorists. Similarly, students of business and entrepreneurial history have long appreciated that — as in the 19th-century case cited by Leland Jenks — it was not the supply of capital in England that was important, it was the horde of American would-be borrowers who pounded the doors of potential British lenders. Yet such historians have also failed to make up packages for the theorists. Perhaps the latter should have read more history and developed their own generalizations, but theorists have never read extensively in historical materials. Perhaps if they did do so, they would become enamored of the facts — and so be lost to the world of theory! Anyway, there has long been a notion prevalent in academic circles that a theoretical hypothesis, however shaky its bases, is somehow superior in intellectual quality to a historical finding, however broad and well supported by evidence; and the deduction has followed that historians should study theory, but theorists may be excused from immersing themselves in facts.

At all events, I have attempted to extend a bridge between history and theory, slight though it may be in this noteworthy area — a bridge that is evolved from historical materials, not derived from assumptions. (So also in some measure had been the theory with which Professor Schumpeter's name is associated and to which, obviously, I owe much.) And I am encouraged the more to make public my rash ideas by recent remarks of my similarly minded friend, Walt W. Rostow. He believes to see a direct positive correlation between advances in economic theorizing and economists' confrontations with practical problems; now, in the post-World War II period, they have been attempting to deal with economic growth (although, as it seems to a historian, under procedures transferred from the handling of statical affairs); and so Rostow is hopeful for the future. Also my friend goes on to urge economists to take account of "the biological strains" in their intellectual "heritage"; and conceivably economists may be forced in the end into the study of economic evolution, and much more deeply than the present-day computation of historical time-series. Perhaps they may yet return to the problem of "the trees in the forest" which Marshall mentioned fifty or seventy-five years ago. In the subsequent complex of theory, stocks of capital and labor, now so precious in economists' model-building, may come to be viewed as no more significant — though no less so — than stocks of finished goods in manufacturers' hands.

The present volume looks forward in yet another way. Economics has been, it seems, wandering ever further during recent decades from most other social sciences. In the present dosage type of economic theorizing, books of theory can be written with scarcely a mention of businessmen, indeed, with human beings noted only under such vague agglomerations as "labor" or possibly "management." And I offer the present book in the exalted hope — perhaps permitted of a professor emeritus, no longer responsible to dean, faculty or students — that it may serve as a first stone in yet another bridge (or possibly better the first section in a traffic circle) to bring together economics, business administration, sociology, and history, and incidentally, in a sense, to restore economics to the rubric of the "social" sciences. In fact, if economics takes on an evolutionary cast, there seems no area so central for the scientific handling of economic change — stagnation and decline as well as growth — with all relevant factors brought into the models, as entrepreneurial history — business administration dealing with economic forces over time within a framework of social institutions and cultural themes. It would not be economics reduced to a series of algebraic formulae, but it might well be economics more useful to decision-makers concerned with long-run problems in business, in government, and in society.

The study of variant entrepreneurship and of the same "economic factor" changing over time is just beginning. We can as yet attempt no entrepreneurial history of a single country, and we can scarcely compare entrepreneurship qualities in any two countries at any given point in time. Correspondingly, any effort to see uniformities in historical details is younger still. Changing and variant quality in entrepreneurship has found no place in the theorizing about economic productivity, movements of international trade, and the like. Yet nothing seems closer to many questions of economic and social policy, while entrepreneurial history seems the most "practical" of all segments in that discipline. The area of entrepreneurship and its evolution calls out for continued research and for more sustained speculation about relationships of changing flows of information, changing social structures, changing economic conditions, and other forces upon entrepreneurial character and performance.

Arthur H. Cole

Harvard University

CONTENTS

PART ONE·
THE CONCEPTUAL PROBLEM

Chapter I ·

THE NATURE OF
ENTREPRENEURSHIP

THE LATE Professor Harold A. Innis of Toronto used to speak
in the most serious terms of the problem of time in economics. There was the problem of horizons for businessmen, governments, perhaps civilizations; there was the problem of changing perspectives of young folks, of consumers,
of public censors; and, not least, there was the problem of
historical depth in economics — or the question, at least in
his mind, of the competence of contemporary economic
theory to deal with changes through time.[1] Not all economic
historians have been as perturbed as Professor Innis, but all
quite surely would be happy to contribute to the approach
to economics which is not content to consider static or
artificially restricted conditions alone. Perhaps it is possible,
in fact, to build on certain ideas to be found in Marshall,
which in turn hark back to the pre-Ricardian days, and to
bring closer together the disciplines of economics and history.

After all, there is a good deal of history in economics already, if one may be liberal in one's interpretation of that
word. The ideas of going wage, standard practice, consumer
habits, price trends, and many others in the field have historical bases. The business cycle has a time dimension; so
have the readjustments in international trade. All that the

3

economic or social historian proposes is that a somewhat greater variety of *all* pertinent historical facts should be brought into the purview of economists as they evolve their theories of change.

To be sure, economists and historians usually have different concepts of the nature of the time useful for scientific purposes. I have in mind especially the tempo of movement. Economists, at least those of recent generations, have been thinking of short-run movements and adjustments. Even economists who now seek to deal with economic development seem to dislike to change the level of their expectations; they want to find their familiar short-term adjustments. On the other hand, historians, at least those who concern themselves with economic and social change, have to do mainly with alterations that require substantial periods to occur. And many problems of entrepreneurship, even some not directly related to economic development, are matters of slow change. Thus, as Professor Thomas S. Ashton points out, the closeness of the rungs in the English social ladder, which was so important an element in England's eighteenth-century economic success, was the product of centuries of history, a fact that this eminent scholar declares "has not been sufficiently appreciated by those who, looking at English progress in technology and wealth, lightly assume that similar results can be obtained with equal speed (and less social disharmony) in communities of undifferentiated peasants today." [2]

There is a second major divergence relative to time and movement in the attitudes of the two types of student. The economist looks frequently for a terminal point — an equilibrium restored, a readjustment achieved, a limited change previsioned, or "stagnation" or a stationary state attained. The writers on economic development again seem sometimes to speak of that desirable phenomenon as a "one-shot" problem: let's get Indonesia or the Argentine developed and then turn to something else. But historians have open-ended concepts. They look backward to times that are open because the data become so misty; and they look forward to change proceeding continuingly into an indefinite future.

There is also the important difference between the two groups that they do not usually utilize the same raw materials in their labors. The economist feels uneasy, if not baffled, if among the variables which he can imprison within his *ceteris paribus* he cannot place all alterations in the society (or societies) under consideration, even modifications of technology. When economists find themselves required by their specific problem to deal with matters of culture and cultural change, they are likely to regard themselves as "stepping out of their depth"; and they may attempt to limit the problem to something with which they can deal by contending that, for the economist, the question of the process of cultural change is "summed up concretely and fully in the rate of capital accumulation required to effect the cultural changes necessary for development." [3] Other ways of stating the economists' general position is that they want to deal with changes within a given economic and social structure; or they seek to discover fixed relationships between variables in order that forecasting and the further evolution of theory may be promoted. On the other hand, the historian draws no lines around the proper area or "depth" of his considerations. He follows where his problem takes him, if necessary to esthetic appreciation, religious convictions, or philosophic beliefs. Accordingly, he is much readier than the economist to make table companions, if not bedfellows, of social psychologists and anthropologists and all sorts of peculiar citizens. And such will be raising their tousled heads in the ensuing study of entrepreneurship and entrepreneurial history.

5

It does appear essential to specify at the start that the examination of data in this entrepreneurial field, like the examination of data in other areas of economics or economic history, should involve a perspective, a tempo, and a set of apparatus appropriate to the endeavor. Such was allowed the study of bimetallism in the past, or that of the business cycle, or even monopolistic competition. It is especially worth noting that in these several cases variant dredgings of historical facts were allowed. In the study of entrepreneurship, rather extreme degrees of dredging seem essential; that particular research excursion becomes blended with an exploration of entrepreneurial history. Accordingly, one may not inappropriately contend that we, as economists, who quite properly are interested in entrepreneurship, are not "as economists" really out of our depth in pursuing the inquiry into whatever territories it may lead us. There is no logical requirement that economics be limited to the handling of data of today and this week, or the phenomena merely of the market place.

The Concept of Entrepreneurship

Entrepreneurship has enjoyed a number of definitions which have varied to some extent according to time and place. In the days when the creative aspects of the entrepreneur were first being recognized, he was referred to as a "projector." [4] The modern term came into use in England only in 1878, when it signified a "director or manager of a public musical institution" or "one who gets up entertainments," [5] although thirty years earlier John Stuart Mill had actually mentioned the word as a French term in a footnote to his *Principles,* in which he expressed regret at the lack of an English equivalent.[6] Recently the word has frequently been employed to differentiate an active businessman from a slow-moving one. Thus, in his description of the bazaars at Beirut, Professor Dalton Potter of American University introduces the dichotomy of "chandler" and "entrepreneur" (not hesitating to draft the latter term), the former to cover the retail dealer who carries on a passive trade in traditional goods and the latter one who "makes a market" for new varieties of items.[7] This last practice approaches a distinction which Dr. Redlich and others are disposed to make between "entrepreneur" or "enterpriser" and "manager" — of which more shortly.

In this book, entrepreneurship will be used in two senses, although the context of each use should make the particular meaning obvious. Usually, the word will be employed to mean the function or activity. Here I shall have in mind the purposeful activity (including an integrated sequence of decisions) of an individual or group of associated individuals, undertaken to initiate, maintain, or aggrandize a profit-oriented business unit for the production or distribution of economic goods and services. The aggregate of individuals which together and cooperatively develop the decisions might perhaps be denominated the "entrepreneurial team." It is really a team in the senses (a) that each person or officer plays a particular position or represents a particular aspect of the total enterprise, and (b) that each such person or officer is in some measure a complement of the others as far as the total purposes of the unit are concerned. The team feature is observed when individuals in such a group have to be replaced. If a weak sales manager is succeeded by one quite capable of expressing his division's interest, all the other members of the group shift their positions to some extent. For instance, the chief executive may give hitherto unknown support to the production chief or the personnel manager. A balance is reasserted.

In such activity the goal or measure of success will ordinarily be pecuniary, but that basis may be supplemented by other yardsticks of appraisal. Again, it should be specified that this entrepreneurial activity proceeds in relationship to the situation internal to the unit itself, the social group that really constitutes the unit, and to the economic, political, and social circumstances — institutions, practices, and ideas which surround the unit.[8]

Perhaps it should be pointed out here that while there are a number of people involved in the development of a decision, and while the group may be looked upon as a team, there is no escaping the fact that all the members of such a team are not equals in any administrative sense. The effective element is to some extent compensated for by shifts in the actions, perhaps in the informal subgroupings, of the remaining members. There remains, however, the chief executive, president, or chairman of the board, who undoubtedly exerts more influence than any other individual in the team, and sometimes, depending on personality or force of character, may have almost the power of veto over all the rest. Mr. Chester I. Barnard, president of the New Jersey Bell Telephone Company for many years as well as being a distinguished scholar, once was belittling the real contribution of top executives, asserting that in his job all that he did was to say "Yes" and "No"; but I noted that it was he who did the saying of "Yes" and "No."

Some observers have been inclined, it seems, to take the easy road of identifying the latter variety of figure as "the entrepreneur" of economic theory, even if they have to dip down in corporate hierarchies sometimes to take a powerful vice-president or "take-over" comptroller as the entrepreneur of specific enterprises. I am disposed rather to lean to the other extreme and doubt whether the economists' entrepreneur ever existed in reality. To my way of thinking, when an enterprise had grown large enough or the period of operation extended long enough so that the head of the unit had to share his duties of observation, planning, and execution with one or more other persons, he was in effect sharing his entrepreneurial function; he was moving toward the "multiple" entrepreneur of which I have spoken above. And with the increase in the complexity of relationships surrounding business institutions and an increase in the complexity of data needed to operate such units successfully, the multiple or divided quality of entrepreneurship becomes the most important element.

Although the word "entrepreneurship" will usually be used to indicate function or activity, occasionally I may use it to signify the commonalty of entrepreneurs. By this I have in mind the aggregate of individuals performing that function or carrying on that activity in a given time and place, or even over considerable periods of time, just as one might speak of "knighthood" or "the ministry." Thus, I might remark that entrepreneurship in England has been drawn lately from certain classes of society.

It is obvious here that with the first effort at definition we run into complexities. I am attempting to grasp the economic significance of certain aspects, at least, of business enterprise conceived as social phenomena, and, as will appear more clearly in a moment, I wish to view these social elements as in a state of constant change. In other words, I seek to merge some aspects of the supposedly distinct disciplines of business administration, economics, sociology, and history. In such fearful circumstances, it will surely be wise for me to try to make clear what I believe the operational limitations and implications of the definition to be.

For example, brief reflection suggests the notion that entrepreneurship can be viewed by such a person as a social psychologist as similar to other forms of activity in somewhat comparable relations, such as the statesman in connection with the economic development of a region or a college president in the up-building of his institution. Of the first category, one could cite Alexander Hamilton operating in the early days under the American Constitution, or Julius Vogel in connection with the upsurge of New Zealand in the 1870's and 1880's; of the second, Charles W. Eliot at Harvard or William R. Harper at Chicago.[9] However, limitation of the term "entrepreneurship" to the purveyance of economic goods and services on certain terms seems necessary for purposes of clear analysis, especially relative to motivations and to sources of power.

Cursory examination of phenomena in the area suggests that the term "the entrepreneur" may be construed occasionally in the singular, but usually in the plural — and for two reasons. The first is that decision-making is the critical or key operation in entrepreneurship, and even in single-man proprietorships the head of the enterprise rarely decides by himself, that is, under circumstances where the original suggestion or some later advice has not come from subordinates or staff. Effective administration is a necessary condition for innovation or other creative action by businessmen; and it is true that usually administrative activity must also be shared by the individual entrepreneur. The second reason is that frequently nowadays decision-making in companies is purposefully plural. A president may exist, but he is only one among equals.

Mr. Barnard, Professor Marshall E. Dimock, and others have pointed out the complexities of decision-development in sizable organizations, and the nature of the administrative delegation of powers. It becomes necessary in entrepreneurial study — which is concerned with the business type of enterprise — to keep in mind the two related, really interdependent phenomena. There may be a broad participation in the formation of decision, and there is usually a delegation and dispersal (through the organization) of various types of decision-making, but there is also a seat of major policy decision-making, and decisions from this last source overrule all others insofar as there is any conflict. Nevertheless, all varieties of other decisions are necessary to interpret those that deal with policy as well as routine decisions that repeat interpretations.

Professor Karl W. Deutsch then at Massachusetts Institute of Technology once proposed that entrepreneurial decisions be defined as those made at the risk of not being able to make the same or similar ones again. No doubt decisions of this quality are the most important ones — those which give entrepreneurs sleepless nights and stomach ulcers — but surely decisions of other sorts are essential to the "initiation, maintenance, and aggrandizement" of business institutions. Similarly, the establishment, and change, of an administrative organization for the proper execution of decisions, and the supervision of subordinate units, are necessary for the "maintenance" of entrepreneurship. Hence, as I have suggested, the entrepreneurial function is both dispersed and concentrated. Usually, in speaking hereafter of decision-making and of entrepreneurship, I shall have in mind the "concentrated" or "policy" aspect, sometimes designated as "coordinating" operations, but I shall not mean to imply that the top executive, like the proverbial professor, arrives at decisions in an ivory tower, insulated from ideas that come up from members of their staffs, or that decisions get executed from a single center by some omniscient, omnipresent boss.

This explanation, however, gives rise to another sort of question: what is the difference between entrepreneurship and business in real life and between the study of entrepreneurship and that of business administration? Of the former it may be asserted quickly that the two areas are substantially coterminous. I do believe it economically and socially important to emphasize the time element in the phenomena common to the two concepts, the potentiality of indefinite continuance and of persisting innovational action. These features subsume a multipersonal organization of some sort; and this latter circumstance in turn spells social elements of leadership, effective coordination, human relations, and the like.

Put in concrete terms, my contention is that the individual peddler was a businessman but not an entrepreneur. So also is the man who sits in a stockbroker's office all day, buying and selling shares on his own account; likewise the "dickerer" of Maine record, who, at least in the past, started from Portland or Bangor with money, bought goods from one farmer, and proceeded to swap goods for other goods, until in the end he wound up with a supply of butter or some other commodity easily salable in the city, and hopefully salable for a sum of money greater than that with which he launched the series of transactions! Obviously, however, the actual number of individuals (at any one time-period) who would be businessmen but not entrepreneurs in my differentiation would be small. The corner druggist or any such type of small businessman becomes, to my mind, an entrepreneur as soon as he has to rely on a night clerk to help carry the enterprise, try to satisfy customers, note what customers ask for and cannot purchase, make the right change, endeavor to outdo the store down the street, and so on.[10]

Between studies of entrepreneurship and of business administration as bodies of thought, there are, I believe, two important differences. First is the fact that entrepreneurship is interested in the economic and social significance of business procedures and institutions, whereas business administration must also give attention to their instrumental qualities. For example, scholars in the latter area must consider the best ways of measuring advertising effort, not merely the economic and social consequences of that effort.

And the same sort of distinction would hold true of fitting the best cost-accounting system to given situations, the best procedures for operating advancement from within the organization, and the like.

Second, students of business administration usually accept the nature of the businessman as given, as indeed do most economists. Typically, in both disciplines, the implication holds that the businessman in all cultures and countries now and throughout history has always been, and is, the same. Students of entrepreneurship, on the other hand, are interested in discovering why the American or any other businessman of 1959 has the character that he has, and operates in the manner in which he does; and almost inevitably such students become enmeshed in history, at least to some degree. Here again the inquirer is involved with time: he cannot understand the current businessman in any country — that is, why he behaves as he does — wholly in terms of current fact. He must search into the past for the formative, slowly changing forces. "Entrepreneurial history" is a term convenient for designating that aspect of thought or writing about entrepreneurship, which does not necessarily carry the inquiry up to the time of observation, although it may do so. Business administration, on the other hand, may be looked upon as an operational discipline related primarily to the self-generated policies and procedures of the private enterprises, while entrepreneurship is at best advisory and interpretive. It forms part of a social-cultural area, coordinate with the study of religion or politics or art.

I have, however, ventured down a convenient side road. The point from which I turned was the nature of entrepreneurship within the business unit. I should now point out that decisions are integrated, and that one decision becomes in some measure the basis for subsequent ones. This is an important specific phase of the open-endedness men-

13

tioned above. The entrepreneur looks toward an indefinite future, to a growth, a development, at least a continuation. This integrated quality is especially significant because it suggests that the business institution with which entrepreneurship is concerned has a certain organic quality. And quite surely the growth and survival of the individual enterprise must form an element in the biological schema, which Professor Rostow of the Massachusetts Institute of Technology recently commended to our brother economists.[11]

It should be noted again, moreover, that there is nothing in the definition given above that requires the employment of innovation in the activities of entrepreneurship, at least innovation in the usual sense. A business unit may be "initiated," but that is all. However, innovation is not excluded, and I am inclined to believe that business activity is shot through with novelty — local, industry, individual-plant novelty — and that novelty is unsuccessful in the business world unless the institution introducing it is being maintained effectively. The whole area of invention, innovation, adaptation, and so on, is filled with difficulties, both of concept and of application.[12] Is every child innovating when, for the first time, at least for him, he learns to walk? Was each act an innovation when the steam engine was applied to cotton spinning, to wool spinning, to linen spinning, to silk throwing, et cetera? What is the rise of soft-drink bottling in Iran: an innovation, an imitation, an adaptation?

For our present purposes, however, it will suffice to insist on a few, rather self-evident propositions. Innovations are often unrecognized as such at the time of their introduction, since the innovators are usually attempting to meet a specific situation, and anyway would have little opportunity to survey all comparable situations even in their own industries, let alone throughout the world; accordingly, the intellectual process of spotting and appraising innovations is a *post hoc,*

14

historical one, not one that could have value in the world of business action. The introduction of an innovation in a specific business enterprise at a specific time is often merely one course among several open to the entrepreneur to meet a recognized competitive situation. Whether it is called innovation, imitation, or adaptation, the spread among business institutions of new ways of doing things, from one location to others, from industry to industry, and from plant to plant, is much more important for economic growth than the initiation of such new ways at specific points in space and time. (There is also the effect of an innovation in the proliferation of new business institutions, a multiplier effect, of which more will be said later.) [13]

For my second point concerning innovation, namely, that novelty is successful in the business world only if the institution introducing it is being effectively maintained, I need make no long argument. To be sure, I have to admit that there have been cases where adequate capital or exceptional circumstances allowed invasion of new business forms, new processes of production, and the like. However, the costs of getting the "bugs" out of new machinery are well recognized; the trials of introducing a new product or new system of selling or other major change are no less expensive; and a solidly based enterprise is abler to bear such costs, even more inclined to risk the consequences of incurring them. [14]

Another element in the definition of entrepreneurship presented above relates to motivation. That business institutions should be concerned with money-making need not be elaborated. But it is important to notice, especially over the past two or three decades, how considerably American corporations have modified any rule of financial maximization that may have existed, so that corporate longevity, community relations, or public responsibilities might be taken

15

into account. Especially significant has been the trend over an even longer period in the United States toward a reduction in the sovereignty of the stockholder.

Nor is there need any longer to emphasize, at least in the United States, the existence of non-pecuniary incentives among modern business executives. A score of writers — Robert A. Gordon, Oswald Knauth, Thomas C. Cochran, among others — have expressed concurrent views on this matter;[15] and a goodly amount of thought and writing in the field of business administration is going, and has gone, into the problem of finding substitutes in large business organizations for the older pecuniary stimulus. The unit in General Electric devoting full time to the subject seems inclined to phrase its aim as making entrepreneurs out of managers.

Whatever the immediate motivations, those potent in business seem related to one or another of the psychological incentives of search for security, prestige, power, and social service. Professor Marshall E. Dimock expresses the idea that these incentives form a sequence in the attitudes of individual men through their business lives.[16] They also have some value as a historical series. It may suffice here, however, to point out, as Professor Clarence H. Danhof has done in the case of the search for prestige, that such stimuli or incentives are shared at least through most strata of Western society.[17]

Perhaps, thanks to the existence of the institution of inheritance, security for one's family has counted for more in entrepreneurial circles than many other lines of activity in recent societies. I am thinking of the numberless cases in European experience where business activity has been pursued, sometimes "endured," with the purpose of founding a family. Professor Frederic C. Lane in his *Andrea Barbarigo* gives the impression of return to business every three or four generations in fourteenth- and fifteenth-century Venice in order that family fortunes, diminished by government service and by life on landed estates, might be recouped.[18] Much of the nobility in England and Sweden and Germany stemmed from successful business performance. But neither ennoblement nor landed property is necessary. It is alleged of Latin American businessmen that they persist in business even after one line has been successfully established, taking on successively different lines for the supposed reason of being able to leave a separate factory or store to each child in their families.

To be sure, concern for one's family is not an attitude shown exclusively by businessmen. Other sorts of men from the manorial lord or guild handicraftsman down to the modern factory employee or college professor have shared in this interest. In the family enterprise, however, and in the freedom to divert sizable incomes into sources of security (over time), prestige, and even power of a sort, the entrepreneur has perhaps enjoyed a measure of opportunity that has not been available in most other walks of life.

Internal and External Relationships

The specification that entrepreneurial activity "proceeds in relationship to the situation internal to the [business] unit itself" covers at least three somewhat variant elements. First, there is the legal and managerial form. Quite obviously the form of organization, whether it be proprietorship, partnership, or corporation, makes a considerable difference in the manner in which the entrepreneurial function is carried on, as do also the legal requirements and limitations upon the action of company officers. More important perhaps is the operating form, through which management seeks to attain its objectives. At least this is true: the legal form, and the privileges granted under it, are little affected by the desires of the operating managers of an enterprise; and these legal elements change slowly, usually not in response to managerial needs. The operating framework, however, does lie within the jurisdiction of top management. It can be altered to fit the requirements of the situation; and, actually, it has changed in important parts of various business worlds, especially those of advanced industrial nations.[19]

Second, it is worth noting that the entrepreneurial element in an enterprise forms a team; and no two teams are alike. In fact, individual enterprises have varied characters that change slowly — one strong in a given direction, another strong otherwise. The accession of a Henry Ford II was an event that obviously created a new and different team, but so did the acquisition of Alfred P. Sloan in a less conspicuous spot by a burgeoning General Motors a generation or more earlier. Also, in further relationship to the evolutionary character of entrepreneurial institutions, attention may be drawn to the proposition that no alteration takes place in the higher echelons of management without a reshuffling of the duties and activities of all other members of the team. This is clearly the case when a public-relations director is newly added, or when a somnolent sales manager is replaced by one of vigor and aggressiveness. In any such situation the team, like the bits of glass in a kaleidoscope, becomes something novel. Thus, new features are injected into entrepreneurial practices without an overturn of existing forms, and human groups adjust to change.

Third, and perhaps most important for our present consideration, the "internal" situation within an enterprise is to be viewed chiefly as a group of individuals who, like members of other social groups, interact with one another. In this network of interaction are to be found the elements of role and sanction which provide the mode through which economico-business action takes place, and which, changing over time, constitute a major thread in the history of entrepreneurship. In an appreciable measure, expectations of behavior — what the directors expect of the treasurer, what the production vice-president expects of employees, and so on — become incorporated into company regulations. Other expectations, such as that of his staff anent the behavior of the president, and certain expectations relative to behavior of other individuals, remain outside rule books and company manuals. And both categories, quickly or slowly, are subject to change in response to changing social thought. The proprietor of a department store told me privately that he did things for his employees, and they did things for or to him, which his father, retired but still observant, considered quite shocking.

The relations to entrepreneurial performance of economic, political, and social forces external to individual enterprises are manifold. One phase of the political connection was mentioned above: the legal framework within which enterprises function. The economic situation affects the entrepreneurial aspect in two major ways. That situation defines the entrepreneurial problem through the relative scarcities of the productive factors; and the change in relative scarcities over time, of course, does in fact alter that problem. At one time in the United States, management had to get along primarily with the suppliers of capital or their representatives; more recently it has had to establish improved relations with employees and *their* representatives.

While economic conditions may define the problem for the entrepreneurial actors, they do not necessarily decide it. The latitude of potential, even of likely action, for the entrepreneur is considerable. One aspect is the question of action or no action. When my friend Philip D. Bradley taught South American economic development at Harvard, he used to say that an entrepreneur of that area, at least of some of the countries there, could sit on a mountain of iron ore — and go to sleep! A North American entrepreneur, finding himself in the equivalent situation, would presumably not take rest until he had floated a company to exploit his discovery. As Professors J. Keith Butters and John Lintner of the Harvard Business School pointed out a few years ago, there seems to be a considerable number of people in the United States who annually set about trying their fortunes in businesses when they have much less than a mountain of iron ore to back up their aspirations.[20]

It also appears to be true that entrepreneurs are disposed to set about changing the economic situation as much as they can. Entrepreneurial advantage will tend to impel them in that type of action. The same group of men who established cotton mills at Lowell set up a company, called the Proprietors of the Locks and Canals of the Merrimack River, to develop and distribute water power (which enterprise, interestingly enough, is still going). The Weyerhaeuser Company and other large lumbering enterprises have altered their policies of cutting and conservation so that a limited asset has been changed into substantially an inexhaustible one. Again, our early cotton manufacturers, besides welcoming skilled foreign operatives who could be induced to immigrate, set about training people for the varieties of labor that were scarce. And the same was always true of capital shortage. As my friend Professor Jenks used sometimes to remark about the inflow of foreign capital into the United States, one would think from reading about the export of this capital from Europe that somehow the British and Dutch and Germans were thrusting it down our throats; whereas the important fact is that Americans almost assaulted the foreigners in their countinghouses in order to try to get hands on the funds. In sum, then, not only does entrepreneurial advantage tend to alter the existing complements of the productive factors, each entrepreneur seeking thereby a differential advantage over his competitors, but, over the decades, by dint of individual actions and enforced imitations, it seems probable that the combined effect has been considerable.

Economic forces also have, and have had over the past, an indirect effect. A rising level of economic productivity has meant a higher level of education for management, staff, and employees. It has meant the opportunity to utilize more "unproductive" labor, both white-collar within the plant and expert advisers outside it; and it has meant improved libraries, more professional literature, larger staffs, and more leisure for the staff to take advantage of these opportunities.

These "external" forces offer a particularly important challenge in connection with the launching of entrepreneurial endeavor in specific areas such as underdeveloped countries. Professor W. Thomas Easterbrook speaks of the minimum security elements that entrepreneurship seems to require. A region hazardous to life is likely to be exploited by governmental rather than private enterprise.[21] In addition, a society which from religious or other causes finds material welfare unimportant or money-making improper is hardly a good nursery for entrepreneurship. The theocracy of Massachusetts Bay, for example, was positively hostile to mercantile activities.[22] Professor Alexander Gerschenkron has spoken of the low social status of money-making in eighteenth- and nineteenth-century Russia, and Professor Cochran seems to think that the lack in Spanish countries of the really hearty appeal of getting ahead materially may affect the quality of entrepreneurial performance there.[23]

Moreover, there can be no doubt that changes over time in these external elements have altered the entrepreneurial way of life. Sometimes it has been a lag that has mattered, such as the retention among French business circles of attitudes derived from earlier social regimes.[24] Sometimes it has been an intensification of a pre-existent force, as in the cult of wealth that affected the United States especially in the late nineteenth century.[25]

These external factors yield in large measure the sanctions to which the entrepreneur responds. They condition his psychological development in early life; they sustain his activities throughout his career; they give check to some possible actions and give blessings upon others; and they supply the psychic rewards when retirement comes. These are the elements, much more than physical divergences, that differentiate such a country as the United States or Germany from underdeveloped New Guinea or Paraguay. And they constitute a major line of differentiation between twentieth-century Germany, England, or other countries, and these countries in early times.

In sum, the study of entrepreneurship, especially when viewed as a changing phenomenon, parallels or overlaps studies of various sorts in the social sciences, those of leadership, group dynamics, business operations, prestigious symbols, economic productivity, and the like. It seems to require particular attention to the flow of social thought and the activities of social institutions, which help to shape the form and quality of entrepreneurial performance. It demands the adoption of a pace, or rate of change, and of an open-end path of development that are not common in economics; and it counsels a regard for social, differentiating factors and for economic and social meaning that is usually absent in the study of business administration.

Yet there appears to be an area of inquiry in historical entrepreneurship — an inquiry that carries up to the present day — which does not necessitate the spreading of effort over an unmanageable field, and which can be fenced off in an operational manner. And the area has several attractive

22

features. It deals with phenomena basic to an understanding of the characteristic Western organization of society, which is usually labeled "capitalistic" but more properly should be called "entrepreneurial." The changes in entrepreneurial performance over time, isolated as far as possible from the effects of economic resources, constitute as scientific a basis as we shall secure for the appraisal of the private-enterprise system; and the lessons deducible from the study of nascent and immature economies of the Western past, perhaps even the examination of some aspects of our mature economies, may be of value in the determination of practical policies for the so-called "underdeveloped" areas of the world.[26]

The Entrepreneurial World

Even as a professional musician finds important the appearance of new symphonies or sonatas, the resignations of orchestral conductors, and perhaps the activities of booking agents for winter tours, so the entrepreneurial actors live to a considerable extent in a world of their own. It is not an unintellectual world, at least nowadays, but it will seem strange and perhaps Philistine to those whose worlds are differently oriented — towards the fortunes of Grandma Moses or of mobiles, towards the last novel of William Faulkner, or the new cyclotron at Berkeley.

The elements in the entrepreneurs' world present great variety among themselves, from the officers of labor unions to the effort of certain writers to introduce the term "agribusiness," and from the new rulings of the Federal Trade Commission on unethical advertising practices to the echoes from the nineteenth century which occur in the complaints of discontented stockholders. These different elements impinge upon entrepreneurs in varying degrees at different times, conditioning entrepreneurial decisions, molding entrepreneurial characters, and so on. They also react upon one another in some measure, and the entrepreneurs in turn react upon the forces and institutions that condition their decisions or mold their attitudes. Yet, for purposes of exposition, it may be useful to think of such elements as forming classes or unities, however intermixed they may be in reality.

The outstanding, inherent feature of such elements which has inevitably crept into the foregoing description is that of change: the idea of a *novel* term or *new* rulings, the fact that a critical feature of entrepreneurial life itself is change. The entrepreneur looks back into the past to learn the bases of his successes or failures. He is particularly conscious of what his competitors are doing or have just done and he is constantly planning ahead, what to do tomorrow, next month, ten years from now, and what is likely to have happened in government, in the policies of his trade association, in the capacities of statistical analysis to give him help in forecasting sales. For him life is a flow, and for us the representation of the breakdown of the elements impinging upon him must take the form of a composite of flows, perhaps currents in a stream, except that some of these currents became almost motionless, as it were, for varying periods of time: such currents as rulings of the tax authorities, attitudes of columnists, institutions such as professional associations within business that, at least for some years or decades, take on lives of their own. The image which on the whole seems to me to represent the nature of entrepreneurial experience vis-à-vis the various other elements in our society, elements that are sometimes solidified social units and sometimes mere courses of thought, is that of the logger riding a drive of logs down a stream of numerous currents, which in turn are twisted at times by a curving shore line and broken up by protruding rocks and an uneven river bottom. The rider makes his decisions as to the course to be taken by the lead-

24

ing logs, the mass of logs to be kept from jamming, to be kept away from the shore, all almost literally in accordance with Professor Deutsch's definition, namely, at the risk of not being in a position to make further decisions. Here also every decision conditions every subsequent one, and each is made under new, different, and currently changing circumstances.

For heuristic purposes it is convenient and logical to think of the entrepreneurial main current, the sequence of decisions and actions, as affected in its nature by nearby currents of informational and ideational character. By "informational" I have in mind the constantly changing element of technological and professional data, on the basis of which decisions are made, all that the Germans call *fachmässig*. These data change at quite different rates of speed, from the minute-to-minute reportings of moving prices on commodity or stock exchanges to the almost constant understanding of the nature of the wool fiber. In large measure the data become incorporated into printed documents of one type or another, predominantly periodical articles, annual reports, or books, and these come to rest in libraries. Thus the flow of technical data becomes affected by the semirigidities of reporting agencies and business educational institutions. However, the main point is the continuous stream of data, on the basis of which decisions are reached and policies are executed. All is flux.

Behind the flow of technical data lie the slower wellings of concepts and "sentiments." Thus in the intellectual climate in America of the late nineteenth century and particularly with the leadership of Frederick W. Taylor, individuals of unusual apperception in business and in educational institutions began to believe that "right" or "best" ways of doing things in business could be found, that business procedures need not remain the products of trial and error, rules of thumb, each man to learn only by personal experience. Something approaching a scientific business literature could be initiated. And later came beliefs in special portions of the business field: capacity for forecasting changes in the volume of business, the wisdom of "full disclosure," or the desirability of emphasizing human relations.

Associated with such ideas, and to some extent lying behind them, are yet more general notions, many of them deriving from the more or less distant past, but all being modified as they flow along and interact with other more recent ideas and with the circumstances of modern life. I have in mind such concepts as the dignity of the individual, the desirability of material progress, the commendability of personal achievement, and the like.

Such social motivations — what Professor Cochran calls "cultural themes" — are ordinarily not conscious parts of the entrepreneur's world, but they constitute a portion of his social education, and, in a sense, they all condition each entrepreneurial decision at any given time. Even as the past is summed up in the present, and a man is at least in part a creature of his inheritance, so some fragments of relevant history — the lessons of Christianity, the adventurous spirit of the Renaissance, the objectivity of scientific findings, an intolerance of monopolists — are elements in current decisions. These decisions, in turn, may strengthen the force of such ideas, and so the concepts continue to flow and to condition entrepreneurial life. Of course, the interaction of the ideas with circumstances of the modern world may also weaken the power that they had previously exerted. The force of the stream is somewhat altered.

These cultural themes have a consequence other than affecting the character of individual decisions directly. They exert an indirect influence through institutions which they help to bring into existence; indeed, an important segment of the complex of institutions which I shall later include under the term, "the entrepreneurial stream." In the rise of public accounting firms, counselors in industrial relations, even the internal corporate arrangements of line and staff or of co-ordinating committees, ethical principles or cultural themes have play. And the evolution and increased use of such instrumentalities in turn affect the empirical situation. One stream acts upon another, and indeed reacts upon the first.

Basic in the entrepreneurial world, then, as in the world of art or literature or education, are ideas and ideals, themselves a changing flow, far removed from what is usually regarded as the field of business. Out of such concepts and social themes, with conditioning supplied by the techniques of business operations, derives a changing complement of technical and operating institutions, from schools of business to put-and-call brokers, some of them entrepreneurial units ancillary to larger ones. With the aid of these institutions, and responding in part to the preceding centuries of cultural change, a constantly changing body of entrepreneurs makes linked chains of decisions concerned with the "initiation, maintenance, and aggrandizement" of profit-oriented social units, decisions that attempt to relate the changing supplies of productive factors to the changing requirements of the societies (consumers and governments) within which they are allowed to perform their functions. Obviously, the simile of riders of drives of logs, even riders trying to judge the currents in rivers swollen by spring freshets, is no exaggeration.

Conclusion

Entrepreneurship, at least in all nonauthoritarian societies, constitutes a bridge between society as a whole, especially the noneconomic aspects of that society, and the profit-oriented institutions established to take advantage of its economic endowments and to satisfy, as best they can, its economic desires. What talent will be attracted into entrepreneurial activity, how well this talent will perform its function, and, to a considerable extent in modern societies, even how the national product will be shared — all of these questions are determined by the combination of social and technical forces, most of them changing with more or less rapidity, and all having initial impingement upon, or receiving initial impetus from, the entrepreneurial actors. Nothing that I have learned since 1946 has led me to alter the view which I expressed then: namely, that to study the entrepreneur is to study the central figure in modern economic development, and, to my way of thinking, the central figure in economics.[27]

Chapter II·

THE NEED OF A POSITIVE VIEW

LIKE EVERY TOPIC in the social sciences, entrepreneurship, if viewed historically and if analyzed deeply enough, leads one into nearly all fields of knowledge. One could speculate with Pareto whether mankind is divisible, as it were, into those whose complements of "residues" and whose other endowments destine them to be leaders, and into those whose natures make them content to be lead. One could explore with the aid of anthropologists whether the endeavor to get ahead, to improve one's status in some manner, if not in the ways we know best, is universal in human societies. Or, nearer to home, one might examine by the study of the history of economic thought how it came about that the entrepreneur became almost wholly squeezed out of economic theory.

The student of entrepreneurship who himself carries a historical bias must take note of the rather progressive negation and neglect with which economists of the twentieth century have treated the entrepreneur. Marshall found room for such a figure, even elaborated a particular function that he felt to be dominant in the activities of "the undertaker." Taussig gave evidence of a realization that human beings had something to do with directing the productive process. But as the decades rolled by, only such special areas as monopolistic competition or business-cycle analysis knew the enterpriser or even the businessman.[1] Even as much economic history could be written in the same period with no more than picturesque figures on its pages — railroads "were built" and banks "were organized" — so such a highly regarded text in economics as Professor Paul A. Samuelson's could come to be written without use by the author of actors in this drama, at least in the private section.

Profit-Maximization

The foundation on which modern economists have based their analyses dominated by impersonal forces is essentially that of the "economic man" who "naturally" seeks in an entrepreneurial role to maximize profits. Thoughtful theorists have admitted that this proposition is hypothetical, but they have not called upon other social scientists to prove or disprove the assumption; instead they contend that, if not substantiated by facts, it could be employed safely *as if* true — as a book-publisher might elaborate his publishing list *as if* all of us loved poetry.

The only point that needs to be made in this connection is that this belief in profit-maximization was, after all, only a belief. It was launched, indeed, under somewhat suspicious circumstances, for the author who gave greatest currency to the notion of "self-interest" as influencing "the nature and causes of the wealth of nations" had written a book only twenty years earlier in which he stressed the dominance of "sympathy" in social relations. And, if never supported in the minds of theorists by more than "common observation," or at most a willingness to interpret the course of specific events as sufficiently explicable by the use of this hypothesis, it is entirely logical to contend that this prime foundation of recent economic analysis *could* be supplanted by another

30

contention, the latter based on "common observation," or perhaps now on data derived from research.

Such a transition appears to be under way. Professor Joel Dean has summarized the condition of the basic assumption of profit-maximization as follows: the contention has been "qualified . . . to refer to the long run; to refer to management's rather than to owners' income; to include non-financial income such as increased leisure for highstrung executives and more congenial relations between executive levels within the firm; and to make allowance for special considerations such as restraining competition, maintaining management control, holding off wage demands, and fore-stalling antitrust suits." The concept has, he says, "become so general and hazy that it seems to encompass most of man's aims in life." [2]

A president of the American Economic Association finds the "generally recognized development of a managerial class" — and the rise of an "organizational economy" — to occasion a reappraisal of the "profit maximization" principle.[3] Professor Andreas G. Papandreou raises similar doubts, and former Dean Edward S. Mason's only reply is the expression of a hope that economists will not have to abandon their very useful theorem. These and numerous other expressions of skepticism, uncertainty, and outright rejection leave the observer with the unavoidable conclusion that some fundamental modification of this basic concept is in gestation.[4]

Students of entrepreneurship and entrepreneurial history may well regard this development as an essential first step in the construction of a "positive" theory; it helps to clear the ground. While the hypothesis of profit-maximization commands the allegiance of economists, the latter have a strong logical basis for emasculating the entrepreneur. They may well reason: (a) economic conditions determine the level and variations of profits; (b) entrepreneurs follow the lines defined by the attractiveness of profits; (c) therefore, we need look only at the basic economic conditions; we do not need to concern ourselves with the men who run business enterprises; if John Smith does not have a keen nose for exceptional profits, Bill Jones will have. Hugh G. J. Aitken, one of the originators of *Explorations in Entrepreneurial History*, saw this situation early in his studies, when he restrainedly wrote, "It just is not helpful in economic history to regard business men as mere agents of economic forces . . . It seems to me that this rejection of the impersonality assumption must be one of the basic postulates of entrepreneurial history." [5]

To be sure, such a rejection, even if supported by facts, is only half of the story. It merely opens up a possibility. There remains the obligation upon students of entrepreneurship and entrepreneurial history to demonstrate that acknowledgment of the existence of the entrepreneur has important consequences. Indeed, Professor H. J. Habbakuk once posed the direct question: "What difference does it make that economists and historians pay attention to the entrepreneur?"

Efforts at Reconstruction

One consequence of such attention is to be seen in the endeavors of a few current economists to fit somehow the direction of enterprise, the businessman, the entrepreneur, whatever the agent may be called, into the pre-existing pattern of economic theory. The efforts also seem to show the futility of halfway measures. The recognition of the entrepreneurial function as not determined in character by economic forces causes numerous cracks in the current theoretical structure. Two illustrations will perhaps suffice. One may be drawn from the highly provocative efforts

32

that a group at the Carnegie Institute of Technology has been making: Professors William W. Cooper, Richard M. Cyert, and their associates. Professor Cooper raises the criticism of "traditional theory," that, like classical physics vis-à-vis the nature of the atom, no effort was made to pierce the interior of the firm:

Under the Marshallian and later versions of this theory, the entrepreneur is regarded as operating directly on (more or less) "will-less" factors of production. No method of communication is specified. The "factors" are assumed to know immediately what is expected of them and to adjust themselves without further ado; the entrepreneur is assumed to know instantly what is being done and how he should respond in the face of market criteria. Misinformation, conflict of information, and lack of information are all absent. Nor are there intermediaries present to consult and advise, or to transmit information.[6]

Pursuing the thesis, which he had stated earlier,[7] that "control considerations need to be built into the theory" of the firm, Professor Cooper elaborates a construct of a control system. It is somewhat similar to the circular schema sketched by Professor George Albert Smith some years ago (and reported in *Change and the Entrepreneur*, pp. 13 ff.), and to that more specifically pictured by Professor Kenneth E. Boulding shortly thereafter. Professor Cooper's model, however, contains significant advances over preceding efforts. I venture to present it here.[8]

The nature of the process, as described by Professor Cooper, is fairly obvious. Objectives are stated by the entrepreneur and worked out on the basis of observed (reported?) market conditions; a prediction — a "budget" — is developed; men and processes are selected to carry through the envisaged operations; reporting of intermediate results is launched at once and continued. These reports may lead to a redefinition of objectives, an amended budget, and all this

33

takes place on the basis of standards established by management, the entrepreneur. Redefinition is stated to be "necessary if the organization is to adjust to changing conditions";[9] and presumably so also could the process of prediction, the method of reporting. Even the standards themselves could be revised "to adjust to changing conditions."

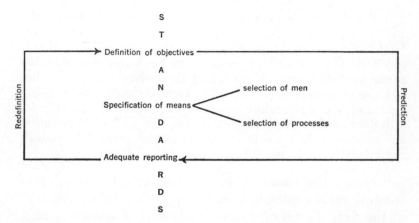

One interesting conclusion which Professor Cooper draws is that the presence of controls "acting through the media of 'willful' agents rather than 'will-less' factors may result in quite different observational behavior than that expected by the economist conducting investigations of business behavior with a model which does not allow for such conditions." [10] The author is particularly concerned with conditions of cost, "administration of equity accounts," and the like; and therefore, he asseverates that costs "may not be allowed to behave; they may, within certain limits, be made to behave." Perhaps others, interested in different aspects of enterprise performances, might wonder whether labor conditions, consumer relations, even natural resources "may be allowed to behave," and whether they may not, "within certain limits, be made to behave."

Professor Cooper was not making a plea for the study of entrepreneurship and entrepreneurial evolution.

Professors Cyert and J. G. March carry the analysis further.[11] For example, they find enterprises to have communication patterns, with "relay points," and that it makes a difference how many such points there are, how long the chain through which communications have to pass, and even the order in which particular pieces of information proceed: for example, data about costs going through a "relay point" occupied by a sales-oriented executive. They hold that the mere size of the decision-making unit is of importance. For example, in a multiple-man unit, each man will tend to hold the belief that the others will conform to known company policies; and therefore innovations have a poorer chance of adoption than in a one-man deciding unit.

They find the use of the budget in businesses important to a proper concept of enterprise behavior. And they see the annual budget not merely as a "prediction," a "schedule," and a "control device," but also as a "precedent." By defining decisions in many features of company action over the succeeding twelve months, the budget thereby establishes "a prima facie case for continuing [the] existing expenditures." There is a sort of dead hand of past budgets!

They also see the existence of "organizational slack" in any sizable business institution. Employees carry various roles other than those for which they are paid: roles of membership in cliques, in their respective families, and so on — and employees, not the company, define the minimum attention that they will give to these other roles. Anyway, here is slack which the enterprise can use to withstand the pressure of unfavorable circumstances and thus bear down upon its costs of operation.

In short, when one looks inside the business unit, one finds reasons to make allowance for willful factors, and really to cast doubts upon the traditional assumptions of rapid, automatic adjustments to profit advantages.

The Endeavor of Professor Burton S. Keirstead

Analysis of a different type is carried in Professor Keirstead's *Essay in the Theory of Profits and Income Distribution* (1953), but some of the same logical features appear: criticisms of previous theories and the elaboration of new ideas pertinent to the field of entrepreneurship, even to entrepreneurship as a historical phenomenon.

Professor Keirstead is concerned primarily with uncertainty and how the entrepreneur can deal over time with that unpleasant feature of business life. He admits that, when one leaves the static model, "the problem of profit maximization becomes more complicated." [12] He sees two sources of profit due to changing circumstances. One is the movement of general conditions, economic and political changes, which, if favorable to the enterprise, result in windfall profits. The other source lies in particular or company conditions; and here profits may arise either from a favorable change in the market for the goods of the enterprise, or from the introduction of innovations, either new processes or new products.

Now uncertainty affects all of these situations; but the author sees experts helping the entrepreneur to prevail against such difficulties. His forecasters can give him a good line on general conditions for something like 12 months in advance, and on particular conditions as much as "100 to 150 months ahead." In the case of large enterprises, with which alone Professor Keirstead deals, the marketing profits seem to him those of an oligopolist, and those arising from innovations to be (temporary) monopoly profits. In general, the author's conclusion seems to be that the entrepreneur may proceed, by aid of his expert advisors, *"as though he were certain,"* even if there really is "objective" uncertainty in the situation.[13]

There are, however, curious lapses in the whole argument, sometimes curious failures to prosecute an admitted limitation. For instance, general conditions are alleged to give occasion for windfall profits in consequence of their influence upon prices; but does this relationship exhaust the situation? The author includes political as well as economic factors in his general conditions, and, if political, why not social and all elements external to the enterprise? Also, whether the general conditions be limited to political and economic alone or more broadly extended, why do the consequences need to be restricted to the effects upon prices? Why are they not regarded as conditioning the whole conduct of the business institution?

Again, the company's experts are viewed as able to help the entrepreneur with respect to market forecasts, but apparently not with regard to accounting procedures, labor relations, public relations, and the like. Why is it not appropriate to corral the company's whole executive team into a relationship with "general" conditions, as apparently Professors Cooper, Cyert, *et al.*, are willing to do?

At one point, Professor Keirstead suggests that with respect to innovations the entrepreneur may well find himself in "unique" situations, where "there is no calculable probability of the hypotheses about the future that he may form." [14] However, are not novel situations, for the particular enterprise or particular region, if not for the business world as a whole, pretty frequent affairs in an entrepreneurial system? Are not many situations more or less unique? Are there really many situations relative to which top executive decisions are called for, for which the entrepreneur can

37

envisage a "calculable probability of the hypotheses about the future," even with the aid of his experts?

The foregoing writers are representatives of the avant garde among economic theorists who, confronted with the world conditions of the postwar years, especially the reawakened interest in economic development, are currently struggling to convert the pre-existent, predominantly static analysis to a really dynamic form.[15]

A call for such a formulation, made recently by Professor Guy H. Orcutt, a well-regarded Harvard economist, indeed carries a framework in which entrepreneurial activity is most readily fitted. Professor Orcutt wants place for "decision-making units," to be sure, families and governments as well as business enterprises — with the decisions conditioned by historically derived elements. As he puts it, "the probabilities associated with alternative behaviors or responses are treated as dependent on conditions or events prior to the behavior." No wonder that he has to label his proposed construction "a new type of socio-economic system."[16]

Where the unhappy theorists may land is no immediate concern of entrepreneurial historians. The chief point for us is that whether the reformers abandon the notion of profit-maximization or not — and Professor Keirstead quite surely does not — they seem bound to become involved more and more with entrepreneurial problems; conditions internal to the business units, the nature and competence of the staff departments, the launching of given activities which admittedly will not mature until a subsequent time-period, and so on. In other words, the new theory promises to take on major features of history; that is, dynamics, and entrepreneurship. When one tries to come to grips with economic change or economic development in a free (entrepreneurial) system, one can hardly avoid paying some attention to the entrepreneur.

The Influence of Economic Development

Quite surely, as an Oxonian recently put it, "economic growth is beginning to reoccupy a central position in economics . . . [a position] that it has not had since Adam Smith." [17] And in such a reorganization of economics, the entrepreneur cannot be neglected.

Certain aspects of entrepreneurial performance seem particularly significant for a form of economics that is really dynamic, and is concerned with unlimited economic growth: open-ended economic development. It is noteworthy, for example, that enterprises which escape "infant mortality" — disaster in their earliest years — may well acquire a zest for survival, perhaps a drive for success, which has but loose correlation with profit conditions. As Professor Cooper remarked vis-à-vis costs, the business unit may be made to behave in a manner that economic conditions alone could not guarantee. An extreme case was brought recently to my attention — that of an enterprise currently brewing beer, although it began life manufacturing automobiles.

Again, business decisions, when not concerned with routine affairs, are not unitary in character, but, as already suggested, are likely to be cumulative or at least linked, each major decision conditioning all subsequent ones, each decision, when carried into effect, being a commitment of some sort. Growth of the individual enterprise is the consequence of a succession of successful, linked decisions. For the decision-makers, especially in an economy where the owner-manager is an unusual figure in the larger enterprises, a number of incentives other than profit-maximization come to influence their actions: aggrandizement of the business unit by strategic moves, achievement, power, public service.

Even as the men who write the books or design the buildings of a given society are the children of many diverse influences, and not infrequently persons inexplicable in terms of existing social forces, so also the operators of the larger business enterprises may not be understood without regard to much more than the existing "complement of the productive factors." They are the products of the culture in which they matured and are currently operating, plus idiosyncratic elements that may lead them to deviate from any norm of their time and environment. Moreover, as Mr. Noel G. Butlin once enjoined the Research Center for Entrepreneurial History, "Whether we are dealing with economic or any other type of change, we need also to recognize the moving character of the entire society and to cast our concepts . . . with this fact firmly in the foreground." [18]

Perhaps ultimately a prediction of Saint-Simon made as early as 1814 will be justified; that the science of society would be evolutionary and historical rather than mechanistic.[19] Surely economists will be driven more and more like Cooper, Cyert, and their friends to study business units as social institutions possessed not merely of communication systems, but of role structures, informal organizations, diversities of group interactions, and the like. And they will come to recognize that, with an ever-moving character of the external society, the social organization that is the business enterprise will also be ever-changing.

The aspiration of the theorists of the current generation endeavoring to deal with economic growth, the difficulties that confront them, and the present state of the relevant theories are revealed in the latest book on the subject by two able young economists, Gerald M. Meier and Robert E. Baldwin, entitled *Economic Development: Theory,*

History, Policy.[20] The authors were trained at Harvard, show a familiarity with relevant modern theoretical materials, and the volume is, indeed, the most historical of the treatises that have appeared on the topic.

Professors Meier and Baldwin are engagingly frank. They offer three major propositions which make evident the magnitude of the task which they and indeed all similarly minded adventurers must face when they explore this territory so long a puzzle to historians.

1. Within the economist's usual framework, the rate of economic development is held to be determined by "the degree of utilization and the rate of increase of the various productive means." The authors have no more to say about the degree of utilization of the factors, although that matter might be of interest to those concerned with entrepreneurship; but they do go forward to remark that "when one attempts to trace the causes of changes among the productive factors, he becomes enmeshed in a myriad of social, political, and economic forces. These forces, moreover, cannot be arranged in any neat hierarchy of cause and effect. All of them are interrelated." [21]

2. After a survey of writers of the past who have paid some attention to problems of economic change from the classical school through the neoclassical, Marx, Schumpeter, and the post-Keynesian analysts, Messrs. Meier and Baldwin reach the view that, except on rare occasions, all these writers manifest quite limited visions: "they limit their analyses to the economic performance of Western capitalism," and, "for this purpose, they make many assumptions about the general sociological, political, and economic nature of this society." [22]

3. Despite the need for an extensive rethinking of appropriate economic analysis, and the drawing upon writers such as Max Weber, Pareto, Sombart, and Veblen, "the

widening of the traditional boundaries of economics, so far, has proceeded only very slowly." [23]

Actually, Professors Meier and Baldwin do little to alter the picture. In considering the "basic characteristics of poor countries," they utilize the four rubrics of "underdevelopment," "backwardness," "capital deficiency," and "foreign trade orientation." They do pay passing attention to the entrepreneur, recognizing that in such backward areas he is operating under conditions of insecurity; but they seem to regard him as essentially a twentieth-century, at least a nineteenth-century, American entrepreneur who chances to have been born in some strange foreign land. And when the authors come to deal with "maintaining development in such countries" — which, incidentally, is a notable section of their volume — they make use of concepts all familiar to recent economic literature: population, capital accumulation, technological discoveries, investment, and the like. Investment takes place without borrowing; changes of all sorts, of which actually only technological ones are mentioned, come into use automatically. Even the problem of "resource flexibility" can apparently be surmounted without human intervention. All rich countries — France, Canada, Brazil, Japan, Germany, and others — seem to be regarded as falling into a single category, and their businessmen all to be cast in the American model.

Still this book and others of its class are noteworthy both for their evident recognition of a dynamic situation and for their attempts to suggest the changes in modern economic thinking necessary to analyze it properly, the requirement of dealing with "a myriad of social, political, and economic forces" of which Messrs. Meier and Baldwin speak. In addition, the volumes are important for their attention to flows. It is the increase of population, the rate of technological advance, the accumulation of capital, and so on, that concern them mostly. Equilibrium is hardly mentioned. Perhaps in the end economists' eyes will come to fix upon the business institutions which themselves are changing and which are the principal channels of economic change, as well as upon the individuals who direct their decisions.

A Place for the Entrepreneur

The validity of the thought that the entrepreneur may properly be regarded as the central figure in economics[24] is subject to argument on the grounds of both logic and fact. In logic the question takes the form: what specific contribution in production is attributable to the activities or ideas of the entrepreneur? And the answer clearly will vary according to the depth of analysis. Superficially, it would appear that there is no net product specifically and separately attributable to the entrepreneur. The contribution of the entrepreneur flows out through the actions of labor, the movements of capital goods, and the conversion of raw materials, even as the contribution of an orchestral leader flows out through the singing of the violins or the beating of the kettledrums. Yet no one would doubt that the conductor contributes something, and that the contribution of one conductor is different from that of another. So, too, with the entrepreneur.

If one examines the situation more fully, however, one finds that, in fact, distinct embodiments of entrepreneurial activity do exist, or may be unmistakably discerned to have existed. The mark of the entrepreneur is shown, and always has appeared, in the organization of enterprises under conditions of economic freedom. Occasionally, economists have not been too clear in their handling of this element in production. For example, Marshall held that organization was an important part of capital, and that "it seems best sometimes to reckon [it] . . . as a distinct agent of production."[25] But clearly there is good reason to view the external and internal forms of operating arrangements, especially the latter, as choices of the entrepreneurial actors, not as determined by the supplies of capital, labor, or land. Sometimes the forms and even the procedures remain oddly constant despite appreciable increases in scope of activities. Thus, Professor Stuart W. Bruchey asserts that a fifteenth-century Italian merchant would have felt quite at home if he had dropped into the countinghouse of Robert Oliver of Baltimore, whose business life covered the years 1783–1810.[26] At other times patterns change rather rapidly, even among business institutions of similar size.[27]

Specific cases dot the histories of companies and the biographies of businessmen, offering the analyst almost unmanageable materials: for example, the well-known cases of Standard Oil's experiments with legal forms, U.S. Steel's endeavors to control the supply of its chief raw materials, or Ford's use of the assembly line. Other data, new but typical, have appeared in publications of the Center, of which several may be adduced here.

1. An analysis of the unsuccessful career of the Stanley Steamer automobile and the relation of the Stanley brothers to the events led a recent investigator to conclude that the failure of this motor vehicle in competition with those driven by the internal combustion engine was not "solely or even principally the result of [the latter's] inherent superiority as a form of motive power." The Stanley brothers were craftsmen and were not interested in production volume.[28] The author concludes that "in this case at least the relative success of the rival innovations depended as much upon the managerial abilities of the entrepreneurs reponsible as upon the technical merits of the alternative forms of power."[29]

2. An investigator looking at the rise of the large "first-

44

class" hotels prior to the Civil War finds that their appearance in the more important commercial centers was due to various forces and to various types of people. No simple formula of businessman's response to profit opportunities summarizes the facts. Instead, the inquirer finds that "the imaginative, bold hotel-keeper, the civic-minded merchant, the architect eager to experiment, the guest who dealt out both praise and adverse criticism — all these have had an important part in the development of the modern hotel." [30]

3. Professor John E. Sawyer of Yale contends that the course of economic development in this country would have differed in timing and probably in significant directions if entrepreneurs had not been susceptible to creative errors, if I may label what he describes as a perfectly logical development out of nineteenth-century American conditions.

Professor Sawyer starts with the two premises "that — leaving the sports aside — most entrepreneurs, like all other social actors, tend to act and react in terms of the social frame in which they are raised and in which they live; and, second, that the American scene [of the nineteenth century] *defined* the entrepreneurial norm in terms of aggressive and creative performance; that it tended to make ceaseless drive and innovation, not deviant behavior, but ideal performance of the [entrepreneurial] role." [31]

To these two basic contentions he adds a third which can be best reproduced in his own words:

. . . in the context suggested, and urged on by the pressures and momentum, even the illusions of the culture, past experience of growth and further real prospects gave rise to exaggerated anticipations of future growth that repeatedly induced entrepreneurs and investors to over-respond to existing market stimuli and in effect over-leap existing economic realities in the scale of their plans and in the scope and timing of investment decisions;

45

and that in the special circumstances of 19th century America their individual and collective over-estimations operated to accelerate the processes of growth and often, in varying measure, produced the results that, *ex post,* made "economic" their initial over-estimates.[32]

The *kinds* of effects in which I believe its presence may be seen vary widely:

— the *timing* of the building of basic facilities, such as transportation, in advance of demand;

— the *magnitude* both of the investment input and the resulting facility available;

— the premature introduction of economies of scale in earlier stages of manufacturing, etc.;

— the resulting lessening of bottleneck limitations in the succeeding phase of growth;

— the tendency to maximize the credit flow and make maximum use of credit available;

— the pressure upon technology — hastening adoption of the new and development of the better;

— the planning and building of organizations in terms of expansion potentialities;

— the quick response available to recovery from the bottom of a cycle (and even the policy of a Frick, investing in depression on faith in future growth);

— perhaps above all the endless daily decisions to buy a tool or make a plan or hire a man, in which the major premise of growth determined the course of action.[33]

To the extent that it worked in an economic sense — that an over-anticipation of prospects in fact paid off in either a private or social balance sheet, we find ourselves on the perilous edge of an "economics of euphoria" — a dizzy world in which if enough people make parallel errors of over-estimation, and their resulting investment decisions fall in reasonable approximation to the course of growth, they may collectively generate the conditions of realizing their original vision. It suggests, historically, a sort of self-fulfilling prophecy, in which the generalized belief in growth operated to shift the marginal efficiency of capital schedule to the right, and in which the multiple centers of initiative, acting in terms of exaggerated prospects of growth, pulled capital and labor from home and from the available reservoirs abroad, and so acted as to create the conditions on which their initial decisions were predicated.[34]

4. Mr. Charles Wilson of Jesus College, Cambridge, finds in William Lever a splendid exemplar of the concept of the entrepreneur which he favors and which was noted earlier: the possessor of "a sense of market opportunity combined with the capacity needed to exploit it." [35] Rarely has there been a career which was so largely determined by the decisions of the actor, and rarely one of which the consequences were more diverse.

To be sure, Lever as a youth found himself in a small soap works operated unprofitably by his father. However, there was no necessity of his adopting and pushing "every kind of advertising — mostly borrowed from North America"; it was his own choice to continue in existence, operating under their own names and often under the direction of their previous owners, the numerous competing plants that he bought out as he prospered, and thereby retained good will in a market where irrationality has always played a considerable part. It was this English-born and English-bred man who wrote at middle age, "I don't work at business, only for the sake of money. I am not a lover of money as money and never have been. I work at business because business is life. It enables me to do things."

And in the end the "things" that he brought into existence embraced a model village in a country where they were unknown, a substantial monopoly of soap production in Great Britain, an international consortium in fats and oils, and new imperial relations of the British government with sources of oil-bearing natural products over a good part of the globe.

47

Statistical Evidence

A more general appraisal of the contribution of entrepreneurship is to be found in a comparison of inputs and outputs in the American economy over the period from 1869–78 to 1944–53, made recently by Professor Moses Abramovitz.[36] It appears that over these decades the input of labor services, including those of salaried management, and measured in man-hours, declined slightly, that the input per capita of capital increased something like threefold but that the national product per capita increased approximately fourfold.

In explaining this discrepancy Professor Abramovitz turns to "the gradual growth of applied knowledge which is, no doubt, the result of human activity, and not of that kind of activity involving costly choice which we think of as economic input." Some of this growth, apparently, is viewed as a derivative of general social change, as through broader education, but in first place appears "knowledge concerning the organization and technique of production," the use of resources, and the like, all of which are features of entrepreneurial character.[37]

Some part of the explanation might well run in terms of the changes (through time) of the entrepreneurial "stream" — to which attention will be given below, in Chapter IV — as well as to the more nebulous matter of the reaction of that "stream" upon society as a whole, that is, upon its mode of thinking, its standards of value, and the like.

Conclusion

In brief, a new era in economic theorizing seems to be dawning, without the fanfare that accompanied the advent of the institutionalists or the lesser breed of "technocrats." The way had been cleared by the decline, prior to World

War II, in the attractiveness under modern conditions of the profit-maximization thesis. With the coming of peace and the need of paying attention to underdeveloped countries, the replacement of the static type of theory with some form of dynamic concept — mock or truly dynamic — became pressing. Already theorists are moving to fill the gap, and, as they do so, they find it useful or essential to make a place for the entrepreneur or the institutions which he utilizes and directs.

The introduction of change through time, however, and particularly of the agent most productive of change, threatens to upset traditional theory in a far-reaching manner. When the tempo of the theory is altered from that of short-run "adjustment," the entrepreneur with his living enterprise, his "creative responses," his capacity to alter the course of economic development by idiosyncratic performances — these all enter the picture and must be taken care of by the theorists. It is possible that an analysis of entrepreneurial phenomena can make a contribution to the evolution of a new concatenation of theories — which would include, perhaps, some elements of Adam Smith, Alfred Marshall, and those in between, together with others directly related to the social milieu in which the economic process takes place. The elaboration of the latter relationships — what Professor Boulding characterized as the "larger" economics — seems to that eminent scholar a "most challenging" proposition.[38]

Chapter III·

THE ELEMENTS IN A POSITIVE VIEW: THE ENTREPRENEUR AND HIS ORGANIZATION

FOR A PROPER UNDERSTANDING of entrepreneurship, it is essential to keep in mind that it is a social phenomenon in several dimensions, if not in several senses.[1] One dimension relates the bearers of that function to the other human members of the groups that make up their particular enterprises, as well as to different persons more or less loosely connected with these institutions. Another relates entrepreneurial units to one another, to form a sort of constellation of entrepreneurship in which individual enterprises constitute the separate stars. And the third dimension relates the bearers of the entrepreneurial function to the economic and cultural milieus in which they chance to be operating, and this may involve relationships indirectly with cultural milieus of the past. Perhaps these three groupings may be thought of as a set of concentric circles, the second enclosing the first, and the third encompassing the prior two. Such a figure is all the more appropriate since the groupings are to an appreciable degree interconnecting, if not interacting, the first even directly with the third as well as with the

50

second. I propose to discuss the first of these relationships in the current chapter.

Certain sources of possible misconception may well be considered at the start. For one thing, an effort to split an enterprise into the entrepreneur and his organization is recognized as bound to result in difficulties. If, as already proposed, an essential element in entrepreneurship is decision-making, and if that process be held to embrace all steps from the initiation of an idea to the implementation of its official reception, obviously the entrepreneurial function becomes diffused through various strata, as has been suggested above.[2] An innovation may have its origin in a suggestion-box or in a president's office. Also, decisions of sorts are made all down the line, even by the surly gateman who fails to pay proper respect to an unexpected director and gets the president into trouble with his board. And, insofar as the entrepreneurial function extends to the execution of decisions and the maintenance of the profit-oriented institution — and surely one cannot leave the entrepreneur in an ivory tower of merely conceiving the possibilities of innovations — that function becomes diffused through the various layers of the establishment. Mary Parker Follett, for example, studied business administration essentially as a form of government,[3] and probably this approach is sound. Accordingly, just as one should not survey the King or Cabinet without including Parliament, or the President without Congress (and perhaps other parts of the whole governmental structure), so one must, at least for some purposes, include the whole administrative business organization when speaking primarily of the top executives. It should also be recognized, however, that in routine matters hierarchies do exist in business institutions, and that, even in large corporations, there is an individual or a group above whom (or which) appeals cannot be made for change or reversal of decisions. For purposes of the current analysis, this individual or group may be taken as *the* entrepreneur, and an effort will be made to examine the relations of this individual or group with the rest of the social unit.[4] Such relations are important. The exertion of leadership toward determined goals, the taking of blame for failures en route, the absorption of pressures to favor one or another of the participants in the joint enterprise — these and other less critical elements are involved in the activities of the policy-clinching, policy-administering center of the organization relative to the remainder of the group.[5]

Second, the term "organization" also stands in need of clarification. One may conceive of sets of relationships involving the entrepreneur and his organization almost as varied (among different cases) and as complex as the structure of physical atoms. However, perhaps a series of concentric circles will again be enough to portray the typical situations. In the first surrounding circle would perhaps be the board of directors or the executive officers of any wholly-owned subsidiary concerns that existed. Farther out would be the suppliers of materials, the sellers of finished products, the officials of related labor unions, the leaders in the local charities, and the like. Somewhere at about this distance would also fall the various governmental units with which the enterprise has relations. Still farther may be the consumers of its products, and beyond them the general public that may have more or less precise opinions regarding the worthwhileness of the particular enterprise. Here any or all of these elements in the organization may come into the discussion, but chiefly attention will be devoted to the individuals concerned directly with the day-by-day operations of the unit.

Third, and perhaps most important, a limitation of the

area of survey must be proclaimed — and for two reasons: the phrase "entrepreneur and his organization" really covers the whole field of business administration, and there is as yet no history of business management in any country. Having had something to do with the 300,000 books on that subject, past and present, that now exist in the Harvard Business School Library, I am all the more disinclined to attempt a summary of the evolution of that management even in one country within a few pages of a single study.[6] It seems necessary here merely to relate certain groups of facts on which historians are pretty well agreed, to the phenomenon of entrepreneurship as viewed by social scientists. I shall then look only at the developments flowing from changes in financial control, at consequences of the increase in complexity of business units, and the evidences of a rising sense of public and of a social responsibility among business executives.

Role and Sanction in Entrepreneurship

It is enlightening to think of the relationships existing between the entrepreneur and the various elements of his organization in the terms provided by sociology.[7] The bearers of the entrepreneurial function are viewed as playing a role in the Lintonian sense; and the execution of the several aspects of the role is stimulated by positive and negative sanctions exercised by the various individuals and groups with which these role bearers have relationships.

Professor Leland Jenks elaborated a schema of this character with special relevance to entrepreneurship in *Change and the Entrepreneur,* which R. Richard Wohl, then a graduate student at Harvard, summarized in the following fashion:

Every sanction defines a status and a corresponding role. The sanction is aimed to regulate a pattern of social relationships. All types of social relationships are structures, and every sanction relates to a particular type of social structuring. It establishes and regulates certain types of expected behavior, and assesses the rewards and punishments that attach to them. It thus creates a typical organization of the motivational structure of individuals. A given individual occupying a position in the social system (status) is presumed to behave in certain fairly set ways in carrying out the functions that attach to his position (role); he suffers consequences (set by sanctions) in the form of changed attitudes and action on the part of those to whom he is bound by social relationships.[8]

And it may be noted that such structures, behavior, and the like apply to economic and instrumental as well as other social relationships. Here, as I see it, is where economics and business administration, sociology and social psychology converge — with a significant admixture of history. The quality of acquired and currently-flowing communication is also important.[9]

A phenomenon such as the preference for short-term commercial paper in the American banking system, the use of pauper children in the early English cotton mills, or the Burlington strike of 1888 can each be analyzed from nearly all the approaches just suggested. The primary questions become: under the existing conditions of technical knowledge, especially the knowledge which the actors in the specific case might reasonably be expected to possess, given the prevailing state of education, literature, and libraries, what economic advantages and disadvantages were believed by the actors to attach, and to have attached to the specific action, and what did the censors of the actors (that is, their fellow entrepreneurs, the political and religious leaders, and so on) think the right action to be — "right" in both the pragmatic and ethical senses? As the performance of an economy in the past can properly be assessed only on the basis of the natural resources and productive techniques

54

known to have been available at that period, so a business practice or attitude of a given situation can fairly be appraised only on the basis of the body of knowledge and the cultural themes known to have existed at the time. A historian, more than an economist or sociologist, is disinclined to deal in absolutes. He is ever expectant of change. But the historian will place the specific event in the stream of changing social institutions and social thought.

Essential Features of Control

A major factor in determining the relations between an entrepreneur and his organization is the nature of the power that put him into his post and that holds him there. Of course, proprietorships and partnerships wherein the entrepreneurial function is linked to financial involvement are the basic and still the most numerous type of business unit here or abroad. They have appeared so commonly in industrially young economies, or in parts of economies where risks were considerable, that some writers (such as Professor Reinhard Bendix in his *Work and Authority*[10] have given them the label of "entrepreneur" and used other terms, such as "managers" or "bureaucrats," to designate the executive heads of large enterprises.

Such units have ever served as fields of opportunity for the many entrepreneurial aspirants that seemingly develop — and have always developed — rather widely in Western societies. Recent inquiries have shown that not a few men move back and forth, into and out of their own enterprises, as fortune smiles and refuses to smile! Proprietorships and partnerships are also training grounds for men to become officers of large business institutions. I suspect that this is a more common phenomenon than is generally recognized. Apparently, through past decades, many top executives of large corporations have always been sons of businessmen;

and the latter were, I believe, the proprietors and partners of business units just mentioned. In other words, small businesses have served as steppingstones for the rise of families from farmer or mechanic or clerk to high business positions.

Enterprises of the independent sort have ever given opportunity to men who were restive under authority. The relations of such individuals to subordinates, work force, customers, et cetera, come closer to being authoritarian than anywhere else in business. Here was the home of the man who as a Colonial merchant did not hesitate to embark in privateering when opportunity offered, or, like Morgan in 1907, could take control of a national financial crisis, and — more recently — threatened to close down his plant rather than try to do business under conditions set by "that man Roosevelt"! Under any conditions, however, mortality is high among such units, and individually they do not survive long. Concrete evidence of the life experience of these enterprises in America is provided by the scarcity of records of goods-distributive houses, from village stores to city wholesalers. Few sets of such records survive in any library or other depository; and yet they have existed in this country by the hundreds of thousands.

A common development from the simple proprietorship is the creation of a family firm. The first step may be the addition of the phrase "and son" when the first new generation is taken into the enterprise. However, many family firms lack revealing names. Such firms have advantages and disadvantages from the entrepreneurial point of view. They sometimes command a loyalty from the active members of the family that adds to their economic strength. Sir Henry Clay reported that family concerns in the English textile trades came through the trials of the 1920's and 1930's better than the nonfamily enterprises of comparable size and type. When the mill was in danger of having to close its doors, all members of a family rallied to support the show. Moreover, there seem to have been circumstances of international trading or finance, where supervision from any single point was difficult, and where devotion to the common family venture may have taken its place. This was true of the Italian banking enterprises, the Rothschilds, the eighteenth-century merchants of London or the American colonies, even some of the twentieth-century international margarine firms described by Mr. Charles Wilson.[11]

It appears that the family firm was most prevalent in France, less so in England, and probably still less in Germany. They are rare in the United States, and perhaps only those of the du Ponts and Fords attract broad attention. Professor David S. Landes indicates that anyhow the family counts for much in French industry and trade, and that, at least in some cases, procedures have been worked out informally within families whereby some of the weaknesses of family succession and family dominance are avoided. The family is sufficiently unified in aspirations so that the ablest, or at least the best available representative, of each successive generation is supported as effective head of the institution; and if there are disgruntled or spendthrift members of that generation, they are persuaded or dragooned into selling their stock to the new head of the show or at least to those who are willing to support the latter's hand. Thus, there is no loss of family control by reason of the sale of stock to strangers, while management is not allowed to deteriorate more than is unavoidable and still maintain the family traditions.

The weaknesses of family firms, enterpreneurially speaking, are the failure of talent to be regularly inherited on the male side, and the likelihood that sons of businessmen, especially successful businessmen, will prefer to pursue careers apart from business — in the professions or in the arts, perhaps. Biological and social forces are antagonistic to the family enterprise. Sometimes, to be sure, marriage helps out. The Whitin Machine Works seems to have prospered in the hands of sons-in-law,[12] and men in the same relation to du Ponts appear recently to have contributed much. But balancing such good fortunes is likely to be the drag on such institutions arising from the necessity of taking care of ineffective members of the family group or of getting members launched in the professions. And then there is always the economic problem that, in cases of distress or of the expansion that competition may make essential, the enterprise can be saved only by giving up financial control.

A successful argument might be presented on the basis that the family enterprise is genetically anterior to the single proprietorship. The former seems essentially a vehicle for the intrusion of an older and more basic social organization, the biological group, into the realm of economic action. In various parts of the world today, from the Near East to Korea, business activity is still severely handicapped by the demands of family obligations. In at least the common Western form of proprietorship, from the medieval itinerant peddler to the present-day corner druggist, the entrepreneur may be looked upon as having shaken free of a normal earlier attachment.

Sometimes, of course, the single proprietorship is extended by the formation of a partnership, while some family firms also take this legal form. But the partnership need not detain us long although it does give some opportunity for the acquisition of added talent. I once knew of a successful wool-selling enterprise in which a Jew and an Irishman were joined. The Jewish partner bought the stock, and the Irish one sold it! A partnership also gives some promise of greater effective longevity, even of continuity, than a single proprietorship if the surviving partner (or partners) take in new, younger folk.[13] And, third, there is surely some added power of sanction from within the enterprise. Economically advantageous or socially meritorious actions are likely to be applauded, and socially disapproved ones curbed. The single proprietorship is the better home for the willful tyrant or headstrong individualist — for the Napoleon or the Hitler.

The Coming of Professional Management

The owner-manager variety of entrepreneurship in its several forms, while increasing numerically, has lost economic dominance pretty well throughout the Western world in what Professor Boulding calls an "organizational" revolution. The facts about the separation of management and ownership, of the rise of salaried executives, even perhaps the mode of life in the large bureaucratic organization with which managers' management is particularly associated, are so well-known that they need not be recounted here.[14] Certain features especially significant for entrepreneurial development, however, need to be noted.

"Professional" management in the sense of effective control by executives with small stockholdings is not limited to large or very large corporations. It will be found in many medium-sized firms, particularly family enterprises that have been converted to "public" ones.

This form of management, at least in the United States, has shown a bias toward the attainment of professional qualities very broadly defined. With less direct involvement in financial results, the professional manager, like the medical man in his hospital, has had an incentive to seek the scientifically best, at least the most broadly approved, methods of operating his adopted establishment. And it may be added that inasmuch as the more narrowly defined professional entrepreneurship that is concerned with stock ownership has penetrated to the stratum of medium-sized enterprises, the more broadly defined professional entrepreneurship has tended also to spread over a considerable portion of the American business system. No change in the entrepreneurial role in America carries as much social significance as this spreading belief in the existence of good ways of carrying through business operations, and the belief that it is the duty of first-class business administrators to discover or learn and to apply such ways.

The rule of professional managers (in the technical sense) has expanded considerably in American industry, beginning with the banks and railroads before the Civil War. There has been some similar development in Germany, to a lesser extent in England, and still less in France. Perhaps it is no coincidence that the progress of an intellectually professional attitude has been registered in about the same proportions.

Surely conditions in the capital market constituted an important factor in the promotion of professional management. In this country the early banks, insurance companies, even cotton mills could be set going through the cooperative efforts of a few merchants or other men of means; but even there professionalism of a sort soon raised its head. The presidency of the commercial banks was usually an honorary position, sometimes carrying no salary at all; the board of directors as a whole or through a committee continued to pass upon investments; but otherwise the cashier came to be the chief executive officer. There is evidence too that as early as the 1840's the stock of such institutions had become widely distributed, and that the officers by no means held control through ownership of shares. The process was, if anything, more rapid in the case of the railroads. To be sure, there was a period in the 1870's and 1880's when certain lines were controlled by such persons as Forbes or

Vanderbilt or Gould through sizable financial investments in the stock of the roads; but these were distinctly the exceptions. The stock of the New England roads was rather quickly dispersed. Even Erastus Corning had little financial commitment in the New York Central or its constituent lines; and any number of roads seem to have taken on early what might be considered a natural American pattern — natural, that is, in the light of underlying economic and technical conditions. There were few men with large personal fortunes, and few of those who wanted to learn to operate so complicated an enterprise as a railroad or other sizable business unit. The trend toward professional management may have had play in the cases of British support of various American railroads, by stock purchase and by loans, when no effort was made, at least in most cases, to try to exercise control over the use of the money committed to the American projects. In many other underdeveloped countries, the British did send managers along with their capital.

The scarcity of capital operated indirectly also in the United States to bring professional management and a separation of ownership from management. Under "general entrepreneurs," of whom Professor Cochran has written,[15] professional managers were a logical development. Later, when investment bankers came to play a prominent role in the procurement of funds, first for railroads and later for the rapidly expanding industrial and commercial enterprises, their intervention was likely to produce the sort of separation of which we are speaking. This was especially true in the hectic 1890's and subsequent years, while the predisposition of the investment-banking houses, feeling themselves to some degree trustees on behalf of the investors whom they had persuaded to place their funds in specific companies, was to seek the best available manager, not to be content with the chance abilities of a large stockholder, let alone the scion of one. In the institutional system of American finance there was a built-in bias in favor of professional management. Perhaps here one should also include the bias supplied by the development of the stock exchange and that of the trend of savings within the country.

The scarcity of capital had affected other relationships in times past. For example, it was fairly common in our pre-Civil War period for the state governments to demand, and receive, the right to appoint government directors to the boards of directors of banks, railroads, or other concerns in which they had invested state funds. Later there were federal government directors on interstate railroads to which the federal government had made land grants. Again, in receiverships the courts of the country appointed trustees to conserve the assets of railroad enterprises; sometimes, in fact, such trustees or receivers operated the lines for years or even decades.

Out of the scarcity of capital also grew the system of affiliations between specific railroads and specific investment-banking houses which was a notable feature of the years between about 1880 and 1930 (and on which the federal Department of Justice largely based its unsuccessful suit against these bankers for violation of the Sherman Act). Pecuniary and other advantages quite as much as pressure or moral compunction kept the ties strong over considerable periods of time. Indeed, the role of the financial houses vis-à-vis all types of American business enterprises seemed so vigorous and promised at the time of his writing to last so long that Professor N. S. B. Gras erected this era as a distinct stage in the evolution of the American economy.

Increase in Complexity

Without stretching the meaning too far, one is probably justified in saying that complexity in business life has increased in the two directions of institutions and ideas. The nature of the former trend is indicated by two facts: a large metropolitan department store buys from something like 20,000 suppliers, while General Motors has 12,000 suppliers who in turn have scores or hundreds of their own. General Motors does its selling through more than 18,000 dealers.[16]

It is revealed also by a recollection of the simplicity of the business life of the American Colonial merchant, who actually did not differ greatly from merchants of that era all over the world. (Perhaps conditions in London were somewhat more complex.) The merchant of that time would probably have *complained* at the paucity of institutions on which he could lean for help, if he could have looked into a reliable crystal ball: banks, insurance companies, freight forwarders, labor exchanges, and scores of other ancillary and service units — of which more will be said in another connection.[17]

Similarly, for the larger enterprises, internal complexity has increased with growth. And this increased complexity of departments and divisions, sales manager and chief accountant and the like, has brought a new creative element into the organization. Typically in the smaller, earlier business unit, the few white-collar people in the office were folk who merely took orders as to what to do. But one does not hire a comptroller or a purchasing specialist or their compeers merely to give them directions; nor would men study to become such specialists if they were to have no initiative. This creativity is strengthened by the greater role of planning in modern business: budgeting, forecasting of sales, training of future executives, the formation of professional associations for accountants, personnel directors, and the like.

To the relatively new notions just mentioned may be added those of market research, inventory control, contingency reserves, incentive wages and whatnot, all of which from time to time come to count in executives' decisions, and all of which change sufficiently with continuing investigations so that the ideas must, as it were, be kept up-to-date. The "advanced management" sessions at schools of business are designed in large part to supply this refurbishing of concepts.

All these types of increased — and increasing — complexities have an important two-dimensional effect. The entrepreneurial function becomes much more that of a co-ordinator than it was earlier, even in medium-sized business enterprises, calling perhaps for the talents of an Eisenhower rather than those of a Napoleon. To be sure, this variety of entrepreneur would do well for his company if he encouraged communication from his subordinates, and if he on his side communicated downward his ideas as to objectives of the business unit. At all events, the increased and increasing complexity of business connections and operations has been a potent force in altering the role of the entrepreneur toward his organization.

Recognition of Public Responsibility

To a degree that is rather surprising on second thoughts, the social responsibilities of business are self-enforcing, that is, through imitation. The economy of any country probably would have progressed less rapidly, and along different paths, if business processes had been patentable: processes such as installment selling, the issuance of company manuals, assembly-line production, the introduction of new forms of depreciation allowances, and the like. And it is also surprising, even astonishing, how many improvements in business procedures are constantly being devised and imitated — and superseded! — inspired in part by the "instinct of contrivance" (which surely Veblen would not have credited to businessmen) and in part by the desire to gain a differential advantage or to meet competitors' prices. A good deal of the purely instrumental aspect of public responsibility, the acceptance of technical as well as technological change, is forced upon entrepreneurs.

Of somewhat similar character, but not quite, are certain new-blown relationships toward consumers. Beginning apparently with the sewing machine, and spreading with the spread of "consumer durables," producers and distributors have provided ever-improving service to purchasers. Again, the rule of *caveat emptor,* and the attitude of sellers deriving from that legalism, have been modified in practice by the concept that "the consumer is always right," by the institution of complaint bureaus in retail stores, by the grant of liberal return privileges, and the like. To some extent, to be sure, these measures have an instrumental quality, as first indicated: service on electric refrigerators and the rest is merely an imitative gesture, inspired by a desire to secure one's share of the market, while it is indeed somewhat more expensive for a retailer to stand up for his rights than to let the consumers sometimes make false claims. Businessmen have found that there is a financial restraint upon perfection. Still, the role of the entrepreneur in many lines of business has been modified over the decades. As he has become less arbitrary with his staff, so has he developed new attitudes towards consumers.

A development of the twentieth century in the public relations of the larger corporations, especially in the United States, has also affected the entrepreneurial role. I have in mind the so-called "full disclosure." Company reports in the United States, especially the annual type, have always been more revealing of company performance than similar documents of other lands. Perhaps our greater geographical distances which made chummy stockholder meetings relatively unthinkable were a factor. Perhaps in railroad matters, American managers had to keep in mind the European investor, actual or potential. In any case, financial revelation was not universal in the nineteenth century, nor persistently on the same level.

A step in a new direction was initiated by a public accountant of English origin, Mr. A. Lowes Dickinson of Price, Waterhouse and Company, at the time of the first reporting from the United States Steel Corporation. Influenced no doubt by the professional status of public accountants in England, Mr. Dickinson urged a generous disclosure of both physical and financial results of the corporation's first year of operations. Judge Elbert H. Gary agreed and carried the question to Mr. J. P. Morgan, who, having in mind his sponsorship of the sale of many million dollars' worth of securities, gave his approval. The example of the Steel Corporation has been widely, although gradually, followed. The New York Stock Exchange has given support to this same practice. Accordingly, more than ever before, American entrepreneurs manifest at least a modest sense of obligation to the public and to public authorities.

The larger area of "public relations" has shown a modicum of adjustment to the same ideas, and this too is a phenomenon of the twentieth century. However, the early version of such relations even in that century was that of attempting to explain, if not to excuse, public misfortunes such as train wrecks or violent strikes. Subsequently came an endeavor to create favorable publicity for companies and their doings. But some public-relations counselors, such as the important Mr. Edward L. Bernays, have tried to make the relationship of corporations to the public a "two-way street": if the companies wished to create a favorable attitude toward them on the part of the public, they should see to it that they had something to communicate that would be accorded a favorable reception.

The increasing regard which American corporations have

recently displayed toward the communities in which they exist, and the greater willingness of enterprises to accept governmental intervention of various sorts, in order to check inflation, to combat depressions, even to prevent monopoly, are also evidences of a greater degree of public responsibility on the part of American entrepreneurial actors.

Changes in Social Responsibilities

Social sanctions playing upon American entrepreneurship have been evident in various relationships over past decades. The general storekeeper was supposed by his customers to run a sort of social club around the well-known cracker barrel, at least in the winter time. From an early period the banker seems to have been under the virtual obligation to dress soberly, to attend church, and to be conservative in his opinions. As late as the 1920's, the sales representatives of Boston investment bankers were expected to wear vests through the hottest days in summer when calling upon clients.

More significant, of course, was the attitude toward employees taken by employing entrepreneurs, and sanctioned by the censors who were important for them: members of the communities in which they lived, their peers in industry or trade, the forceful members of Congress, leaders in the churches, and so on. To be sure, the history of personnel management, broadly interpreted, is yet to be written; what an employee expected to be required to deliver when he took a job from a factory owner or from a "gang-boss," what the employer or boss expected to be delivered, and how rules were changed from time to time by reason of pressures of one sort or another so that satisfactions were increased on one side or the other or on both.

From what we know at present, it seems as though the relations of employer and employee — if one may venture to

67

average out all the employments in all the corners of the country — have come pretty nearly a full turn. At the start, the employees were members of the same communities as the employers, perhaps members of the same churches, or even distant relatives. The mores and protection of the community prevailed, the relations of one human being to other human beings. Today, employer-employee relations, while on a less personal basis, are no less important.

Human relations have followed various patterns in the past. On shipboard, for example, special relationships existed, and before people were long ashore the management of groups was often necessarily conceived in terms of discipline, perhaps as a "residue" from days of slavery, a "transfer" from military practices, or perhaps as an obvious necessity when workers — quite understandably — put their own convenience above coordination of group efforts. The career of William Austin was perhaps a bit extreme but not wholly atypical. At an early age he achieved the captaincy of a sailing vessel, but he was lured to solid ground and placed in charge of the Charlestown jail. From there he moved to head the operations of a New England cotton mill, and finally wound up as a manager of a southern plantation. No doubt the cotton-mill agent was usually a kindly person, perhaps fatherly, towards the individuals of his organization — at least, outside the mill — but he believed in the necessity of discipline within the establishment, discipline trimmed with fines, discharges, blacklisting, and the like.

In time another primary element in employee-employer relations arose, that of loyalty. In an era when business success was believed to hinge much on secret formulae or individual ways of handling materials — a belief that went back into handicraft days, at least as between guild members and the outside world — it was easy for employers to come to think that workmen ought not to move into the employ of competitors. But the notion spread into nonindustrial areas. Charles E. Perkins and his contemporaries were dismayed at the advent of railroad brotherhoods in considerable part because they saw a conflict in loyalties. A workman could not be loyal to his railroad *and* to his union. And this notion of worker-company attachment, if not allegiance, has persisted into modern decades, now converted into pecuniary or quasi-pecuniary terms. Contentment will reduce labor turnover; and so the costs of worker training, loyalty deriving from an appreciation of the purposes of the enterprise, the sense of sharing, will make for greater worker satisfactions and greater productivity.

Dr. Oscar W. Nestor showed in his doctoral thesis that before the twentieth century little was being done for employees in American industry, even in the fields of safety and sanitation. One Alfred Dolge, trying to introduce into this country some of the social insurance schemes that he had known in Germany, did not have much effect. Nor did other employers with modern beliefs succeed much better.[18]

We know that there was considerable subcontracting within producing establishments, especially in the metal trades, and we can guess that one reason for its elimination was the desire on the part of the heads of the enterprises to introduce uniformity of labor conditions, and perhaps to try to increase the sense of "belonging" mentioned above. We can also suspect that employers in the last decades of the nineteenth and the first of the twentieth centuries took from the nativist movement, which goes back at least to the Know-Nothing political activities of the 1840's, some notions about the immutability of the characters of the recently-arrived immigrants. The concept can well have been widely held that the "Wops," the "Hunks," the "blockheaded Swedes," and the like were incapable of intellectual and social improvement themselves, and their children and children's children likewise. Why try to make it possible for their offspring to become doctors or scientists or business executives?

In any case, it appears clear that the first real change in attitude came with World War I and the accompanying shortage of labor. Most of the schemes then devised, from personnel manuals to baseball teams, were abandoned in the postwar depression, but a new start was made in the 1920's, an effort to find out *What's on the Worker's Mind* (as Whiting Williams' book of the period was called), which in turn led to the Western Electric experiment and contemporary concepts.

The major alteration from the practices and ideas of the nineteenth century, no doubt in high measure imposed by changes in labor supply and the growth in strength of labor unions, and probably facilitated both by periods of prosperity and by the somewhat common cause of paid executives and paid employees, has been the development in entrepreneurs of a much greater sensitivity to the aspirations or demands of their human partners in enterprise. As a result of the new dispensation, entrepreneurship in America is in fact called upon to make rulings in social justice — the distribution of the national income — for which its authority seems merely to be the negative circumstance of inaction elsewhere in society.[19]

The quality of social decision to which I refer is highlighted by the data on cotton-mill earnings in New England over the 1825–1914 period, brought together laboriously by Professor Robert G. Layer.[20] The general picture is that production of fabrics per man per hour rose substantially and pretty steadily in the decades before 1860, but millworkers' earnings increased little. The workers secured the benefit of the enhanced productivity, which was, of course, not due to proportionately increased exertions on their part, through the lowered cloth prices which they shared with other consumers, and perhaps in somewhat increased stability of employment which the lowered cotton-goods prices helped to assure them through improved competition for the consumer's dollar. On the other hand, earnings and productivity seem to have moved more closely together in the post-Civil War era, especially after 1880, although the basic data on productivity here must be admitted to be much less satisfactory than those for the pre-1860 decades. All one can say is that it *looks* as if the workers in the later period were awarded an important share of the increased productivity that came from technical advances of all sorts.[21]

Something of the same situation obtains relative to the yet more recent "productivity increases" of wages covered in various union-management agreements. Perhaps management in some or all of these cases has the blessing of federal government conciliators, and of course they yield largely because of union pressures. They may actually have the tacit endorsement of our present public censors and public opinion, but concretely they are placed in a position where they are saying in substance that the needs of the workers are greater than those of the consuming public, our export position, the stockholders, or the managers themselves!

To be sure, entrepreneurs have always had some share in the making of such decisions. The New England cotton-mill operators, for example, were participating in the years before 1860. It appears, however, that the "productivity" angle of the recent wage bargains is in large measure fictitious, at best perhaps a hoped-for incentive. There is the difference that, whereas competition among cotton mills prevented much of the gains due to enhanced productivity from sticking to the fingers of the mill owners, today there is less competition among wage-earner groups, and enhanced "productivity" wages do stick to the fingers of the beneficiaries. Presumably, this is all to the good. I am not arguing the merits; I am merely pointing out that management has become a vehicle or agency for the improvement of labor conditions in a degree not evident earlier.

The Nature of Roles and Decisions

Two general features of the relations of entrepreneurs to their organizations deserve special note: the influence of history, and the degree of flexibility. One impact of history upon the role and sanction system is evident in phraseology used by Jenks or Wohl.[22] "Status," "expected behavior," "bound by social relationship," and the like all imply existence and activity in the past, like the businessman's "standard practice" or the economist's "consumption habits." Past years or decades or even centuries have established a pattern of mutual expectations — actions, rewards, punishments — which constitutes a social structure; and social structures permit the entrepreneur to function, and allow production and distribution to proceed.

History is involved in another way as social patterns are worked out. As already suggested, decisions by entrepreneurs are reflections of the experiences which, over the past, have impinged upon the decision-maker or decision-making group.[23] Thus, the Quaker merchants who determined on a one-price system of retailing were summing up a specific religious development. Mr. Frank W. Abrams, who did much for the employees of the Standard Oil Company (New Jersey) during his administration as president of the company, is likewise reflecting the ideas and aspirations which from the Pilgrims down have helped to establish American cultural themes, and are now still molding them.[24] Therefore, it can be said that 1959 decisions are never made on the basis of 1959 data alone; the hand of history rests on each decision-maker, in part by reason of his direct relations with a given culture, and in part, at least, by reason of his connections with a specific system of entrepreneurial roles and sanctions. The entrepreneur is a social animal, not a machine to calculate the probabilities of profits.

If this role and sanction structure is historically based, it is also to some degree flexible. After all, it is man-made, except insofar as the limitations of man's basic nature and the world's limited resources play a part; and what man has put together, he can alter. The notion of "law," reasonably common in economics, is foreign to this approach.

Change and the potentiality of further change are implicit assumptions of the philosophers of business who observe and comment upon the current trends. Thus the thoughtful Charles C. Abbott, dean of the graduate school of business of the University of Virginia, recently laid out a program for businessmen:

The administrator must seek to serve the people for whom he is responsible. If he is to accomplish things through people, if — in Lord Beveridge's phrase — he is to get "common men to do uncommon things," he must try to supply them with goals they are willing to accept. He must endeavor to furnish them with what they need to do their jobs — whether tools, policies, or attitudes. He must seek to remove their frustrations. He must seek to give them the satisfaction of accomplishment. He must search for ways by which they can advance and develop their potentialities.[25]

Professor Peter F. Drucker places even heavier burdens upon entrepreneurs of the current and future generations. "It is management's public responsibility," he writes, "to *make* whatever is genuinely in the public good *become* the enterprise's own self interest";[26] or, as Adolf A. Berle, Jr., interprets Professor Drucker, the corporation must solve "two combined enigmas, both political: that of achieving functional harmony between the corporation and society and that of achieving harmony between the corporate activities and prevailing ethical ideas."[27]

Mr. Berle himself sees a social "revolution" already well forward to fulfillment. Competition now operates, he believes, "within far narrower limits than classical economics contemplated." And the reason is clear, "at least to political scientists":

Few of the major segments in a community really want a regime of unlimited competition in the modern community — neither the great corporations, nor their labor, nor their supplier. Fundamentally, they all want, not a perpetual struggle, but a steady job — a job of producing goods at a roughly predictable cost under roughly predictable conditions, so that the goods may be sold in the market at a roughly predictable price.[28]

And Professor Thomas C. Cochran, a business historian turned philosopher, gives the most complete analysis:

The managerial ideology [of the earlier 1950's] so emphasized education, cooperation, and success through personal relations, and disapproved so strongly of egotistic individualism, ruthless dealings with competitors, and any quest for high profits dangerous to long-run security, that the managerial creed . . . [of the period] seemed to be in a transition stage toward a rationale for a political rather than an acquisitive culture, toward a doctrine in which the goal was to achieve a position that conferred power and prestige, rather than personal wealth.[29]

Cochran correctly deduced the consequences of such changes:

Once the *major* aim is transferred from extra profits for stockholders to the welfare of the organization, the critical step has been taken in the direction of a new social adjustment. Planning comes to be in terms of how the organization can best adjust to general social trends so as to insure survival over many years, how it can continually raise the compensation of its employees to sustain loyalty and morale.[30]

He observes a noteworthy parallelism in the goals of modern "managerial enterprise" and the modern welfare state; and he ventures the prediction that future historians looking back on the course of the movements of these two trends in the first half of the twentieth century may find the change as important as the end of feudalism, the rise of world trade, or the beginnings of industrialism.

Conclusion

The relationships of the entrepreneur to his organization may advantageously be construed in terms of role structure. To do so confers at least two major gains. For one thing, the technical, economic, ideational, or other elements concerned in the "initiation, maintenance, and aggrandizement" of profit-oriented enterprises, which constitute an area of primary interest to the economist, can be reduced to the same denomination, as it were. The factors of economic growth — discovery of mineral resources, investment of capital, and social approval of money-making — are conveniently located in one and the same model. Again, there is a merging of "micro-" and "macro-economics." The ideas and conditions that characterize the whole society are seen to penetrate and affect the individual enterpriser. And, perhaps as an extra dividend, the forces important in both society and a single plant are notable as heavily freighted with history. An understanding of the economic system, at least in its realistic, evolving character, and through the creative responses of its chief Western actor, the entrepreneur, must be interdisciplinary, involving both social science *and* history.

Chapter IV·

THE ELEMENTS IN A POSITIVE VIEW: THE ENTREPRENEURIAL STREAM

MATURE ENTREPRENEURSHIP is likely to conduce to an economico-social situation which affects more than the "initiation, maintenance, and aggrandizement" of individual business enterprises. And the situation is not readily subordinated to a consideration of entrepreneurial actors responding individually to the social milieu — men, institutions, and ideas — in which they chance to be located, a subject that will concern us in the succeeding chapter. What I have in mind here is, primarily, the interaction of entrepreneurial units.

Perhaps a simile will help to convey my meaning. A composer or a baseball player might possess exceptional talent, but his contribution to the entertainment of the nation would remain rather minor if his performances were restricted, respectively, to his family parlor or his own sand-lot. Music as a social phenomenon nowadays means, when viewed realistically, everything from symphony orchestras to arrangers of FM broadcasts, and from publishers of musical scores to manufacturers of disc recording apparatus. And correspondingly baseball means all sorts of supporting and fulfilling elements: producers of equipment, talent scouts, architects of baseball parks, schools for umpires, and whatnot. So, likewise, with entrepreneurship.

I have chosen to call the entrepreneurial concatenation of this sort a "stream." I have done so to emphasize the circumstance that, predominantly, the actors in the various actions are endeavoring to produce changes in the pre-existing situation. We are concerned with individuals caught up in a flow, not men performing repetitive actions in a static system. We want to learn, as it were, how the whole fraternity of log-riders manages to perform in a manner more productive than if each rode alone, relying solely on his hands and his native instincts.

The Elements of the Entrepreneurial Stream

Of primary importance for the proper functioning of an entrepreneurial flow is a beneficent climate of social opinion, a changing climate, to be sure, but one that does not discourage the flotation of new enterprises, especially enterprises that can reasonably anticipate an expanding desire for their goods or services, and a climate that still attracts talent into the area. Desirable also, of course, is relative freedom from government intervention in the form of favoritism, government monopolies, and the like, even freedom from major monopolistic conditions within the private sector.

For purposes of exposition, it is convenient to conceive of business institutions as forming a hierarchy based on function. Colin Clark publicized the threefold division of primary, secondary, and tertiary; that is, extractive, manufacturing, and service industries. This breakdown may be useful for some purposes but not particularly for ours. Utilizing more fully a functional analysis, one can make the divisions of primary productive, ancillary, and service industries. In the first category would be lumped those industries that are usually labeled extractive, manufacturing, and construction. In the second would be mainly the purveyors of equipment, providers of information, disposers of waste products, and so on, for the first. And in the third would fall transportation, marketing, financing, and advice. (For completeness of coverage, one would have to make a place for establishments that serve consumers at the latter's instance: automobile repair shops, cobblers, and the like; but they are negligible for our present purposes.) For other ends, other schema may be preferable. For our analysis, it appears best to conceive the extractive, the consumer-goods manufacturing, and the construction industries as the main stem, and the other industries and professions as ancillary or secondary to them. In turn, of course, a railroad company, a department store, or a management counselor has a network of relationships: suppliers, advisors, et cetera.

Beyond business enterprises, one must take account of affiliated institutions that not only increase the complexity of entrepreneurial relationships but also make a contribution to entrepreneurial performance; for example, trade associations, schools of business, libraries, even governments in their promotive activities. Insofar as these associations, schools, and so forth, provide avenues of communication, means of joint public relations, or the like, they are tantamount, logically, to service institutions.

As a contrast to the stream or system that I have in mind, one need merely look at the American Colonial merchant-manufacturer (for example, the Browns of Providence) from the vantage point of the sophisticated present. We find that they had to assemble their raw materials and equipment themselves from farmers and local handicraftsmen; they did their own banking, carried their own insurance, often provided their own transportation facilities; they had to rig up their own private network of correspondents to gather news of markets and prices; and they had to get along without libraries or schools for the training of either staff or successors. And if there were two, three, or a half-dozen manufacturers, or two, three, or a dozen merchants, they provided little more than duplicate units of self-sustaining operations; there was no system of *other-supporting* relationships, no creatively related hierarchy of business institutions.

In a modest degree, it may also be useful in the ensuing analysis to have in mind the sort of breakdown by qualities which Professor Danhof suggested some years ago and to which further reference will be made: innovators, imitators, Fabians, and drones.[1] I would be inclined to use a somewhat broader basis for classification than that which Professor Danhof employed, that is, readiness to accept new procedures and new lines of production. However, the notion of variant grades or qualities of entrepreneurial capacities is the important feature.

The Contributions from Structure

While an appraisal of the entrepreneurial stream could proceed on several bases, its relationship to long-run economics, especially to economic growth, seems most important. Here one may subdivide the evidence into two types; that concerned primarily with entrepreneurial structure, and that concerned especially with the flow of information.

In the first category, the play of entrepreneurial initiative may first be noted. With young men acquiring as they mature the conditioning of a permissive, even encouraging, culture, there will always be entrepreneurs waiting to take advantage of new opportunities, from the largely imitative effort of starting a new drugstore in a burgeoning suburban center to the setting up of a specialized counseling firm for hotel management. The lure of accomplishment or of the dollar is by no means wholly in the direction of higher profits of established enterprises; it also stimulates the invention of new links in the entrepreneurial network. (The projector of supermarkets kept trying even though his idea caught hold slowly.) The evolution of the economy does not have to await a decision by the central planning soviet. Also the new producing or ancillary institutions will probably come under the guiding hand of *young* men, operating their own small or medium-sized enterprises and eager to make their mark.

Economic growth is promoted also by the organic character of the entrepreneurial institution — that is, that the latter has some similarities to a "tree," as Alfred Marshall remarked, and not to a machine or an algebraic formula. A recognized quality of chemical manufacturing establishments is their bias toward expansion. At the end of the processes necessary for the production of item A, there are waste elements. By adding a little in the way of new raw materials, and carrying out a few further processes, item B can be produced; but there still are waste elements that can be used up by adding, and so on and so forth. In other manufacturing activities, the steps in change may take the form of developing new, and sometimes unanticipated, products like the famous Scotch tape or the Polaroid camera. An unusually interesting case was that of the Lever soap people when they set up a subsidiary in Africa to supply the English establishments with groundnuts. After a few years the subsidiary had elaborated a life of its own: plantations, steamships, import trading into Africa, and the like. And our large corporations manifest similar characteristics. When Frigidaire makes electric stoves, Hotpoint makes refrigerators, et cetera.

Another way in which economic growth is promoted through entrepreneurial action is in the propulsion of a form of multiplier. For example, a shoe manufacturer decides that, instead of tying together pairs of shoes and throwing them into gunny sacks, he will put each pair into a cardboard box. His innovation pleases retailers and customers; he needs more boxes than can be turned out by the old processes; new machinery is devised, perhaps new machines to make the new machinery; possibly a new trade magazine to serve the makers of shoeboxes, or the makers of shoebox-making machinery; and so on. Or, to take another example: the growth of a railroad system promotes a whole circle of chain reactions running off in a number of directions: production of rails, development of special equipment to roll the rails, development of special equipment to test the state of rails that have been a considerable time in use; production of ties, or special track- and tie-laying apparatus, or special tars for variant soils; railroad magazines; compilations like Poor's *Manual of Railroad Securities;* and so on.

And, if entrepreneurship supplies a device for the seizing of opportunities, it also furnishes a mattress on which unwise adventurers may fall. In a way of speaking, enterprises hardly ever die completely! Or, to put it another way, "new" enterprises are hardly ever wholly new! When a hotel changes hands, there may be nothing novel under the new management but a new face in the back office and silverware with new initials. When a cotton mill is sold, it may appear as a statistical unit in a reporting of new establishments, but there may be the same machinery, same employees, same bankers, and same selling connections. Entrepreneurship provides a built-in conservation of trained capacities, sunk capital, and implemented business relationships.

This sort of exfoliation seems more than the economist's "division of labor" or his "external economies." The significance is perhaps best grasped by contrasting a primitive entrepreneurial economy, where each tub stands on its own bottom, with a mature entrepreneurial one with a structure of mutually supporting institutions, in addition to those that compete directly and indirectly. Possibly the significance may also be grasped by contrasting the concept of strata of mutually supporting business institutions with the arena or pit of cutthroat contention, which is often the picture conveyed by nonbusiness observers as valid for all the business world as, of course, it is for some segments at some times.

There is an interaction between institutions which seems to me circular or cumulative in character. Take the case of a management advisory unit. Some enterprising person has the courage, probably based on his particular personal experience, to set himself up as a counselor on marketing or labor relations, perhaps on management problems of all descriptions. He secures some clients who prosper as a result of his advice and, in consequence, they tell their friends. To supplement his talents the expert brings in new men. They give even better advice to clients, who turn out more or better goods thereby and tell more friends, and so on. The same may well be true of any ancillary institution: for example, an advertising agency, a credit-reporting enterprise, or an industrial research bureau.[2]

Quite similar are the relationships that can come to exist between business units and educational or information-purveying institutions: schools of business, business-reference libraries, publishers of business journals and business books. It seems worthwhile to separate this fourth element from the third because of the nature of the data which are interchanged. In an adequate degree, the difference is between business units being aided to do better what they had been trying to do before, and their being urged to do things because they *ought* to do them, or to do things in new ways because this is how these things *ought* to be done.

Here again, there is circular action. An instructor from

a school discovers a novel practice or attitude in a given concern and he writes up the situation, or persuades the businessman to do so, for a business periodical. Other businessmen contribute ideas, their friends on the business-school faculties modify the notions, and gradually an improved practice becomes established and instruction at the business schools becomes improved, so that *future* practitioners of business will learn one more "right" way to perform.

A similar circular action could be elaborated (a) between business executives and their trade associations and (b) between company specialists — controllers, time and motion engineers, and so on — and their professional organizations. The latter type may have the greater long-run influences, since the impact is upon individuals at least one remove from the pressure of financial return.

Two features of the foregoing circular or cumulative interactions deserve special note. One is that these interactions are for the most part "built-in." They are not the sort, like technological innovation or courtesy to consumers, that take their initiation from the free-will decisions of individual businessmen. The interactions mentioned above are in the nature of propensities internal to the system, the type of situation analogous to that which Adam Smith had in mind when he wrote about an "invisible hand."

Second, these interactions seem to constitute relationships in which business is enabled to "lift itself by its own bootstraps," as it were, almost to create something out of nothing! Actually, of course, they are merely instances, like so many in science and art, of the creativity of the human mind.

This aspect of the matter seems to me theoretically very important. If these concepts are valid, there is here a variable acting through time which is not encompassed in the economist's "productive factors" as usually elaborated. It is something that the evolution of the entrepreneurial system brings incidentally into existence, a sort of Archimedean screw spontaneously devised.

I venture to think that Professor Allyn A. Young had something like these phenomena in mind when, writing many years ago in one of his best essays which is, in fact, concerned with economic growth, he said:

The mechanism of increasing returns is not to be discerned adequately by observing the effects of variations in the size of an individual firm or *of a particular industry* [italics mine], for the progressive division and specialization of industries is an essential part of the process by which increasing returns are realized. What is required is that industrial operations be seen as an interrelated whole . . . The division of labour depends upon the extent of the market, but the extent of the market also depends upon the division of labour. In this circumstance lies the possibility of economic progress, apart from the progress which comes as a result of the new knowledge . . .[3]

If Professor Young did not indeed have auxiliary business institutions in mind, his concept does seem to fit the case. Advertising agencies, personnel advisors, machine builders, producers of office equipment, and the rest may be regarded as forming "specialized" industries. They do represent the investment of considerable capital, even when there is little to show in the way of physical assets, and in the aggregate they do provide a considerable market for the products of the primary industries. I would merely add to Professor Young's analysis that, when the "progressive division and specialization" of industries are viewed from the higher level of social action and when these developments are conceived — and properly conceived — as normal elements in a mature entrepreneurial system, these developments will be seen to be built into the system. One can expect such exfoliation in business structure just as one can anticipate exfoliation in botanical specimens. Such an evolution is natural to an entrepreneurial system; and this potentiality is one important element which differentiates such a system from a governmental one. Birth in governmental bodies is a difficult and slow process.

Finally, and especially significant for our particular purposes, it may be noted that the evolution of the "stream" (or perhaps system of interrelated flows) outlined above has altered somewhat, and undoubtedly complicated, the role structure of entrepreneurial actors. Now such actors cannot concentrate their attention upon their own staffs and their own enterprises. They must take proper advantage of, but not be misled by, counseling "experts": machine builders, bankers, comptrollers' institutes, college professors. And insofar as they do seek and accept aid from outside specialists, particularly from outside advisors, they are — as suggested above — putting aside the role of Napoleons vis-à-vis the members of their organizations.

The Gain from Communication

A second feature of interunit interaction is the communication apparatus among entrepreneurial units, a feature that has also played an important part in the promotion of economic growth in Western economies, especially in the United States. This is not the place to attempt to frame a history of economico-business literature, even for the United States alone, where the output has been largest, or of the institutions which have served as channels for the dissemination of business thought.[4]

Briefly, it can be reported that in the experience of the United States there have been three distinguishable eras since the country gained its political independence. Over the first fifty or seventy-five years there was precious little business literature of any sort issuing from the country's presses: a few manuals on bookkeeping, often reprintings of

English texts; a few vade mecums on commercial law; and Niles' *Weekly Register* which, for the most part, informed the businessman merely about what was going on in Washington. Of institutions there were only the coffeehouses, a few mercantile reading rooms, and the stock exchanges in various cities.

If we disregard the growth of organs purveying business "intelligence," such as the prices-currents, the *Journal of Commerce,* and similar newspapers, we find in the next period (from about 1825 to 1885) mostly the rise of industry literature. *Hunt's Merchants' Magazine, The Bankers' Magazine,* and the *Railroad Gazette* were just about what their names betokened. So also were the *Iron Age,* the *Textile World,* and the like, which were launched by publishing entrepreneurs in the years just before or the decades after the Civil War. This was an era when knowledge was, in a sense, partitioned off by industry. To be sure, these periodicals indulged in few interpretive articles about their particular industries. At best they were *fachmässig* — professional, in a way of speaking, concerned with technological changes, new products, alterations in the tariff, new establishments, and not much else. Such monographic literature as appeared was also industry-bound, if I may use the expression, chiefly books on materials and processes in industry.[5] There were, moreover, few institutions to facilitate communication: young trade associations, local chambers of commerce in the older cities, subscription and a few public libraries (although I fear that these institutions paid little attention to the "professional" needs of businessmen), and, toward the very end of this period, the social science associations. Accordingly, such progress as occurred in management, and such progress of this type as was reported, could not very easily move from one segment of business to another.

It is the last fifty years that have been productive in the improvement of media of communication within business. The evolution should perhaps be recognized to have begun in the 1880's or thereabouts, when certain speculative thinkers, American and English, and engineers in particular, began to grasp the notion that there were uniformities in business, maybe "laws" of a sort. "Natural law" was then a dominant element in at least American idea patterns,[6] and its influence may have provided ready acceptance of the notion stemming largely from engineering circles, even if the engineers were not directly affected by it. Curiously enough, the Industrial Revolution in England had not provoked ideas about the uniformities of business. The country seems to have maintained the mercantile, if not the artisan, point of view, the basis of success being the learning of a certain skill or the tricks of a certain branch of trading. An English author has asserted that, even in the primary field of accounting, the mercantile form of double-entry bookkeeping was not converted to industrial purposes until the closing decades of the nineteenth century. In cost accounting, the French appear to have made starts in the earlier part of that century, before the British, although they too did not carry the study far.

At all events, general business periodicals such as *System* and functional ones such as *Industrial Management* or *Marketing* arose, while books took on similar objectives, thereby expanding the horizons of businessmen. A wholesaler in leather need no longer think his vocation to be primarily confined to the recognition of differences among skins of different origins and divergent treatment; he had common ground with the wholesalers of paper or textiles or other commodities. So also with the accountants and the purchasers, those responsible for advertising or the forecasting of business conditions. There was opportunity for what more recently has come in the social sciences to be labeled "cross-fertilization."

In this period came also the institutions which, better than those which had preceded them, could serve as vehicles for the cross-industrial transmission of thought. There were the professional associations, and there were the schools of business. Probably one should add the large corporation, since here were, in daily communication, people trained in marketing, production, accountancy, and the rest; and, with the tendency of the large modern corporation to overleap industrial lines, there was less likelihood of limitations arising out of industrial conditions, supposedly peculiar industrial circumstances. However, perhaps the professional associations and the schools of business were the most influential instruments for the dispersion of knowledge.

Because no one had cast business operations into terms of functions, the earliest professional bodies were connected with activities ancillary to the main lines of primary producers: for example, engineering and banking. Even in the accounting field the first group to organize was that of the public-accounting practitioners. But in the twentieth century all sorts of functional experts have coalesced into such professional associations: purchasing, advertising, credit analyzing, controlling. These institutions have generally possessed two characteristics: they have been compounded of local units which, in addition to the national body, have held meetings for the reading of papers and discussion; and usually the national organization has published proceedings of meetings, a regular periodical, or both, while sometimes a large local unit has distributed material presented before its members. Inevitably industrial or local provincialisms have been broken down, and a more or less abstract "business-ism" or business-administrational point of view has been promoted.

The schools of business have contributed to the same result, although, of course, in a different way. Their graduates have carried such a point of view out into business, proclaimed it in their own activities, and — as another type of built-in, circular action — have tended to look with favor upon other graduates of the same sort of school coming into business with similar prepossessions as to the nature of business operations. Again, the research and writing of professors and doctoral candidates of these schools have extended the influence of this approach to business administration. Indeed, one of the early creative thinkers in this field, Arch W. Shaw, was a businessman who came to Harvard in 1910 to see what Harvard's new school of business was all about, and stayed to assist Dean Gay and to write on the functional analysis of business procedures. And periodicals such as the *Harvard Business Review* and the business research studies from almost every school of business have universally contributed to the same end. Finally, the professors in such schools have been called by "practicing" businessmen to give advice upon specific business problems. Here, through direct contacts, the academic approach of generalizing about all branches and operations of business could have immediate consequences upon the thinking of business managers and their staffs.

Third, but not unimportant in their own right, have been the publishing houses. The contribution of some such institutions has been implied in the references to prices-currents, commercial newspapers, and trade journals. Beyond the establishments that initiated and issued such periodicals I have in mind the publishers of business monographs: McGraw-Hill, Ronald Press, and the like. These houses, which would analytically fall into the category of "service" institutions in the classification proposed above, have actually been creative in this "service." They have sought out possible authors; they have proposed and produced new varieties of books; and they have tried to sell their business books as widely as possible among businessmen. Of course they did, but obviously here again has been a "built-in" promotion of economic progress. What was good business for these publishers was socially advantageous — at least insofar as they did not oversell their clients(!) and insofar as their books proved to carry sound counsel to businessmen.

If one adds the growing volume of government publications useful to business practitioners, the large body of financial "services," the specialized organs such as Dun & Bradstreet reports or the *Official Airline Guide,* and the rest, it becomes apparent that modern entrepreneurship, at least in a mature economy such as the United States, is almost literally floating on a stream of literature! One sometimes wonders how the top executives in America find time to do anything but read!!

At all events, the growth of an entrepreneurial system in a country may lead to the evolution of a business literature of manifold elements. The latter development will, in turn, exert a constructive power, abetted by the entrepreneurial ambitions of periodical and book publishers in the field, and by the professional associations that transmit information about such literature or information from it.

A further process by which this flow of information may have significant impact is through the "leveling-up" in the quality of business units. If, to employ the Danhof terminology, more of drone character can be converted into Fabian, more Fabian into imitative, and so on, the general average of productivity would be raised, and output per entrepreneur or per employee man-hour increased.

Finally, and as a sort of footnote, I should add that the evolution of business literature has brought a considerable change in the entrepreneurial role, at least in mature entrepreneurial societies. Professor Danhof says that one class of early American agricultural enterprisers was derided as "book farmers." Probably early railroad operators or early industrialists would have been similarly held up to scorn if they had utilized data out of printed sources. Surely the American entrepreneurs throughout the nineteenth century wished to be known as practical men. In the railroad field, for which alone we have any substantial survey, Professor Cochran found little evidence that his "railroad leaders" of the 1845–1890 period utilized the professional literature of their day, even the *American Railroad Journal*.[7]

Today a real entrepreneurial problem is the control and proper utilization of the ever-swelling flood of business information of all types, from changes in international competition to possible uses of electronic computers. The role of the businessman is coming dangerously close to that of an academic scholar, except that the former still "has to meet a payroll"!

Competition and Monopoly

Not all relationships among entrepreneurial units are socially advantageous, of course, even when they may hold advantages of greater or less duration for the enterprises involved. Almost all of the actions taken have at least a partial motivation in the general desire among business units, as indeed among human beings, to control the environment with which they must interact.[8] Almost all of the leaders in business units also make manifest the interpretation of their social role made by the then-existent group of entrepreneurs in the particular region or country. Some types of action have only minor effects upon the production stream, though they may be fairly widespread. In the early days of industrialization in England and the United States, for example, employers in various segments of industry proclaimed the enticing of skilled workers from one another to be one of the cardinal sins. We have no evidence about the extent to which the employers lived up to their self-inspired ordinance; but the formulation of the concept is interesting as one of the earliest spontaneous structurings of the entrepreneurial role among industrial leaders. Of late years, at least in the United States, there appears to have been no such condemnation of enticement relative to any type of employee from engineer or atomic physicist to company president.

Another variety of self-imposed rule among entrepreneurs of nearly all countries is that one may speak enthusiastically, if not ecstatically, about one's own products, but should not denigrate or belittle the products of one's competitors. It is not good form even to attempt to lure purchasers from possible outlays that are only indirectly competitive: for example, "Reach for a Lucky instead of a sweet." A recent effort by the manufacturer of a cigarette without a filter-tip to combat all varieties with the latter equipment with the slogan, "Smoke for real," did not last long. At all events, advertising has always and universally — or almost so — been single-directional, if I may use the term: it has spoken well of Antony, not ill of Caesar.

A third matter is perhaps, strictly speaking, an internal policy — internal to the individual enterprise — but it is a policy adopted largely with other, possibly competitive, enterprises in mind. I refer to the efforts of corporations over recent decades to keep executives from leaving their doors by the grant of pensions or stock-purchases contingent upon the officers remaining with the company. Often such rights are forfeited by withdrawal of the executive on his own initiative. To be sure, devices of this sort may be looked upon as mere substitutes for the family or blood ties that once helped to keep an executive staff together; but, insofar as they immobilize talent and prevent it from moving to a situation where it would be economically more productive, as might be indicated by the current salary and not be mirrored in the accumulated benefits, the practice is socially disadvantageous. Perhaps, with the attraction of much young talent into the field of business and with the leveling-up of the quality of instruction in the numerous schools of business, it is not of much real social consequence that interunit executive mobility has been cut back over recent decades. The anchoring of executives to specific enterprises, to be sure, does have effects upon the phrasing of the entrepreneurial role. The professional manager, no less than the erstwhile family executive, becomes a one-enterprise man. (And perhaps entrepreneurial monogamy is good.)

Actions of a different sort have to do with the endeavors of entrepreneurs to secure preferred positions in their industries, perhaps partially or fully monopolistic places. Of course, it would be inappropriate here even to attempt to suggest all the types and varieties of efforts that are related more or less closely to such activities: exclusive rights to specific lines of trade or manufacture, privileges as "purveyors to His Majesty," patent rights, monopolistic and oligopolistic situations, and the rest. A library of books has been written on the different aspects of the subject. A few comments will have to suffice.

One important element is the almost universal endeavor of entrepreneurs to acquire a quasi-monopolistic, if only temporarily quasi-monopolistic, position. Businessmen are not unique in this characteristic, of course. When Dame Myra Hess with her piano or Cary Grant with merely his mobile face strives for artistic excellence, they are in reality trying to secure such a quasi-monopolistic position. They desire to be preferred — and perhaps secure larger compensation — when, respectively, a pianist or an adult male motion-picture actor is demanded. The same is true of Emerson's imaginary entrepreneur who made the "better mouse-trap," the Carrier Corporation when it brings out improved air-conditioning apparatus, or the Narragansett Brewing Company when it begins to sell its beer in "king-sized" bottles. Innovations are often introduced in efforts to secure a differential — that is, a temporarily quasi-monopolistic — position and, as Mr. Knauth has said, "Innovation is nearly constant in business." Since innovations, especially if they are imitated, contribute to economic development, it seems to follow that the striving for monopoly is socially advantageous.

Such activity is one facet of entrepreneurship's effort to control its environment. Perhaps one could even go so far as to say that there are two varieties of response by entrepreneurs to the uncertainties imposed by increasing competition; one is to gain ascendancy (that is, control) over one's competitors, and the other is to let them live and arrange for a sharing of the market. Vigorous entrepreneurship is like the man who, confronted with disease, says in substance, "They can't do this to me," while the weak type may be compared with the man, similarly attacked, who calls in nurses and doctors and medicines and tries to lean on others in his illness. In the experience of American business, entrepreneurs have sought monopoly at many times; in the spermaceti-candle manufacture of Colonial days, in the salt mining of western Virginia, in getting the best (and first) railroad line into Chicago. Even in the "combination movement" of the late nineteenth and early twentieth centuries, an effort to get into control of supply rather than to divide the market seems to have been dominant. Industrial pools or cartels represent the alternative form, sometimes carried, it seems, to the form that the most disadvantageously located and the least efficient unit of the industry is allowed to make a profit.

If endeavor for differential, quasi-, or fully monopolistic position be regarded as a normal element in the phrasing of the entrepreneurial role in a fluid economy, it does not follow that free and unlimited exercise of this effort will be socially desirable. Only in the most primitive societies is the sex instinct not curbed by law or custom or both, even though that instinct is rather useful for the continuance of the unit. In the United States it took some time to develop a philosophy and a technique of control over business. As Dr. Lee Benson has pointed out, there were precious few persons, even as late as the 1880's, who pretended themselves or could be looked upon by others as possessing expert knowledge of the "railroad question" of those decades.[9] So also the Sherman Act was a crude instrument for the settlement of the "trust problem." Not unnaturally in the circumstances, businessmen reacted in a rebellious manner.

I believe it to have been a sound development of the last few decades that leading businessmen, all who really count in the monopoly question, have come to accept limitation upon monopolistic conditions as a permanent and socially advantageous phase of governmental activity. They resist extensions of the government's concepts — for example, that mere bigness is evil — but they have come a long way since 1890. Acquiescing in governmental "interference" has become a normal element in the role of the American entrepreneur.

Conclusion

Appreciation of the significance of the entrepreneurial stream, especially the potentialities of creative action within it, seems essential for an understanding of entrepreneurship viewed as a changing phenomenon. The entrepreneur cannot be studied merely within his own enterprise, nor can the social meaning of entrepreneurship as a whole be appraised properly if inquiry is similarly restricted.

To historians and economists, the notion of such a stream offers a variant element in helping to explain economic change. The "structure of the economy" may be viewed, not as such-and-such industries of such-and-such magnitudes, or as equivalent bodies of matter that mysteriously do move, but as a fecundly built, interacting complex of largely self-serving, profit-oriented business institutions, with service attachments not necessarily self-seeking. And this complex, which is, of course, always a changing one, seems to have importance for the explanation of economic growth. The degree of its evolution in various countries may help to make evident the basis for differences in national productivity.

Chapter V·

THE ELEMENTS IN A POSITIVE VIEW: THE SOCIAL CONDITIONING OF ENTREPRENEURSHIP

THE ACTIVITIES of the individual entrepreneurial unit have a separateness, a life of their own, to a far greater extent than could be exposed in the foregoing discussion (Chapter III). These activities constitute the whole area of business administration, about which whole libraries of books and magazines containing discussions of accountancy and bank management, advertising, public relations, and a thousand other themes have been assembled. Yet into these operations, and the changes in their character, forces from outside the field of business seemed to penetrate, and quite naturally, since business is a social phenomenon and could hardly fail to be affected by the society in which it thrives.

Similarly, the concatenation of entrepreneurial units, moving through time and changes, was seen (Chapter IV) to have an instrumental character of its own, indeed to suggest that the whole is greater than the sum of its parts. Yet here too the analysis could not be completed without paying attention to influences from the whole societies, influences that modified the forces or altered the direction of these superunit interrelations.

There is good reason, therefore, to turn one's eyes to the more general, the broader-ranging, elements in human societies to see how they affect entrepreneurship in all its forms and relationships. We shall be concerned primarily with three problems.

First, we must consider the circumstances under which entrepreneurship comes into existence. Societies have carried on quite well without the use of entrepreneurs, and some do still. We need to look at the conditions that are conducive and those that are retardative to the appearance of the entrepreneurial form of production. We should study also the circumstances that favor and those that check the extension of the scope of entrepreneurship within economies. Professor Gay thought at one time that there was a "rhythm of history": that there were periods of increasing "freedom" for entrepreneurship, followed by periods of increasing restraint upon its activities.

Second, we must note that just as there is no necessity in any society's choice of the entrepreneurial form of productive organization, so there is, of course, no necessity in the choice by individuals in a given society of the role of entrepreneur. The institutions of entrepreneurship must compete for talent with other social institutions, the entrepreneurial role with other roles of that society; and it may well be that the performance of individual economies under the entrepreneurial system is in no small way affected by the quality of talent that is attracted into business.

In the third place, we must be concerned with the manifold relationships of the rest of a given society with the entrepreneurial segment, and with the changes in these relationships through time. These connections pertain to the motivations, the modes of conduct, and the effectiveness of entrepreneurs — the "why," the "how," and the "how well" of their actions. And the connections take one into religious, educational, political, and other phases of life in the given societies.

The Appearance of Entrepreneurship

Professor Easterbrook has contended that entrepreneurship as society's chosen instrument of production is the exception in the world's history, really pretty new when projected against the centuries of household, communal, and state enterprise. Professor Gay, in his "rhythm of history" just mentioned, implied that at neither point of the oscillation between state and free enterprise did the alternate form wholly disappear. Professor Gerschenkron is disposed to think of economic development first, and then of the entrepreneur as the child of that development; and he finds the Parsons-Jenks scheme ineffectual in explaining origins, having in mind his native Russia, where the intellectual, social climate was always hostile, but where, nevertheless, entrepreneurs appeared and flourished.

Little research, even by anthropologists, has gone into the matter of origins. Professor Cyril S. Belshaw does report from his examination of South Sea folk that "where indigenous peoples feel that it is in their capacity to produce for a market that is within their reach, without domination or double-dealing by outsiders, and with every step of the process reasonably well delineated, it is seldom that they do not take up the opportunity." [1] Dr. Redlich has suggested the possibility of entrepreneurs appearing in the agents connecting two nonentrepreneurial systems: for example, the serfs who transported surplus grain from the manor to the burgeoning town. Professor Sylvia L. Thrupp finds opportunities for the advent of entrepreneurs in the existence of famine conditions, the fiscal problems of princes, and the need for more or better sacramental wine. [2]

Rarely have entrepreneurs had to struggle against more

adverse forces than in seventeenth-century New England and in nineteenth-century Russia. Professor Bernard Bailyn describes the conflict of the Massachusetts merchants against the theocracy that then controlled the young colony — and the 158-page will of one merchant, Robert Keayne, who tries there to defend himself from the attacks upon him during his lifetime, essentially for embracing mercantile pursuits.[3] In Russia the entrepreneur was "despised by the nobility and the intelligentsia." The good life implied "tilling the land, which belongs to God, and receiving the divine blessing of its fruit" — not craving for riches and laying up treasures on earth. "In innumerable adages, fairy tales, and songs, the wisdom of folklore insisted upon the unrighteous origin of wealth." [4] But, in both instances, entrepreneurship took root and grew.

Since Weber it has been common practice to look to Calvinism as a factor particularly favorable to the introduction and increase of entrepreneurs, at least at one remove: Calvinism encouraged the accumulation of capital, and capital is prerequisite to entrepreneurship. Calvinism was viewed also as directly promotive insofar as it adjured men to be zealous in their "calling" and encouraged them to look on achievement as indicative of their favored place in God's sight.

Calvinism, however, does seem to have counseled a cautious form of entrepreneurship, careful and pedantic, hardly the seedbed of great changes. Professor James S. Duesenberry finds nothing in the Protestant ethic to account for the innovational activity which is characteristic of Western capitalism, and he expresses the belief that entrepreneurship of that sort was an offspring of the Renaissance.[5] And Dr. Jelle C. Riemersma reports findings in his research that give circumstantial support to Professor Duesenberry's conjecture. The strictly Calvinist Dutch merchants who launched the East and West India Companies of the early seventeenth century did not, in their personalities, "conform to the type of the ascetic, frugal, and calculating Protestant." They were instead "men of splendor and bold action." Moreover, Dr. Riemersma cites the German writer, Paul Koch, as having found similar traits among the entrepreneurs of Basel and of Frankfurt-am-Main.[6] A broad effort to explain the rise and expansion of entrepreneurship would probably be couched in terms of promotive and retardative forces, with a further breakdown of minimal and superminimal conditions.

Professor Gerschenkron is surely correct in stressing the primary requirement of economic opportunity. Entrepreneurship did not flourish in the hard conditions of the Middle Ages; it was peripheral to other forms of economic organization. It does not flourish today among primitive peoples living near the margin of subsistence. Production and distribution there must be closely controlled by those who clearly have only the welfare of the community at heart. Even where entrepreneurship has evolved, to some extent, as with the merchants of various Middle Eastern countries, economic conditions must at least be permissive before the phenomenon spreads to other lines of business activity. To be sure, the situation need be no more than permissive; one quality of the entrepreneur is his ability to perceive latent economic opportunities and to devise their exploitation. Typical among nineteenth-century cases is that of Charlemagne Tower, who saw the potentialities of the iron deposits of northern Minnesota and, at the risk of personal bankruptcy, succeeded in bringing them into production.[7]

Similarly, social toleration is important as a minimal condition. In France the nobility of the sixteenth and seventeenth centuries were permitted to engage in trade under specific rules without the loss of their status.[8] Serfs in nineteenth-century Russia were allowed to leave the estates to which they were legally attached, and to carry on various sorts of entrepreneurial activity.[9] However, as in the case of economic opportunity, the minimal conditions were not too restraining. Here personality factors seem sometimes to have "cut through the cake" of customary disapproval. Such factors are said to have accounted in part for the innovations of the Industrial Revolution in England. In somewhat similar fashion, Lebanese merchants in Jamaica are reported to have shrugged their shoulders at public obloquy and led the way to economic revival in the face of disapproval by the old aristocracy and its followers.[10] Innovators are sometimes represented as lonely men who, by their "hard cutting edge" or their boldness, have isolated themselves, at least temporarily, from their fellows.

Entrepreneurs must also be provided with minimum securities of various sorts, as Professor Easterbrook has contended. Perhaps such securities of person and property are the concrete evidences of the minimum of social toleration just mentioned. Andrea Barbarigo and other Venetian merchants of the fourteenth century sailed on trading voyages only under governmental protection.[11] So also did the Spanish galleons that traded between Cadiz and the New World in later centuries. Business in nineteenth-century England was under a handicap because, in the law of libel, statements of businessmen's financial positions could not be broadcast as were their American equivalents in Dun & Bradstreet's reports. The broadcaster was liable for damage if his statement, though true, caused loss to the person reported on. Again, English merchants have, in the post-World War II years, proceeded with some hesitation in their exports to the United States because the import regulations of the latter country were so complex, and so often executed with seeming arbitrariness.

However, the minimal conditions of encouragement and of security are appraised, and have always been appraised, by individuals with different inheritances and different experiences in life. Perhaps there are, and always have been, individuals with a propensity to entrepreneurship, men to whom the support of hazards is an exhilaration, who place exceptionally high values on accomplishment or on the "carrot" of monies to be spent in conspicuous consumption, who find a challenge in leadership, and so on. Quite likely the variation among men in these entrepreneurial qualities is not sufficient to cancel all the difficulties noted above, but those with the strongest propensity in this direction may well place a considerable discount on the supposed obstacles.[12] For them the threshold will be low. They will appear as the innovators, the "sports," the "deviants," the breakers of customary habits of thought and behavior.[13]

Incentives in Entrepreneurship

Above the minimal conditions range circumstances that are more promotive of entrepreneurial zest and capacity. The economic environment may be especially favorable. Such seems to have been the situation at various points in the world's history: when the Italians were exploiting the Mediterranean basin; when the discoverers had opened the New World; when the technological improvements of England's eighteenth century put her temporarily in a cost-differential position; or when American merchants turned their backs to the sea and began to taste the sweets of our western resources. Quite obviously a large carrot had effects.

So also did numerous other circumstances. "Pax Britannica" reduced various uncertainties. The adaptation of corporate organization to trade, and much later the introduction of limited liability, helped to smooth the path. The Heralds' College in England is alleged to have been pliant in the registration of coats-of-arms submitted by rising businessmen who desired such a symbol of distinction. In Sweden the prospering group of iron masters actually were unable to break through the more rigid social organization of the country, but, as elsewhere, they at least gained the position of a distinct upper class.[14]

This matter of noneconomic stimuli to entrepreneurial achievement is very important. It can be regarded as an expression of the almost universal human desire for prestige. This brings us close to the anthropologists, to some ideas in Thorstein Veblen's writings, and to all who seek social progress in any line through the erection of a "Hall of Fame." [15]

A different, somewhat broader construct is supplied by Professor Parsons, writing as a sociologist. As phrased by Professor Duesenberry, the position is as follows:

> The unique force of money income as a motivation in our society appears to arise from the fact that the social recognition and the self-respect achieved by an individual are largely dependent on the degree of occupational success which he achieves . . .
>
> It follows that a society can achieve a high degree of economic efficiency only if its social structure is such that a very high degree of social recognition is bestowed on the achievement of occupational success . . .
>
> An ethic which places a high valuation on occupational achievement is a necessary condition for economic development but it is not a sufficient one. The criteria for occupational success must be such as to encourage the active searching after new ways of doing things.[16]

One cannot properly contend that social esteem is the only impelling force. The Calvinist leaders in Amsterdam's mercantile world around 1600 — men like Uselinx — were not accepted as social equals by the established Northern merchants, but they persisted. And perhaps it is no coincidence that they were chiefly responsible for launching the East and West India companies in Holland, that is, that they became business "mavericks." [17] The record of the Jews in business is sparkling evidence to the same proposition. So also was the white man in many yellow, black, or brown communities, although here perhaps the exploiter from Europe or America might be regarded as one living by values imported in his person rather than by those that were prevalent in the land of his activities.

Yet social ideas congruent with entrepreneurial aspirations and social structures respondent to entrepreneurial success must be given great weight in an analysis of the operation of entrepreneurial systems. For Europe the residual elements of the older social system, and the diversions of ambitions and efforts which such residues provoke seem to be of major importance to such observers as Professors Tibor de Scitovszky,[18] John E. Sawyer, David S. Landes, and William N. Parker.[19]

Professor de Scitovszky draws a contrast between the situations in Europe, especially England, and in the United States. In the former areas, "the existence of a feudal aristocracy and landed gentry set a social pattern, which to achieve was the ambition of the newly rising capitalist [entrepreneurial] class." The British entrepreneur of the nineteenth century "wanted to outdo his rivals, not in the scale of his business or wealth, but by being admitted to high society and by becoming a member of Parliament or alderman in his native town. Such ambitions restrained the ruthlessness of industrial warfare and diverted a good deal of time, energy, and money from business."

On the other hand, the landed aristocracy of the eastern

United States, such as it was, lacked both the wealth and importance "to set social standards; politics . . . carried little social distinction and could not satisfy social ambition either; and society life, set up in a few Eastern cities by the business class itself, encouraged . . . money-making by adopting wealth as its sole ranking principle." So the American businessman found in money-making, besting his rivals, and enlarging his business "his only ambition and pastime. Only when he was already a spent man would he turn his energies to spending and enjoying his wealth." [20]

Professors Sawyer and Landes have dealt mainly with France. There they find the residues from pre-Revolutionary times to affect various elements in the entrepreneurial world: the tastes of consumers, the attitudes of owner-managers to employees, or the hopes of businessmen for early retirement and devotion to things of the spirit.

Professor Parker observes that in Germany business achievement commands respect only when attained on a large scale, where it will be rather obviously comparable with the contributions to the welfare of the nation, of the army officers, or the bureaucrats. [21]

An entrepreneurial history of the United States would need more strands of analysis than those suggested by Professor de Scitovszky, and some of these additional elements will appear in subsequent discussions. For the present purpose, however, certain forces appear worth specific mention.

One is the religious situation. The struggle in New England, to which reference has already been made, settled one aspect of American business life: it would be secular in character. Perhaps it is important that thereafter there was an increasing number of competing sects, or that these sects were mainly those called "Protestant" in Anglo-American terminology. Quite conceivably our economico-business evolution would have been appreciably different if we had chanced to have secured an official church and if that organ had emphasized the inconsequential character or riches on earth. But that is all speculation.

Surely a dominant folk hero in the United States has been the man who gets ahead, and of such persons no one has outranked the man who rose from rags to riches by his business operations. This social skewness was not any American invention. Literature issued in England from the seventeenth century onward carried the same theme: for example, Thomas Powell's *Tom, of all Trades* (1631), James Donaldson's *Undoubted Art of Thriving* (1700), or later merely *The Art of Growing Rich* (1796).[22] There were perhaps English antecedents of the Horatio Alger type of fiction, even the type with which Alger's name has been allied, although he did not actually follow the formula.[23] However, the American infection with the disease was deeper, and the zest to excel in business success has nowhere been more intense.

In addition to circumstances deriving from economic, religious, or psychological factors, there are developments within the area of business operations and perhaps some political elements, which should be taken into account in explaining conditions within entrepreneurship that conduce to better-than-minimum performance. In other words, there are various influences playing upon the entrepreneurial actors of any period in almost any land, to which the individual performers respond in varying degrees according to their inheritance and previous training.

Out of these circumstances, Professor Danhof drew his classification of entrepreneurs already noted: innovating, imitative, Fabian, and drone.[24] He was examining merely commercial farmers of the 1820–1870 decades, and he used principally the test of speed in innovation to establish his classes. However, numerous social "themes" — to use Professor Cochran's term — affected the farmer's attitude toward the adoption of new methods of cultivation, new crops, et cetera; and classes of roughly corresponding character could be rather readily conceived that would take more elements into consideration.

The main points here, however, are that we are dealing not with an either-or phenomenon but with a more-or-less. That the more-or-less performances derive from a number of elements, of which the talents attracted into business and the relation of the possessors of such talents to the surrounding society, are the most important factors. Such variations in endowments and responses are a sufficient explanation of variant business success, and an alteration in the ratios among such classes of entrepreneurs as innovators, imitators, sluggards, and sloths through education or better communication is one means of raising the aggregate production of an economy, one means of attaining economic progress.

Development of Variant Types

Even if economic and social conditions may be generally favorable, and at least some entrepreneurs are willing to battle the hazards, not all such promoters of economic change turn out alike. There are, and always have been, certain forces that condition the character of such bearers of the entrepreneurial role.

Sometimes it has been governmental intervention that helped to establish the pattern. In the French printing trade of the sixteenth and seventeenth centuries, for example, the number of opportunities was limited by guild decree, and one qualification for entrepreneurial action seemed often to be a willingness to marry a deceased printer's widow! But happily such monopoly conditions, with such dire consequences, did not widely prevail.[25]

In Canada in the early nineteenth century, success seemed to require a combination of political and business skills, at least in canal construction.[26] In the United States throughout that century, many industrialists had to know how to secure support of congressmen in tariff matters; and, even more recently, the businessman in many Latin American countries is supposed to rest easy only if he has a relative in the top echelons of government.

A different type of entrepreneur may be observed in a number of cases of frontier economy, a type which is rarely found elsewhere. A man may reach a primitive community almost accidentally. Having launched one business enterprise, he becomes involved in the economic development of the town or region, and to facilitate the operations of the first line of business, he enters a second line, then a third, until he winds up with a diversity of enterprises under his control. Such a person was Cadwallader Washburn of Minneapolis. He moved from Maine to Minnesota to seek profits in the virgin forests there, but, having started lumbering, he soon found it advantageous to control the water powers at St. Mary's Falls. Next he saw the opportunity to establish a gristmill and supply the growing population of the region with flour, and before long he needed a bank to help in financing his undertakings. Finally, when the existing railroads threatened to raise rates inordinately — at least as he saw the situation — he started the construction of a railroad of his own.

Certain eastern areas provided examples of the phenomenon in our Colonial period, perhaps the Pepperells of New Hampshire, surely the Browns of Providence Plantations.[27] Men or families operating in this manner appear in a number of communities as economic development moved west: for example, the Pillsburys, also of Minneapolis and the McGees of Kansas City. Sometimes the type reappears in a newly expanding community of the East. Such were the Bordens of Fall River, Massachusetts, whose history was traced by Professor Robert K. Lamb in his doctoral dissertation.[28]

One is even tempted to think of a sort of "intensive" frontier, if one may borrow a term from the economists. What I am suggesting is that the frontier entrepreneur, like other frontier characters examined by students such as Professor Samuel D. Clark of Toronto, exhibited a considerable degree of individuality.[29] They were innovating, at least in a territorial sense; they followed no observable pattern of proceedings; and sometimes they won the disapprobation of their fellow townsmen or their equivalent — as, for example, when some of the Browns hoarded wheat at the start of the Revolution or the Bordens sought to monopolize the economic opportunities of Fall River. So, likewise, one could contend that when railroad men or industrialists began to break contracts with their local communities and commenced to employ practices that, to say the least, were arbitrary and self-centered: for example, instituting blacklists against undesirable workers, such entrepreneurs were isolated from their fellows, enjoying the anomie of frontier conditions. They had moved out of the controlling influence of one set of sanctioning individuals and had not yet come into the circle of influence of a new set. To some extent also, the robber baron variety of entrepreneur resembled the frontier enterpreneur in a propensity to spread his activities into numerous lines and to need no one to tell him right from wrong. Jay Gould was no pale shadow of Cadwallader Washburn.[30]

The evolution of a somewhat complex economy (foreign commerce, sizable coastal towns, opportunity for the sale of foodstuffs in the latter) led to the rise of agricultural entrepreneurs. By the close of the second war with Britain, there was a considerable body of farmers in the eastern states whose chief objective was the preparation of cash crops; they had become commercial farmers. It was in connection with the study of these producers that Professor Danhof presented the classification of entrepreneurs noted above; but at least two or three specific peculiarities of these entrepreneurial figures deserve mention. First is the origin of innovations.[31] Almost wholly new tools and apparatus, new farm animals, and new field crops were presented to the farmers, not originated by them. Occasionally, as in the case of merino sheep, a novelty was brought to the country by a person who, although in government service, chanced also to be interested in agriculture. Sometimes American farmers traveled abroad and brought back knowledge of foreign agricultural practices and the like. Chiefly, improvements in farming in this country came from builders of agricultural equipment, seed or plant importers, and editors of agricultural journals. At most, the farmer entrepreneurs helped in the improvement of the equipment or the testing of new crops after the initial steps had been taken.

Second, these agricultural entrepreneurs were extraordinarily subject to delusions of a speculative character, delusions that can readily be named "agricultural crazes" or "fevers." The "merino mania," the curious efforts in the 1830's to grow the *moris multicaulis* tree (for the feeding of silkworms) as far north as Maine, and the "hen fever" of the 1850's are typical of a number of quasi-hysterias that swept the country in the pre-Civil War decades.[32] While the movements did not lack beneficial results to American agriculture (since not only merino sheep but Berkshire hogs, broom corn, and various varieties of wheat reached the country's farms in this manner), they are significant in the present connection for two reasons: they indicate the breadth and intensity with which the cultural theme of getting ahead and seizing the main chance had come to dominate the country; and they point to the importance of information, or its lack, in affecting the decisions of entrepreneurs. There were "crazes" in American agriculture after 1860 — the Belgian hare, the silver fox, various types of wheat — but the epidemics were less prolonged and less severe, and the difference may be attributed to the influence of the national Department of Agriculture, its agencies, and the corresponding state units.

In the third place, agricultural entrepreneurship is noteworthy in that interunit cooperation instead of interunit rivalry tended to prevail. Manufacturing industry, at least through the nineteenth century, put much store by its patents and by its secret processes; but, typically, agriculture shared its successes. A farmer who had secured good crops by use of a certain rotation did not hesitate to spread the good word at the county fair or, if he were literarily inclined, through his favorite agricultural periodical; and so also with the use of a new seed, and so forth. Perhaps the bent toward secrecy on the industrial side was a nonrational residue from the earlier form of manufacturing organization, the handicraft system with its guilds, imported with the earlier skilled factory workers, if not with the hand workers who came over in our Colonial days, but the bent may have had a perfectly rational base. In most manufacturing lines, there was an advantage to the individual enterprise if it could protect a differential in costs deriving from an innovation, whether the innovation was really new or was one borrowed from another economy, which could be preserved through secrecy. In agricultural enterprise there was no such advantage. The individual farmer could secure a differential cost position through innovational activity, but in most agricultural situations no local group of producers would turn out enough of any crop to affect the price in the market. Hence, the advantage in costs secured by one farmer could be shared freely with his neighbors without loss to himself. In any case, the difference in entrepreneurial objectives between farm and industrial units is worth noting.

Some of the foregoing features seem to have characterized European agriculture in the nineteenth century, although from the entrepreneurship point of view European agriculture has been studied less than American. To be sure, the agricultural holding in Europe has always been closely involved with the family system of the several countries, while, with the wider dominance of tradition, there has been less room for fevers. Yet on the whole conditions seem to have been similar: improved agricultural implements have come from the machine-building industry; there have been some "crazes"; and the agricultural producers have been willing to share experiences with their "competitors."

If anything, this similarity has tended to diminish over recent decades. American "commercial" farming has tended to become ever more commercial, really industrial in character. There have been rather numerous cases of the use of the corporate form in agricultural production. Capital in the form of agricultural equipment, irrigation works, and fertilizers has been ever more heavily utilized. Not long after the arrival of "steam on the farm," organized labor made its appearance there. And information in the form of market reports and the trends of legislation began to flow more regularly and more abundantly to the farm. The larger agricultural units (for example, wheat farms run by graduates of agricultural colleges), getting market and other information at least daily by radio, and equipped to handle their operations with scarcely any "hired hands," are not essentially different in form from the "push-button" factory of manufacturing industry. Progressive entrepreneurship can be found in either area.

Evolution of Industrial Entrepreneurship

The examination of the advent of industrial entrepreneurship in communities that had previously been agricultural or commercial or a mixture of these two presents considerable difficulties. The process has been going on for so many centuries in so many circumstances that generalizations must be rather limited in character. Thanks to the research work of Dr. Redlich, it has now become clear that European nobility, far from being an indolent group everywhere and always, saw many of its members active in introducing both mining and manufacturing industry into their territories. It is possible that this was the manner in which a development policy of a Maria Theresa or a Frederick the Great became implemented, at least among a portion of their subjects. The monarch would express the thought that fulling mills or added nail production would be good for his country; nobles desiring to curry favor with their sovereign would hear such opinions expressed; and at least some of them might have the resources and the enterprise to erect the mill or the nailery in the hope of a smile or some more substantial favor from their king or queen.[33]

Another source of entrepreneurial talent or direction in industry was surely the merchant groups in a number of countries. It was this group in England that reached back, as it were, from their selling offices to gain some control of the manufacturing process through the putting-out system. Nearly everywhere it seems to have been the merchants who took active parts in the development and operation of railways, especially as investors and as members of boards of directors; and frequently in England and the United States it was the mercantile persuasion that put its capital into factories and gave its talents to their direction.

The commercial influence may perhaps be held responsible

114

for a number of specific developments. For instance, the peculiar form of organization in the New England cotton-textile industry seems to have a strong mercantile flavor. The real control of the factories was in the typical case not exerted at the mill itself but in the office of the "treasurer" in Boston. The treasurer did have charge of the financial affairs of the company, sometimes of several mills, but he also was responsible for the purchase of raw materials and the sale of the products, obviously mercantile operations.

Dr. Lee Benson has contended that the practice of the American railroads of charging what the traffic would bear, of giving rebates, et cetera, derived from the fact that merchants of the seaboard were so important in the development of the railways of that area.[34] And the railroad practices were, in part, imitated in the public-utility industries.

One might also suggest that the banking entrepreneurs of the eastern cities, and subsequently their fellow bankers of the western cities, were strongly influenced in their ideas of sound banking practice by the merchants who often collaborated in the founding of such institutions and often dominated on their "discount committees" and boards of directors. Commercial banks were assuredly commercial, at any rate in the eastern cities; and once institutions of this character were given public sanction, they could be utilized for the needs of farmers and small manufacturers only at risk to their solvency in "bad times." "Intermediate credit" and federal land banks came only in the twentieth century.

There is also evidence pointing to the early dominance of the mercantile group in all forms of business, even after industrialization had made considerable progress, and of the continuance of a mental attitude, subsequently still, in the curious history of cost accounting. Bookkeeping on commercial transactions by double entry dates as far back as the fifteenth century, perhaps the fourteenth; a description of it was printed in 1494, and the first exposition of the mystery in English came before the end of the sixteenth century. Some industrial development was already under way in England. There was a further, rather notable expansion — usually spoken of as the Industrial Revolution — in the eighteenth century; but there was no book published in England that gave a conversion of double-entry bookkeeping for industrial cost purposes until the end of the nineteenth century! Actually, there appears to have been some employment of cost accounting in English (as well as in American) manufacturing industry before that time, and it is also noteworthy that the United States took the lead in the development of thought in the field of cost accounting. The circumstance is, indeed, peculiar that commercial accounting should have dominated the business world for so long a period after manufacturing, mining, and various forms of transportation had grown important in economic output.

As manufactures spread, a new element entered entrepreneurship, when men with technical skills set up shops — enterprises that often grew into sizable factories. These men were usually neither engineers nor academically trained. They possessed useful instincts or had acquired a practical skill. Boulton knew how to work iron; much later Michael J. Owens had a way of handling molten glass, while Samuel Slater, the Scholfields, and numerous other mechanics had learned the tricks of the new textile machinery in England, and were minded to set up their own mills in America. A large majority of the individual small establishments launched in England, on the Continent, and in the United States during the early phases of industrialization were quite surely the projects of mechanic entrepreneurs.[35]

Not infrequently, however, the mechanic was aided by association with a businessman. Partnerships (real, although not always following the legal form) between an inventor and a person familiar with manufacturing and especially with commercial matters were often arranged and often successful. Such was the collaboration of Boulton and Watt; likewise that between Lowell and Moody, in the American cotton manufacture; and there have been many others in British and American industry. Inventors have been rather notoriously poor businessmen, especially in the marketing aspects of their operations. A merchant or someone with commercial abilities often could complement the imaginative work of an inventor.[36]

Another organizational form by which the earlier merchants, at least in the United States, could influence the course of industrialization, indirectly if not directly, was that which Professor Cochran has called "general entrepreneurship." With funds assembled by successful mercantile ventures, individuals such as Nathan Appleton or John Murray Forbes made investments in cotton manufacture or the railroad world. But they had a controlling interest in more than one enterprise in the field of their selection. The operating decisions, many of which were by no means unimportant, were left to the heads of the mills or railroads, but the "general entrepreneur" kept in his own hands what might be called the strategic decisions, especially those involving important commitments of capital or the distribution of dividends: whether to expand production for the oncoming season, whether to purchase a connecting railroad line, and so forth.[37]

Professor Cochran seemed disposed to think of the general entrepreneur as shortly yielding place to the investment banker. It appears, in fact, as though this type of entrepreneur has returned. For a while men in business tended to remain within single industries — W. H. Vanderbilt in railroads, Carnegie in steel — although, even in that generation of men there were exceptions, such as the senior Rockefeller, who bought iron mountains in Minnesota. More recently, however, both here and abroad, the activities of Howard Hughes, John Hay Whitney, the notorious match king Krueger, and others offer the implication that the general entrepreneur may be a recurring type.

Still another type of entrepreneurial actor has been the engineer.[38] It appears that for a number of decades men with engineering training were by no means convinced that they ought to turn their hands to the mere making of money; they were professional men like doctors or clergy. This attitude, however, did not prevent some engineers like Whistler's father, for example, from entering the business of managing railroads, and apparently a goodly number broke away in the last years of the nineteenth century and in the twentieth. A typical case was that of Mr. William E. Nickerson, a graduate of the Massachusetts Institute of Technology, who took the idea of a safety razor when it was hardly more than an image in the mind of King C. Gillette and converted the dream into a reality. He thought through and worked through the practical problems of manufacturing a satisfying, foolproof article for world-wide consumption.[39]

More recently engineers have seemingly become still more common in the ranks of top management in all sorts of enterprises, but chiefly in manufacturing, transportation, and public utilities. Possibly the modern bias toward industrial research and toward an increase in output has derived in part from the presence in high places of men with such training. Surely, Thorstein Veblen would have expected such a development.[40]

Migration of Entrepreneurship

The geographical movement of entrepreneurship raises a host of interesting problems on which relatively few data are as yet available. The earliest form of movement was undoubtedly that of commercial entrepreneurship out of Italy or Flanders to various points of the Mediterranean basin, to towns along the Baltic, even to the underdeveloped area of England. Some forms of financial entrepreneurship tended to follow. And at a later date there was a somewhat similar movement out of Europe to India, America, and points around the newly-opened world. While such developments meant much economically, it is uncertain whether they meant much entrepreneurially. There were undoubtedly some converts to entrepreneurial life among the peoples into whose countries the merchants moved — Germans, Swedes, Englishmen, Indians — but neither forms of organization nor manners of doing business seem to have been much affected. Presumably, the first type of business literature can be credited to the expansion of commerce, the mercantile manual such as Pegelotti's of the fourteenth century, and numerous others after printing was invented. And there were indirect effects — for example, the extension of the silk and wool manufactures in Italy, tin mining in Wales — with some consequences upon entrepreneurial techniques. It is just impossible yet to generalize.

More important, at least to us in America, was the transfer of skills and procedures across the Atlantic in our early days, but thus far it is not clear just how and by what notable steps the American entrepreneur became significantly different from the English, or different from what the English entrepreneur had become in the decades since we attained our economic (perhaps our entrepreneurial) independence. There had also been some transfers of entre-

119

preneurial skills to French, Spanish, and other colonies, but less than from England to North America.[41]

The United States, Canada, Brazil, and other parts of the New World benefited in the nineteenth and twentieth centuries from other transfers such as the migration of European talents, or what Professor Oscar Handlin might label "ethnic" factors in entrepreneurial change.[42] Here one runs into uncertainties when attempting to suggest the results of such movements. It does seem probable that the German immigrants to the United States, who brought with them the production of scientific instruments, optical glass, and the like, injected an appreciation of exactitude into American manufacturing methods which had previously been lacking. Perhaps the machine-tool and the automobile industries benefited greatly. I have sometimes thought that the developments in the Passaic wool manufacture were symbolic of the merger of German and American procedures and ideas. There were two firms set up there by German manufacturers, Forstmann & Huffmann and the Botany Worsted. They desired to produce fine worsted cloths especially for women's wear. In Europe such goods were turned out with much hand labor, but labor was expensive in America, so German persistency, German fondness for high-grade, nicely-made goods, and American facility with machine tools yielded a combination factory where goods as fine as the handmade were manufactured by predominantly machine methods.

The influence of the German immigrants — manufacturers and workers — remains largely conjectural, however, and we can speculate with even fewer facts with regard to the contributions of the Dutch and the Italians, the Jews and the Greeks.

No less uncertain have been the experiences of other countries of the Western Hemisphere. If the Germans imparted a notion of accuracy to United States manufactures, did they make the same contribution to the Brazilian? Or was industry there not sufficiently advanced? And did the Italian immigrants into Brazil remain Italian, or did they become Brazilians in entrepreneurial characteristics?

It is alleged that when one goes to Morocco or Iran or even France, one does business on terms imposed by the local businessmen; in Iran, for example, only after several calls and several cups of coffee. How long, then, can an American firm proceed in a pattern devised by American entrepreneurship, after it has tried to settle into French or Scandinavian or Venezuelan business life? Is entrepreneurship transferable between nations? If so, to what extent and under what conditions?

The transfer of entrepreneurship from West to East has, oddly enough, attracted more attention than that of movements within the West itself. We are beginning to know something of what was involved in the industrialization of Japan[43] and what has been happening in India. The latter case is perhaps the clearer and neater. In brief, the course seems to have been as follows: management skill was scarce; capital came almost wholly from England; Englishmen of executive ability were placed in charge of "management agencies," which by stock ownership controlled several manufacturing or marketing enterprises; native Indians began before separation to imitate the British, especially the Parsis in Bombay; and now a large part of Indian business is operated by management agencies staffed and owned by Indians.[44]

Stages of Entrepreneurship

It is a common practice among economists, and not uncommon among historians, to treat the entrepreneur or the businessman as if he were always the same sort of person reacting to changed conditions always in the same manner, and there are a few not unimportant instances where change has been slow indeed, such as the foreign merchant over the centuries or all proprietors of small shops in any country. Note has already been made of differences among entrepreneurial actors of various countries operating at given periods. I have given implications also of changes in the character of performance through time. At least in a country such as the United States, these changes have really been important for appraising the character of the entrepreneurial system. We know that science and medicine, even teaching, have improved over the decades and centuries. Has entrepreneurship?

It is obvious that divergencies in character among entrepreneurial figures in so large a country and over so many different industries, including those of immigrants whose length of residence in the United States varies tremendously, must be considerable even over a brief period. However, I believe that typical characters can be observed in the relevant data, rough "averages" of a sort, if not "ideal types." [45] Indeed, I venture to offer two sets of composite characterizations.

In the first series of figures, particular emphasis is placed upon the quantity and quality of information on the basis of which entrepreneurs of successive time-periods made their decisions, decisions on whether to go into business, what to buy, sell, or produce, how to do it; and second, upon the complexity of the web of institutions and personalities with relation to which they had to move. Accordingly, three types or grades of entrepreneurial characters can be distinguished, which may be labeled rule-of-thumb, informed, and sophisticated, or, in more elegant terms: empirical, rational, and cognitive.[46]

Once thus stated, the trichotomy will be hardly more than

common sense to a business or economic historian. A couple of illustrations will demonstrate the very ordinary character of the concept. At one stage the merchant had to operate on price data supplied him by some more or less reliable correspondent, data which might be anywhere from a week to three or four months old. At a later period he had "prices-currents" to rely upon, and, if he took the trouble, a series of prices of related commodities and of his primary interests extending back in the files of the *New York Shipping List* or equivalent local periodical. Still later he could secure for many goods prices transmitted by telegraph, perhaps presented in the form of an index with secular trend and seasonal variation eliminated. Again, in the matter of techniques: at one time it was the entrepreneur's own bent as a tinkerer, or the skill of the local blacksmith, that both promoted and limited the design of apparatus. Then came the period when foreign machinery tried out abroad was imported, sometimes in the minds of immigrating workmen, or later when apparatus was described in trade periodicals and purveyed by specializing machine-builders. More recently the layout of the producing unit with a preconceived rate of output will first be envisioned, and then machinery, assembly lines, and so on, designed to suit the planned production.

I have also proposed a variant scheme of "stages."[47] Here I tried to add elements that I had not previously utilized as bases for differentiation: namely, the horizon which the entrepreneur seems to have had in his mind, and the location of the effective sanctioning bodies. (To be sure, as the economy expands in complexity and in territory, the "fit" of any single term as descriptive of the whole becomes steadily poorer, as I have just suggested. All the thirteen states were nearer alike economically in 1790 than Pennsylvania is akin to Nevada at the present time. Also, there has come an increasing diversity in the size of business enterprises.)

At all events, I now suggest that we think of entrepreneurs at successive periods as being predominantly community-focused, industry-focused, and nation-focused. As already intimated, the sources of information can be readily cast into categories consonant with this threefold breakdown. For the importing and exporting merchant as well as for the small manufacturer, the bulk of information came from the community in which he carried on his business, if, against the news that he received from his foreign correspondents, we take account of the gossip that he picked up from other merchants,[48] the data that he needed to plan the import side of his business, and the information on ups and downs of trade, methods for collecting foreign debts, and the like, all of which he needed to conduct his enterprise. In later decades information tended to become channeled into industry streams, both technical books and, particularly, the technical, commercial, and personal news carried in the *American Railroad Journal,* the *Iron Age,* and similar trade journals. Professor W. Rupert Maclaurin has sought to establish that the success of specific groups of entrepreneurs has been no little affected by the circumstance that they were operating in an industry which chanced to be open-ended or chanced to be closed. He has in mind that certain industries happened to receive the names of processes (for example, "chemical" or "electrical") whereas others happened to become labeled as "cotton textile" or "coal mining." The first type has tended to expand into a greater variety of product lines and to invest more heavily in technological research. They have manifested stronger and more continued growth potentials.[49] It is obvious that recent decades have brought increasing interest in the national market and a corresponding advance in the number and importance of such periodicals as *Business Week, Fortune, Tide,* and the like, while counseling organizations, schools of business, and the information services of the federal government aim predominantly toward purveying data of national import. While most enterprises, to be sure, continue to produce for and, especially, to sell to a local or at best regional market, still, to a greater extent than ever before, information about national conditions is available to the local operators, styles are national and no longer local, and a national credit structure ties together all parts of the country.

When I suggested the new trilogy, however, I had in mind more than the stream of information. I was thinking also of the changing locus of effective sanctions. In the early days of handicraftsman, general storekeeper, or substantial town merchant, the people that counted for him, in commendation or criticism, were undoubtedly his neighbors, especially perhaps the local minister, school teacher, lawyer, and those of his own vocation who had retired from business life before him. Robert Keayne wrote his long will in an effort to justify his commercial career to his neighbors in Boston. When Nicholas Brown thought to forestall on flour at the commencement of the Revolutionary War, he hid his stock over the state line in Massachusetts. Eli Whitney seems to have been nearly as pleased at the effects of his manufacturing operations upon New Haven as the consequences of his invention upon the whole South.

Subsequently, it seems to me, there was a period when the man's enterprise and the industry of which it was a part bulked largest in his thoughts. The head of a mill or mine, even if it was a small establishment, was more withdrawn from his neighbors than the local handicraftsman or merchant, and as manufacturing enterprises grew larger and sought new sources of water power, their proprietors became yet more isolated from their kind. These entrepreneurs became conscious of themselves not merely as businessmen but as railroad men, cotton manufacturers, or coal-mine operators. In part this consciousness was promoted by the exigencies of the pertinent techniques and of the particularized marketing operations, but also soon by the specialized trade periodicals that conveyed predominantly industry, not national news. Accordingly, there tended to be "in" and "out" groups. A person might excuse himself for an action as the head of a manufacturing enterprise which he would not think of taking as a citizen of his community: for example, allow workmen in a men's hat factory to breathe the air laden with rabbit's fur, even though he realized that they would succumb to tuberculosis within a few years. And the head of a railroad or a bank would look to other railroad men or bankers for approbation, not to businessmen in general, let alone other civilians. From such circumstances arose blacklist practices of early manufacturers, the robber-baron features of railroading, even the high-handed financial practices of the insurance companies as late as 1905. For some decades, partly because of the wide public approval of wealth-getting and of wealthy individuals, of which mention has been made above, there was no adversely critical censor group. Critics there were, of course, such as Henry Demarest Lloyd or Henry George, but they failed to develop a sufficiently large following, especially among the elite groups of the country.

Already in the later decades of the nineteenth century, agencies of the national government from Congress to the Bureau of Corporations were taking interest in domestic business affairs to a degree hitherto unknown (the possible regulation of railroads, the possible curbing of monopoly, the possible reduction in producers' freedom to market any sort of food and drug), because internal commerce had become national; state lines had become unimportant in that regard, and state governments were powerless to promote adequately the general good. Also, with the muckrakers had sprung up a group of public censors, more numerous and more widely heralded than ever before; and, for the most part, these writers and later-day columnists spoke for the nation, not for the city in which particular newspapers chanced to appear or certain evils chanced to be observed. Journalism had become nationalized. Correspondingly, businessmen came more and more to judge their fellows by something more than industry standards. Tom Girdler, Colonel Sewell Avery, and Mr. Frederick C. Crawford of the Thompson Products Company were appraised on some such abstract basis as what was good for business in general. And leaders in business might look, perhaps hope, for recognition from national institutions: the National Association of Manufacturers, the United States Chamber of Commerce, the Committee for Economic Development, the advisory board to the Secretary of Commerce, even a place on the Board of Governors of the Federal Reserve System or a Cabinet post. With many enterprises aiming at a national market and indulging in national advertising, with their executive talent drawn from all quarters of the country, surely the larger concerns were nation-oriented; and these larger companies set the tone for many enterprises of lesser size.

A reflection of the foregoing changes may, I think, be seen in the conclusions drawn by Professor Sigmund Diamond in his *Reputation of the American Businessman* (1955) — a book of value in various connections.[50] He found the successful business leader of the early nineteenth century appraised at his death in terms of such homely virtues as hard work, thrift, and ambition: in other words, the virtues appropriate to the community. On the other hand, he was drawn to see corresponding business leaders a century later appraised in terms of the economic system; in other words, in terms of the whole nation. To be sure, more than this single shift in spatial basis is involved, and Diamond does not find men extolled or condemned in terms of specific industries. (Perhaps the latter connection would have appeared if the author had handled more cases.) At all events, I venture to see confirmation of my own hypothesis in a study pursued with quite a different objective.

Doubtless a sequence of stages could be worked out for England, France, or Germany when we know more of the entrepreneurial histories of these countries. For the moment, however, it is sufficient to realize that entrepreneurs in probably every area have changed in character over decades or over centuries. It may be convenient for historians to have such shorthand designations as I have tried to provide for the handling of American data; but it is a matter of convenience only. The important element is a realization of a continued and continuing change over time. To be sure, it is also possible to use concepts such as those described above for purposes of international comparison; for example, one might place certain countries in the "rule-of-thumb" or the "community-focused" category, others in the "sophisticated" or "nation-focused." It is possible, however, that inaccuracies would develop in international comparisons since one country's rule-of-thumb entrepreneurship might be much more primitive than another's; and so for other stages. Classifications can be put under too much pressure.

Nonetheless, an analysis of the evolution of any economically mature nation will quite surely reveal that entrepreneurship has not stood still. In ways not related to the supply of the economist's "productive factors," at least in any close manner, but in ways that have relevance for expanding national income and for economic development, entrepreneurship has advanced, even as medicine or mathematics. The creative force of human intelligence has not been screened off from the area of business.

The Other Side of the Coin

No one whose memory runs back two or three decades will labor under a belief that business was ever perfect. Of course, neither is the law or medicine, even the ministry; but business has had a disproportionate share of actors who, even by the standards of their times and discounting the occasions when they were merely outwitting one another, must be set down as performing society a disservice, if not behaving as outright rascals. The question here, however, is how and in what degree the entrepreneurial system as such promoted or contributed to this condition, perhaps after an indeterminate discount for the average weaknesses of human nature, in the face of the institution of private property. After all, there have always been robberies elsewhere in Western societies other than those that took place in business.

The combination of a monetary basis for appraising success, the differential operating advantage to the individual entrepreneur in having net profits larger than those of his competitors (enabling him to shade his prices, inaugurate a special service to customers, et cetera), and the prestige deriving from higher than average profits both as regards plant expansion and as gained through personal expenditure weighs heavily upon the individual proprietor or the members of a partnership, perhaps a bit less so in the latter case, as suggested elsewhere.[51] As businesses increase in size, these forces appear to become less vigorous, especially if the executive office becomes, in fact, multiple and if it turns professional. When the concern grows large enough, quite surely all ordinary forms of dishonesty just do not pay. There is still the occasional Krueger or Coster, and there are searches, at least by ambitious members of company teams, for special advantages with governments of local or larger scope; but it appears to be the general opinion of people who have been close to business over recent decades that morals within business have been steadily rising. This could be due in part to institutions within business itself; for example, the public accountants who, employed by the corporations themselves or egged on sometimes by the stock exchange or the investment bankers, inspect the books of enterprises and actually bring pressure — direct pressure on behalf of financial improvements, but indirect pressure in favor of other reforms. We have no reliable data, however, on what Professor Edwin H. Sutherland has labeled "white-collar crime," no data on any variety of entrepreneurial sins, especially no time-series, and one can merely report impressions.

Another charge of considerable age pertains to the supposed influence of business life upon the nonmoral elements in the businessman's character. He was charged with being ignorant of all but his business, yet domineering and self-satisfied, a man ranked low on the basis of "culture." Perhaps through the decades businessmen have typically been more Philistine, more interested in their own narrow path of life than some other groups in their contemporary societies; but no more interested than musicians in theirs, or artists in theirs. We have no objective standards and no objective data. All that appears reasonably certain is that the entrepreneurial mode of economic organization has not made businessmen more Philistine. Perhaps, even by the literati's standards over recent decades, it has given the typical businessman indirect encouragement to become less so. Not much more can be, or perhaps needs to be, said.

The entrepreneurial system may be subject to hostile criticism on account of its deprivation of freedom, although whether it is more restricting than other modes of economic organization may probably be doubtful. I have in mind two features of modern business life, especially in the United States. One is the effort of corporations to check the movement of executives from their ranks. They do not want to lose a good comptroller or a good vice-president in charge of sales; indeed, any officers in whom they have invested time and money for their training. So pension plans, stock-purchase schemes, and the like, in part recently promoted by high personal income taxes, are evolved in the effort to buy loyalty, at least to make certain that loyalty will not lack proper reward. With the diminution of movement, there may be some economic loss in that men do not move to positions where they might make larger contributions to the national dividend; and with this same diminution of movement, there may be some personal frustrations, even despite the carrots of future enjoyment held out by the various retirement rewards.

Another sort of restriction derives from the sanctions of an entrepreneurial system that is, as it were, "laced" with zeal of one sort or another. Apparently the Latin Americans, to some extent the French and English — but probably not the Germans — have escaped the increased tempo and rising pressures of American business life. There was a time, even in this country, when business pace was leisurely. My notion of the Colonial merchant of Boston, Philadelphia, or Charleston is that he walked down to his countinghouse about ten in the forenoon, spent a couple of hours gossiping with friends, repaired home for a midday dinner and nap, and, unless he had a ship in port, did not bother to return to his shop. Also a typical merchant would retire from trading as he reached forty or thereabouts and devote himself to good works and his family, as long as his doctors could keep him alive (which, of course, was not too long, on the average). I fancy that some fragments of this mode of life persisted down perhaps until the 1880's, even on the east coast, and perhaps a little longer in some parts of the west. At all events, it seems that over the past seventy-five years businessmen have been prisoners of their own ideologies: they ought to work hard; they ought to keep busy as long as they physically could; and so on. Perhaps businessmen have gained real satisfaction in doing what gave them a sense of accomplishment, if only by acting as their peers expected them to act; but there may have been some frustration, and there may have been some economic loss. The compulsory retirement plans instituted by the larger corporations, and the programs in the same type of enterprise to conserve the health of their executives, seem to argue that American businessmen carried "the strenuous life" to excess, from their own, their companies', and the economy's points of view.

Frustrations, even wide-flung grief, seem an inevitable feature of interenterprise relations in an entrepreneurial economy. Dr. Redlich has written of this feature as the "daemonic" quality in entrepreneurship: commercial farmers in one region ruining commercial farmers in another, one corner druggist driving his competitor across the street into bankruptcy, the entrepreneurs in the trucking business performing so effectively as to occasion distress among entrepreneurs of the railroad industry, and so on throughout the length and breadth of the economy. As I have suggested elsewhere,[52] the entrepreneurial system operates to minimize the economic loss; but there are undoubtedly heartaches and worse, as the lesson of personal failure is driven home. Indeed, this phenomenon has been so widespread and long-continued, that we all speak of cutthroat competition as if we took life as lightly as Benevenuto Cellini of a fine spring morning.

Finally, we should perhaps note the serious problem of bureaucratic rigidities in business. It is quite possible that entrepreneurs may be held partly accountable for the evolution of large business units; the pursuit of differential advantage led them progressively into operations of increasing scope. And in such organizations the benumbing effect of size can be seen. Men lose their initiative and drive because sooner or later most of them see the dimming of prospects of substantial advancement, although, of course, others find comfort in being taken care of throughout their lives, as some men do in the army. Men become motivated by rivalries and politics within the organization rather than zeal for effective performance in service of the whole enterprise, while as a result of advancement by seniority, a logical development of bureaucratic life, men reach the high points in their careers at ages when they have already begun to lose some of their intellectual keenness and surely have lost much of their zest for reform, with all the headaches that reforms inevitably bring. Large corporations are alive to this problem; their stock-purchase plans for executives, their health programs, and the like constitute one means of combating the evils. Outside of individual companies, the policy of the American government against bigness in our enterprises operates to limit the difficulties, although it was not formulated with that result in mind. Entrepreneurial zest thrives best in small business units.

Conclusion

Economics has always claimed to be a social science. A brand of economics that paid adequate attention to entrepreneurship would be such a science par excellence. The entrepreneur's relations to his organization constitute one level of social phenomena; the interconnections of various entrepreneurial units in a stream of activities involve another level; and here in the "social conditioning of entrepreneurship" we have glimpses of an over-all, interpenetrating relationship. For those who like similes, one might think of a river vessel. Groups of people are busy in the several salons and cabins; the passengers and the crew form a unit of sorts; while the natural elements — water, wind, and sun — exert their respective influences upon all.

Obviously, this social conditioning involves a variety of factors, from education to economic resources, and from governmental administration to ethnic coherences. We are concerned with the impact of cultural forces upon the formation and performance of social groups out of which flow the goods and services desired by society. Our procedures and range of considerations would not be different if we were trying to account for the evolution of our educational system with its state universities and its Fulbright fellowships, its honorary degrees and its parochial schools.

However, it is only by giving attention to such a broad assemblage of factors that one can hope to give answers to such questions of prime importance for a study of economic development as: how did the system of production get into its present form? What makes it operate in the way that it does? Is the performance getting better or worse? What is likely to happen in the future? Present-day economics is not geared by its traditions, its methods, or its objectives to deal with such questions. In a Western world devoted dominantly to private enterprise, only a type of economics with a time dimension in which entrepreneurial activity is the central thread can hope to render enlightening answers.

PART TWO·
ENTREPRENEURIAL REALITIES

INTRODUCTION

THE EXPLORATION of a new field in the social sciences, at least of a field with a historical dimension, proceeds by alternate steps of empirical inquiry and tentative generalization. Thus it has been with entrepreneurial history. Prior to the drafting of *Change and the Entrepreneur*, there had been a sizable amount of empirical research, much of it in Germany, some in the United States, some elsewhere. Very little of it, other than that of Sombart and Weber, utilized hypotheses or employed frameworks appropriate to our study.[1] Generally, it took the form of company histories, businessmen's biographies, and industrial or local histories with many personal data.

This body of information was subject to interpretation by the first endeavors at generalization, those of the German writers, and particularly that of Schumpeter, who had built a theory of economic development on the nature of entrepreneurship as he conceived the latter. The work of Barnard and Parsons in sociology was also available and useful, and to this mass it was possible to add comments offered by speakers at meetings of the Research Center in Entrepreneurial History at Harvard, including some by Mr. Barnard himself. Data from these several sources formed the basis for the first tentative findings in *Change and the Entrepreneur*. This volume, issued in a form that manifests its preliminary nature, was published in 1949.

In the meantime, *Explorations in Entrepreneurial History* had been launched, through the initiative of two young men connected with the Center, Hugh G. J. Aitken and R. Richard Wohl. The periodical was intended as an organ of discussion for the relatively small group of scholars, some in Cambridge and some elsewhere, who had displayed interest in the subject. Before long, however, it came to publish reports of research findings, not merely theoretical speculations derived from previously available data. In the years since 1949 there has been a host of other publications more or less concerned with our themes: from Charles Wilson's study of Unilever to Miss Mabel Newcomer's statistical data upon the social and educational backgrounds of American business leaders, and from Gordon's *Business Leadership in the Large Corporation* to the articles in the new *Business History Review*. Not least important have been the volumes sponsored by the Center and the written or verbal communications of individuals who have been connected with that institution: Redlich, Landes, Sawyer, Easterbrook, Rosovsky, the young men mentioned above and the senior members, past and present. Now appears a proper and convenient time once more to survey the field, and I have ventured above to give what seems to me the theoretical structure of the subject.

In contrast with the situation in 1949, it is now also possible to present concrete data upon entrepreneurial history, the analysis of actual occurrences, selected to illustrate various phases of the whole experience. To be sure, the material must be condensed into vignettes, but it is hoped that the portrayals remain accurate ones. While I have drawn much of the data for the ensuing vignettes from books or periodical articles, many of them written by persons connected with the Center, I have frequently put my own construction upon events or conditions elaborated by these authors, seeking to relate their findings to the entrepreneurial theory presented here. Much of the material comes out of *Explorations*. There are four or five divisions of the descriptive essays: the relations of entrepreneurship to social classes, relations to primitive economic conditions, to technological change, to the different forms of business organization, and to government.

In the actual exploration of any scientific area, endeavors to discover and state uniformities observed in the concrete data — generalizations of greater or less magnitude, typical situations, or noteworthy representative personalities — become appropriate and useful for further exploration. Such is the major purpose of these vignettes.

Section 1 ·

ENTREPRENEURSHIP AND
THE SOCIAL ORDER

VIGNETTE 1: THE ARISTOCRATIC ENTREPRENEUR

Prefatory note: The development of the research activities summarized in the ensuing essay is almost wholly a contribution of Dr. Redlich, who inspired and supplied an introductory statement to an issue of *Explorations*[2] devoted solely to this theme. In addition to encouraging others to put together their thoughts or to launch new inquiries in the area, he has made investigations himself, and prepared précis of his findings. Others had done work earlier on portions of the field, but in no systematic fashion and without the concepts stemming from an appreciation of entrepreneurship. A particularly useful study, despite such limitations, is that of Dr. Charles A. Foster, entitled "Honoring Commerce and Industry in Eighteenth-Century France," which was presented as a doctoral dissertation in history at Harvard in 1950.[3]

The image of the businessman prevalent in the United States is so strictly that of a man of middle-class origins, if indeed he did not rise in the Alger tradition from "poor but honest parents," that there is a danger of entrepreneurship being viewed in such terms. It is useful, therefore, to inquire whether entrepreneurs have always been, or really need to be, of that stamp. European economic development in the early modern period has been couched so largely in terms of burghers, guilds, and town activities that one is tempted to ask whether other elements should not be introduced, especially with respect to mining, agriculture, the iron industry, and the like, which evolved outside the towns. A contribution to better understanding in both fields derives from an appreciation of the aristocratic entrepreneur.

As the student of entrepreneurial history examines data from the late medieval period onward relative to super-burgher cases of entrepreneurial action, he finds in fact that he must put bounds to his observations in order to secure sufficient focus. He must set aside consideration of kingly entrepreneurs — such heads of states as Gustavus Vasa, Peter the Great, or even Duke Julius of Braunschweig.[4] Again, it is unnecessary here to consider the ups and downs of noble fortunes. Professor Lane mentions such movements in fourteenth- and fifteenth-century Venetian life (see his *Andrea Barbarigo*) and Dr. Foster speaks of the same phenomenon in connection with seventeenth- and eighteenth-century French nobility. Nor need one take notice of the important phenomenon of the ennobling of successful entrepreneurs of the bourgeois class. Finally, we may set aside those noblemen who functioned as military enterprisers — organizers, equippers, and managers of aggregations of armed men that could be hired for the making of war.

That entrepreneurs of noble lineage were important to economic development cannot be doubted when the relevant data begin to be rounded up; moreover, the lines of activity in which they were engaged from about the fourteenth to the eighteenth centuries are surprisingly diverse. Many nobles, of course, lived on country estates, but they sometimes also had town properties. In any case, they did not confine their activities to the exploitation of natural resources that chanced to be in their possession. Quite a few appear to have taken active roles in wholesale commerce, often foreign trade. Others carried on manufacturing in the towns, although perhaps less often than in the country.

Dr. Foster notes that as early as the tenth century four noble families seem to have had a monopoly of glass-making in Brittany. Those with landed properties advantageously situated for water shipment often turned their attention to commercial agriculture. For example, Dr. Redlich mentions the evolution of the *Gutswirtschaft* in eastern Germany which shipped grain to the growing towns of western Europe. Professor H. J. Habakkuk writes of the "improving" noble landowners of England in the seventeenth and eighteenth centuries when the towns provided a nicely expanding market. Those with landed properties were also likely to take up mining if their lands contained minerals or coal underground. The counts of Mansfeld, for instance, had almost a monopoly of the mining and smelting of copper in Germany in the sixteenth century, and Dr. Hermann Kellenbenz speaks of the notable Holstein entrepreneur, Henrich Rantzau, who owned no less than thirty-nine mills, establishments that produced lumber, paper, flour, oil, and powder, and manufactured articles from iron, copper, and brass. In Spain, Portugal, Sweden, Germany, Poland, and Italy there were others.[5]

It will be recognized as not unnatural that the degree of activity, and success, among the nobility of a given country differed markedly. Of course, there was at any one time in such a country as France a very considerable diversity in the economic positions of individuals who could claim noble status. There were nobles with extensive lands and with monies available to loan, and there were nobles who, perhaps with a sword around their waists, walked sadly behind the plough on their small plots of land. Undoubtedly, also, there was something of the diversity of initiative that Professor Danhof thinks to see among the American commercial farmers of the early nineteenth century.

On second thoughts, if not on first, it seems quite logical and natural that the nobility should engage in actions of the foregoing types, particularly under monarchs who were interested in strengthening economically their kingdoms or dukedoms or empires. "Sanctions" of effect were chiefly those exerted by such a monarch, and they were perhaps more effective with the nobility than with the burghers of the towns. If the king of Sweden suggested that it would be a good thing for the country to have more powder mills, what would be more natural than for some nobles to seek royal favor by attempting to set up powder mills? Or as I suggested above, if Maria Theresa chanced to mouth the hope for more cotton-cloth production within her empire, would not some nobles be likely to seek to satisfy the Empress in this regard? Thus perhaps mercantilistic or cameralistic policies with respect to domestic manufactures were carried out administratively.

Entrepreneurs among the nobility seem to have had two types of advantage, although these appear to have varied considerably from place to place and from time to time. One was exemption from the payment of certain taxes; and the other was the possession of rights to serf labor. The importance of these conditions would, of course, depend upon the degree of internal or international competition in the commodities produced by the nobility in their enterprises or on their properties. Perhaps it was on account of such circumstances that everywhere the nobility was forbidden to engage in handicraft activities and in retail trade.

One difficulty was that shared by all who sought to promote or execute economic advance in these decades — the paucity of information as to what to produce, how to produce it, what to try to sell abroad, how to get it there, and how to get payment. Probably it is appropriate to speak of these noble entrepreneurs of the early modern period as "community-bound" — at any rate, "locality-bound" — as one might also speak of the Colonial merchants of New England. A few books on mining had appeared in the sixteenth and seventeenth centuries; very little on manufacturing of any sort; some manuals on commercial practices, weights, measures, and monies of European countries; no current commercial journals or the like.

Presumably information of varied sorts was purveyed by travelers. One type of traveler has interested Professor Karl F. Helleiner of Toronto as a possible source of innovations, at least of ideas new to particular areas. This is the quasi-scholar, quasi-humbug, such as the self-styled Count de Saint Germain, who moved from court to court in the seventeenth century, living by his wits, proposing economic changes, spreading ideas. Dr. Redlich suggests also that the alchemists as a group (of whom the Count was one), who likewise moved about more than most men of the period, could supply considerable technological knowledge. And the higher ministers of the several courts could have taken upon themselves to provide both basic and current data. There is, for example, the case of the travels of a son of Count Karl Otto Haugwitz of Austria in 1754 and 1755 through Italy, Hungary, and most of Germany, accompanied by a technical assistant.

One further source of information or perhaps one further medium of information has been suggested by Dr. Redlich as interesting in itself but particularly significant as evidence of one peculiarity of aristocratic entrepreneurship. This is communication among the nobility itself. Apparently, like commercial farmers almost everywhere around the world, they had no practice of secrecy about methods or processes or successful innovations as was true in the same period, and at other times, among handicraftsmen and manufacturers, even to a considerable extent among merchants. The "improving" landowners and farmers of England or the United States reported their crop achievements in agricultural journals and broadcast how they thought that they had accomplished the noteworthy gains. So also presumably an aristocratic owner of a copper smelter or slitting mill would quite surely find pleasure in telling a visiting aristocrat how he operated, what processes he employed, where the skilled workmen were to be procured, and so on. Practices of this sort cannot, of course, be proven, but surely they correlate with the sanctions evident in other aspects of aristocratic behavior.

Beyond the matter of technical and commercial information — to say nothing also about the problems of executing the actions called for by such data — there were at certain times and places legal restrictions to be overcome, hostilities to be surmounted, perhaps particular social roles to be carried through because of public prejudices or anticipations. (In the present state of our knowledge, we can hardly be more specific.) Apparently, the nobility everywhere in Europe was free of legal restraints until the sixteenth century or thereabouts. Outside of France the members of the class could do what they wished in business, except handicraft work and retail trade. Perhaps, on the other hand, the latter restraints derived solely from moral considerations, things that fighting men should not demean themselves to do. Quite generally, the aristocracy lost status if it soiled its hands in work.

The times of change in France seem to have been different from those elsewhere in Europe. Moreover, the data supplied by Dr. Charles A. Foster enable one to trace the nature of the experiences more closely than in any other country (ex-

145

cept England, to which none of these matters applies). Briefly it may be stated that after a gradual expansion of noble activities in various lines of business, Louis XI, the great bourgeois king reigning in the fifteenth century, confirmed to the nobility freedom to engage in any activity of a commercial or mechanical nature. With his death, however, a reaction set in which before the end of the sixteenth century had interdicted practically all forms of business to members of the noble class.

Another reversal took place in the seventeenth century, partly in procedure and partly in reality. Quite surely both Richelieu and Colbert encouraged the nobility to take active roles in the economic upbuilding of the nation. Quite surely also there was some evasion or disregard of such decrees as still stood on the statute books, with public sentiments on the subject varying appreciably from region to region of the country. In the meantime, a system of official relaxation of laws in specific cases had grown up. In this manner the noble could escape *dérogeance,* that is, action by which he would lose the rights and privileges attaching to the nobility as such, especially, it seems, the exemption from certain taxation. At the beginning of the new century, specifically in 1701, an act was passed especially concerned with wholesale commerce. Immunity from *dérogeance* was assured to all nobility that chose to engage in such commerce by land or sea.

Despite the apparent general and special relaxations of the rules, French aristocrats going into business in the eighteenth century went to troubles that seem to reflect fears of being subject to *dérogeance.* They would insist that there be written specifically into *lettres-patentes* a clause covering avoidance of such a state. Again, the practice became quite common for nobles to use straw men or false names — *hommes de paille, prête-noms* — in partnership agreements and subscriptions to stock. While a vagueness appears to have persisted in the law, the noble still feared to find himself in a stultifying position. As Dr. Foster remarks, the noble would have to base his case for greater freedom "either actively or passively upon the principles of economic liberalism, which in the last analysis would spell the end of the system of privileges, and indeed of an essential element of the organization of society of which he was a member." [6]

The aristocratic entrepreneur, then, flourished rather widely for some centuries in Europe; he was active in a number of important lines of economic action; and he undoubtedly contributed to the economic development of the area. Despite support at times and in varying degrees from chiefs of state, the form of entrepreneurship did remain primitive in character. Its position at law and in public opinion was clouded over from time to time; frequently, if not usually, the business activity was incidental or distinctly secondary to other roles; and it never grew vigorous enough to promote or devise vehicles of information flow that manifested any substantial advance toward the sophisticated forms of the nineteenth and twentieth centuries.

VIGNETTE 2: THE PERSISTENCE OF SOCIAL RESIDUES

No one has seen more clearly the relations of entrepreneurial character to the nature and operations of the particular social system in which it exists than Professor Sawyer.[7] There are, he writes, "observable national differences in entrepreneurial activity," which he feels "cannot be accounted for in terms of economic factors alone, or in terms of the hero in history, the distribution of genes, or any simple psychological reductionism." In seeking explanation, one must turn to "the system of goals and values, the scale of social rankings, and the pattern of conduct that are 'institutionalized' in the particular society." [8] To be sure, these social

147

elements change through time; for example, when a successful or unsuccessful war gives its backlash, when a Colbert or an Alexander Hamilton influences governmental attitudes, or when a group of robber barons makes manifest how unpleasant some varieties of businessmen can be. So also do the economic circumstances change — the domestic market, the international connections, and the technological situation, any of which may themselves stimulate entrepreneurial action. And again there seem to be social institutions and habits of thought, hierarchies of status, educational practices, et cetera, which last beyond the economic situation that gave them birth (or that at least found them innocuous in terms of economic welfare), and which become deterrents upon the business change that altered economic opportunities would otherwise have encouraged.

Analytically there are three or four elements to be considered separately in a discussion of the impact upon entrepreneurial performance of social systems of variant characters. One of these elements is the acceptance of change. Here one must turn to the anthropologist for the full story, but it appears that societies could be rated variantly, from reluctance to accept economic change to eagerness to promote that change. A society will not tolerate entrepreneurs if it objects to innovations and novelties.

A special form of change important for entrepreneurial performance is that of social mobility. To be sure, a sort of crypto-mobility may suffice for a time, as when a Russian serf accumulated money in the hope of buying his freedom or when he could employ free men to do his bidding. But a greater degree of persistent recognition was better. The Heralds' College in England is alleged to have stimulated entrepreneurial action in that country by providing heraldic shields for successful businessmen who desired to possess coats-of-arms. And in a society such as the United States where wealth opened practically all social doors, entrepreneurs and social movement were found together.

A third element is the toleration of making money, of activity in business. In various societies of the past, the merchant or the businessman in general has ranked below such social figures as the clergy, the soldiers, the teachers, and the professional men as a whole. In other societies, activity in business suffered qualitatively. Men in business maintained low thresholds for the frequent or continual intrusion of art or literature, family pleasures, or just long daily siestas. They sought to retire as early as possible in their lives to participate in "more worthwhile" actions, and tried to make possible the movement of their children into the more honorific posts and activities.

Fourth, one might differentiate materialism, conspicuous consumption, obvious accumulation of property, and the like. A society might tolerate a wealthy class if quite unmistakably on the whole it used its wealth in the service of the country; it might adopt a different attitude toward the activity that brought such wealth into private hands if the possessors built themselves gaudy palaces or indulged in conspicuous profligacy.

And there are still further factors that must be taken into account in explaining such phenomena as an Oriental entrepreneur strongly preferring relatives as members of his staff, a French industrialist disliking to drive competitors out of business, or an American entrepreneur being content to assert that business is his life, really a soul-satisfying career.

Professors Sawyer and Landes have independently examined the situation in France and given substantially comparable reports of their findings. It is unnecessary here to attempt to reproduce their materials.[9] A few fragments from their analyses will serve to illustrate the diversity of the forces involved.

Professor Sawyer finds present-day survivals or residues from the "formally stratified hereditary social order" of earlier days, a society based on a seigneurial, agricultural economy, in which property was tied to family and status, political and legal authority tended to be personal and particularistic, and communal relationships counted for much.[10] And Professor Landes finds that business enterprise in France typically "is not an end in itself, nor is its purpose to be found in any such independent ideal as production or service. It exists by and for the family, and the honor, reputation, and wealth of the one are the honor, wealth, and reputation of the other."[11] Something of the dominant attitudes of the earlier period seems to have persisted also in consumption habits: while the American consumer is characteristically content to secure merely more goods, whether similar to his neighbor's or not, the Frenchman's conspicuous consumption takes the form of individualized items — as if he were feeling, "These were prepared according to my orders for my particular pleasure." In short, the French business world, at least that of larger units, would ideally be constituted along the lines of an aggregate of manorial estates with loyalties, personal responsibilities, and community dominance, largely unchanged.

But Professor Sawyer finds French entrepreneurship conditioned also by another set of residues, those of a society that drew its inspiration from "Liberty, Equality, Fraternity." Out of this complex, seemingly, certain tendencies derive which support predispositions of the earlier society: a higher valuation on personal relationships than on material advantage, as revealed in the French system of goods distribution; or the willingness to "live and let live" in the relations among competing enterprises.[12]

All in all, one gains the impression of substantial variance between French and American entrepreneurship in just the elements that make for creativeness, vigor, long-range planning, and the like: that is, in "the system of goals and values, the scale of social rankings, and the pattern of conduct," that are institutionalized in the two countries.

Somewhat comparable studies have more recently been made of Germany and India, Japan and Jamaica.[13] I venture to call attention to the situation in England. Already I have cited Professor de Scitovszky's appraisal of the influence upon entrepreneurship in England of objectives derived from the hierarchical structure of English society with its important bases or manifestation in land-holding.[14] I would add a second influence.

If the country in England was dominated by king and aristocracy, the towns were not; and the merchant power in the towns persisted over so long a period as to leave its stamp upon modes of English thinking — to bequeath residues that affect present-day entrepreneurial performance in that nation. Professor Thrupp has portrayed vividly the position of the merchant class in medieval London. The economico-business literature from the fifteenth century onward reveals the hegemony of commerce, even above agriculture or finance. It is perhaps significant that even through the nineteenth century "commerce" was a term much more common than "business," and signifying the same thing; that the first books that attempted to deal scientifically with business carried the word "commercial" in their titles; even that Charles Wilson's recent definition of entrepreneurship turns on the ability of a businessman to recognize a market opportunity and to have the ability to exploit that chance.

That Englishmen should have taken a hundred years after the industrial changes of the eighteenth century to convert commercial accounting to industrial uses might be viewed as a not unnatural result of the mercantile domination. So also might be the slowness with which advanced education for business has taken hold in England, and writing in the field also. In commercial life, the size of units is typically small, and success depends greatly upon personal contacts and upon intimate knowledge of goods. One could not really "teach" business; it was necessary for each apprentice to "learn" it for himself. Even the dominant character of English banking, with its reliance largely on short-term commercial paper, and the tardy development of a universalistic investment banking system may, likewise, be conceived as consequences of the socio-economic order of English urban communities.

Perhaps with Professor Danhof one may pursue the analysis in terms of prestigious evaluations.[15] One may prefer to utilize the "structural-functional" approach that stems from Professor Parsons. Or, indeed, one may select to "look merely at the facts," as in Dr. Redlich's essay on the many paths to entrepreneurship. There can be no doubt that "observable national differences in entrepreneurial activity" at any one time — or for that matter changes in entrepreneurial activity in a given nation through time — "cannot be accounted for in terms of economic factors alone" or in any other simple "reductionism," and that most widely potent is (and has been) the "social order" of thought and institutions.

VIGNETTE 3: THE SERF ENTREPRENEUR

As Henry Rosovsky suggests in his excellent article on the Russian serf as entrepreneur,[16] the phenomenon is likely at first blush to seem a paradox. "The serf and the entrepreneur are rarely coupled, and most frequently orthodox economic theory almost separates them by definition. Serfdom implies a condition which ties the individual to the soil and makes him subject, more or less, to the will of his owner. The entrepreneur is thought of in terms of activity, courage, and enterprise — a Schumpeterian figure, not a carry-over from mediaeval times." Yet Rosovsky finds thousands of serf-entrepreneurs in Russia at the time of emancipation (1861), with no few playing rather important roles in the industrial development of the nineteenth century, and many thousands more being useful in the operation of the Russian economy of those decades.

Among the individually more prominent serf entrepreneurs might be specified men by the names of Grachev and Garelin, who were resident in the village of Ivanovo, which is located about 180 miles north of Moscow. This village had been a center of linen-cloth manufacture from the early seventeenth century — an activity promoted by city merchants. Serfs became operatives in these establishments, and out of these workers, perhaps particularly out of the skilled printers, arose men "touched by the entrepreneurial spirit," as Rosovsky puts it. By 1798 Grachev was employing 120 persons in his cotton-cloth plants. In addition he was engaged in the older linen-cloth manufacture, having 90 looms in his village establishments and keeping another 400 busy on a putting-out basis. Garelin was similarly occupied, but seemingly on a somewhat less extensive scale. A goodly number of the employees, incidentally, were also serfs, so that we have the curious combination of serf entrepreneur commanding serf workers!

Compared with such men as Grachev and Garelin, the thousands mentioned above were individually unimportant. They seem to have been largely self-employed: tailors and candlemakers, storekeepers, locksmiths, and free-lance carriage drivers. If inconsequential individually, nevertheless they counted for much in the aggregate, as noted above, in making the economy operative. To be sure, Rosovsky does not hold that, even adding all grades of serf entrepreneur together, one could claim that they bulked large in the Russian economy of the preliberation decades. The economy was very heavily agricultural, and the chief urban element was the group of merchants. It is noteworthy, however, that a few of the serf entrepreneurs prospered enough to be reckoned millionaires, and that in some cases they had free merchants working for them, occasionally holding property for them in areas where ownership by serfs was forbidden. The phenomenon reached fairly deep.

How can one explain such a development? Rosovsky suggests the impact of several factors, most of them non-economic. There *was* an expanding market for manufactured items in Russia, with the growth of population and the improvements, however slow, in transportation facilities, while, for such men as those specifically named above, a special advantage derived from Napoleon's sack of Moscow: Ivanovo was far enough away, but not too far. Again, the expansion of the towns and cities, in part the result of the inflow of other serfs, constituted part of the increased market for goods.

Serfs were allowed off the properties to which they belonged — in some degree, it seems, were encouraged to leave — by reason of the commutation of labor dues, which by the eighteenth century had become common in certain parts of the country, in the area north of Moscow in a ratio of three to two. Under the straight labor-dues system, the serf had no incentive beyond getting through his obligations to his lord as quickly and easily as possible, and returning to his own small plot, if he had such. Under commutation, there was opportunity, at least for ambitious serfs. They might work off their money payment quickly and have any further earnings for themselves. Indeed, they might dare to look forward to purchasing their freedom from savings out of their activities, and, if not for themselves, then perhaps for their sons.

The ambitions of money-paying serfs were doubtlessly aided by the upward trend in commodity prices which occurred in western Europe in the eighteenth century, and probably affected Russia in the same period, as well as by the special advance in prices over the French Revolution and Napoleonic years. Money dues set at one date could become less burdensome at a later one, and the serf payer would have more of his income left in his hands.

The agreement of lords to commutation of labor dues appears to have stemmed from two or three elements. Certain lands, such as those north of Moscow, were ill-suited to agricultural activities, especially under the inefficient serf system. There was a possibility that some other mode of using the serfs might prove more advantageous. Moreover, in the eighteenth and nineteenth centuries the lords found their expenses rising, perhaps in part as a result of the increasing commodity prices mentioned above, probably more as a consequence of changes in urban and especially court life. As a result they needed more available cash. Some of them had tried to utilize serfs in manufacturing units set up on their estates, but this arrangement had proven futile. The serfs selected to work in the shops were no more efficient than on the land, probably less so because they disliked the requirement of learning something new, and the denial of work that all the others in their status were performing.

Finally, a sort of negative factor should be noted. Serf entrepreneurship sometimes continued to exist, after it had once evolved, because particular lords refused to release serfs even after the latter had become capable of paying liberally for their freedom. The wealthier nobles found less advantage in accepting such payment than the less well-to-do. And there were some who refused release because that act would serve only to lower their own status. Such a lord was the member of the Sheremetev family who owned Ivanovo and controlled many serfs, including Grachev and Garelin.

Perhaps there was even an administrative element involved for some nobles. A serf entrepreneur who took other serfs into his industrial establishment, or even engaged them to work for him on a putting-out basis, frequently undertook to cover the money payments which these other serfs had committed themselves to pay the lord. The serf entrepreneur became in substance a dues collector.

In short, it appears that, given the various circumstances of eighteenth- and early nineteenth-century Russia, the advent and continuance of serf entrepreneurship constituted a "natural," at least a wholly expectable, phenomenon. Indeed, it seems that the phenomenon may not have been restricted to Russia. Dr. Redlich reports the discovery of evidence that serf entrepreneurs existed in parts of Austria and in German Silesia.

These cases do give support to two features of entrepreneurial thought in general: (a) talent for entrepreneurship will be found in all strata of individual societies, a conclusion that is supported by the data already presented upon aristocratic experience, and those offered elsewhere concerning handicraftsmen, merchants, occasionally professional men; and (b) entrepreneurial endeavors will rise through crevices in societies made rigid by tradition or force. The NEP episode in Soviet Russia tends to support this view.

Actually there appear to be aspects of the earlier Russian experience that convey color or overtones to what seem normal social manifestations of entrepreneurial life, at least in communities that are not heavily weighted with Calvinistic values. For example, the successful serf entrepreneurs indulged in "conspicuous consumption," as have newly risen entrepreneurs elsewhere. Turgenev tells of such a serf, who possessed a two-story brick residence — rarely to be found in a Russian village — and who served good dinners, at least on occasion, complete with champagne. These entrepreneurs also, again like new bearers of the role, could become severe disciplinarians. They bore down hard upon other serfs who had not been so fortunate (or so ambitious) as they. They seem even to have attempted to put obstacles in the way of others following in their footsteps. The Russian serf entrepreneur, then, may be accepted as truly a species of the same genus as the Dutch merchants with their lovely town houses, the first large American industrialists who desired to impress their contemporaries in almost all ways, or the early English cotton-mill owners who could be cruel toward orphan children.

Section 2·

ENTREPRENEURSHIP AND
UNDERDEVELOPED AREAS

VIGNETTE 4: ENTREPRENEURSHIP IN PRIMITIVE CONDITIONS

Perhaps some day scholars will think it worthwhile to spend time in attempting to trace and catalog all sources of entrepreneurship, all the situations in which the activity has taken first root. As already indicated, Professor Thrupp has suggested three possibilities as common in western Europe: local famines, the financial necessities of princes, and the provision of sacramental wine; and Dr. Redlich has thought of the opportunity of becoming business intermediaries that came to serfs or other peasants who transported grain or other goods from manors to the rising towns.

Whatever the initial impulse, there seems to be a period in the economic development of most areas when entrepreneurship lacked the strength to stand alone. Professor Easterbrook would say that the minimum measures of security had not yet been provided.[17] Actually, the phenomenon seems more general in character. Sometimes it appears that the uncertainties of financial return yield consequences not essentially different from the hazards of life, theft, or similar misfortune. At any rate, there are numerous cases in history where the state has stepped in to provide securities that appeared to be necessary to induce entrepreneurial action. It might take the form of naval escort to Venetian merchant vessels of the fourteenth century; it might involve the release to such an entrepreneurial organization as the British East India Company of powers that in most other situations the government kept in its own hands;[18] or, in nineteenth-century America, it might take the aspect of "mixed" enterprise, the state furnishing some of the capital, all of which might be lost.

The Canadian fur trade offers an excellent example of the impact of hazards of various sorts upon the mold in which entrepreneurial endeavor was carried on. Here the evidence was assembled in Professor Innis' *Fur Trade in Canada,* and analyzed anew in Professors Easterbrook's and Aitken's *Canadian Economic History.*

From the earliest days of French possession, merchants of Quebec and Montreal were desirous of dealing in the commodity. Indeed, furs constituted practically the sole item that could be exported from the interior of the country. And it was a commodity with some fortunate characteristics: it enjoyed a steady, if somewhat inelastic, demand in Europe — a demand that grew continuously, it seems, but could not be made to expand by modest price reductions; and it was an item that provided relatively high value in relatively small bulk, a fact that had influence in more than one direction. It facilitated the movement of the goods once they had been secured, but it also encouraged the continued spread of trapping activities over more extended areas of the wilderness.

On the whole, the marketing elements in the trade were difficult for the Quebec and Montreal merchants to overcome. The turnover was slow. A couple of years might well be needed between the assembling of goods to be exchanged for furs, and actual realization from the sale. The friendly

Huron tribe of Indians had initially been utilized as collectors of the furs, but they soon had to become middlemen between the merchants and tribes more remote. In repeated warfare, the Iroquois disputed the role of middleman with the Hurons, and the Indians resented in some measure the efforts of the white men to introduce greater system into the business, especially when *coureurs du bois* and *voyageurs* began to reach back closer to the sources of supply. Occasionally movement of furs was impeded by the unwillingness of a given tribe of Indians — a settled plains group, for example — to participate in the transportation of their catch.

By the eighteenth century, moreover, the British traders operating from Albany, New York, were cutting into the business of the Canadian French. They had support from the Iroquois. Also the British possessed the advantages of shorter lines of communication with Europe, cheaper manufactured goods to barter with the Indians, and West Indian rum, which was not only less costly than French brandy, but widely preferred by the Indians over the latter form of liquor.

Last, but not least, the French government recognized, quite as well as the local merchants, that furs were the only immediately available source of income from its North American hinterland. Therefore, it sought to use the commerce in furs somehow as a source of government revenue.

An important consequence of all these circumstances was that the trade in Canadian furs was free of government or other control only over short intervals. Licenses to engage in the business were usually required; the government endeavored to enforce a monopoly of purchase from dealers; it undertook military action in support of its plans; and the like. Moreover, when the British essayed an attack on the French hunting grounds more direct and more organized than that maintained by a few merchants in Albany, it took the form of the chartered Hudson's Bay Company, although at the time (1670) English public opinion was turning vigorously against such enterprises with exclusive privileges. Perhaps the form was justified in this case; at least it is true that the company declared no dividend for seven years. Again, it is noteworthy that, after 1763 and the reorganization of the trade under the British flag, it was not long before the fur-trading firms of Montreal were agreeing to "join their stock" and soon were setting up a "North West Company," which exercised over much of the next decades an effective monopoly of the business. In 1821 the Hudson's Bay Company absorbed the North West Company and again secured a substantially monopolistic position.

In short, the physical and economic conditions of the Canadian fur trade fostered a relationship to government and a type of entrepreneurial organization quite different from that which was common in the more southerly thirteen colonies. The elements of insecurity in these conditions seem to have been most decisive. The manner in which entrepreneurial activity is carried out — to some extent the manner in which it *can* be carried out — is a derivation of many forces. Sometimes a "free" entrepreneurial system is feasible; often it is not.

VIGNETTE 5: THE PIONEER ENTREPRENEUR

The "underdeveloped," but rapidly expanding, areas of the United States produced the jack-of-all-trades and the "tinkerer" in its handicraftsmen; they stimulated also the blacksmith who could turn his hand to a considerable variety of tasks; and a somewhat comparable entrepreneur arose in the same regions. This pioneer entrepreneur is to be found in eighteenth-century New England and progressively across the country with the opening-up of successive regions.

The Browns of Providence Plantations, as Professor

Hedges has labeled the family, constitute a striking case.[19] The first Brown of note was a merchant of Providence, dealing at wholesale and retail in a diversity of goods. He trained four nephews, John, James, Nicholas, and Moses, in whose hands the family's fortunes rose. Soon they had a distillery to manufacture rum out of the molasses which they were importing from the West Indies; they set up a ropewalk to supply their ships with cordage; they took a brief interest in the slave trade; they were leading figures in the manufacture of spermaceti candles and in the creation and operation of the "trust" that attempted to control the market for such candles. In addition, they established the Hope Iron Furnace nearby, and in fact provided the metal for the iron railing that for decades surrounded the Battery at the tip of Manhattan Island. Before the close of the century, they were in the China trade, owned cotton mills, and had at least a finger, probably more, in banking and insurance. To be sure, they were not active in all of these lines of business at any one time, and some of their operations may be viewed as steps in the transference of mercantile capital to domestic manufacture. There were four brothers, and later their sons and partners, involved in the total experience, although for the most part the brothers went into activities jointly; but the record is a notable one. The entrepreneurship was diversified in objectives, or perhaps subjectives!

A few decades later the case of Erastus Corning could be cited.[20] Admittedly there was some connection between his two major lines of activity, his hardware business and his interest in the railroads stretching westerly from his hometown of Albany, New York: his store sold rails to the railroad companies. However, he seems to have taken a creative attitude toward the railroads, much more than was necessary to foster the market for his iron, and in the end expended much time and energy as president of the New York Central Railroad. In addition, he invested in western lands, became involved in the construction of the canal at Sault St. Marie, helped to create and then served as president of a savings bank, and was concerned in local charities.

Further west, and later, Cadwallader Washburn will serve as an example.[21] Washburn came from Maine to Minnesota in the 1850's, together with a number of other men interested in lumbering.[22] Successively he became interested in lumbering, in the operation of sawmills and the sale of their output, in the waterfalls at Minneapolis, in flour-milling machinery, in banking, and in the development of the rapidly growing city. At one stage he set about the planning and construction of a railroad, because he thought that those then serving Minneapolis were conspiring to exact excessive rates on his goods and those of his fellow citizens.

The McGees of Kansas City, thriving especially in the 1860's, will serve as my final example.[23] The first real blooming seems to have been connected with the outfitting business in the 1850's, but previously the family had had contacts with a flour mill, a distillery, a sawmill, a tavern, and a general store as well as the almost inevitable land speculation. Later the McGees apparently had fingers in many lines of business development in the thriving city.

Actually, one encounters this phenomenon fairly late in the evolution of the eastern United States, as new centers rose. One such case was investigated years ago by Robert K. Lamb, who studied the development of Fall River. This advance did not really get launched until the founding of the Fall River Iron Works in 1825. From that base the intertwined Borden and Durfee families expanded into cotton textiles, commercial banking, the railroads that touched Fall River, and real estate. Professor Lamb came to argue the importance of the group as the source from which individual entrepreneurs often seem to derive much of their strength, and the importance of the community.[24]

The phenomena described above relate to the phase or stage of entrepreneurial evolution that I have ventured to denominate "community-focused." [25] Here it seems to have been the opportunities offered by the area of residence that tended to condition the bearers of the entrepreneurial role. Also these pioneer entrepreneurs frequently became leaders in the business evolution of the city, identifying themselves with the community and finding satisfaction in its prosperity. At a later date businessmen were led to specialize in given industries, and to think of themselves as primarily associated with the rest of that industry, less with the community in which they were located and less with such unexploited opportunities as it offered.

VIGNETTE 6: THE OVERSANGUINE ENTREPRENEUR

Professor Sawyer has called attention to the contribution of error to economic development, although he used rather more careful language.[26] Professors J. Keith Butters and John Lintner spoke a few years ago of the sort of psychological compulsion that spurred men to set up their own enterprises;[27] and the statistics of concerns that do not survive their first birthdays appear to confirm such a hypothesis. Anyway, it seems that cold, rational calculation of risks and chances of success has never controlled the launching of business enterprises, especially in economies that have been undergoing rapid or reasonably rapid growth under conditions of free enterprise. To be sure, there undoubtedly have been numerous businesses begun under unsound economic conditions which have survived and prospered by dint of supernormal exertions and ingenuities of their entrepreneurs.

In Professor William W. Cooper's phrase, they have been "made to behave."

Henry Noble Day's career will serve to illustrate the sort of "error" in business mentioned above. Perhaps because his contribution to American economic evolution was slight, and because little remained behind after his business activities to mark his passage, he is all the more valuable to us. The record is not distorted by subsequent reconstructions deriving from successful achievement. The case is the more important to us, however, by reason of the imaginative and painstaking work of research that his biographer, Professor R. Richard Wohl, carried through. As a result of his labors we are able to see Day the promoter projected against the background of the social thought and sanction patterns of his era and community. No biographical sketch, at least in the field of entrepreneurial history, more fully interweaves historical data and sociological theory.[28]

The chief events in Henry Day's life are rather quickly told. He was born in a small town in Connecticut in 1808, and spent his youth in New Haven, living in the house of his uncle, who was the president of Yale. Henry attended the college, graduating in the class of 1828. After sampling the professions of teaching and law, he turned to the ministry, studied further at Yale, and ultimately wandered almost by chance to Hudson, Ohio, a small town thirty miles south of Cleveland, which was then the seat of Western Reserve University. Henry Day was to teach sacred rhetoric at the university.

Now at Hudson in the 1840's two things happened to Day. He found his duties at the university so simple that he had time for journalism, and soon took responsibility for the local newspaper. Second, and partly as an indirect result of the first circumstance, he was caught up in the railroad fever that was then afflicting that portion of the country. In fact, he rose swiftly to become the promoter of a group of railroad lines that should convert Hudson into an important rail center, tying the roads of the East with other lines that would sooner or later reach the Pacific Coast, and a promoter of stores and other business structures that would be appropriate for such a transportation center. Perhaps it was inevitable in all the circumstances that this delightful dream should not last long. The bubble broke in 1854. It required a year or two, even with Day's help, for the interested parties — and the courts — to distribute such assets as survived. Once this was accomplished Henry Day accepted the headship of a "female seminary" at College Hill, near Cincinnati, and did not touch business again.

Now, there are actually many interesting facets of this story, even if Henry Noble Day cannot be regarded as important by most standards and even if Hudson never has grown to be a Chicago or even a Cleveland. For one thing, it will be obvious to all who know American history passably well that Henry Day was the prototype of "boosters" and local promoters who appeared — and disappeared — in thousands of American communities over the decades of the nineteenth century. It was in part by reason of these Henry Days that the country grew.

With most such individuals, however, it is impossible to reconstruct with even plausible evidence the thoughts and emotions with which they carried through their self-imposed tasks. It is fortunate that a satisfactory documentation does exist in the case of Henry Day, and happily Professor Wohl recognized its unusual quality. I venture to introduce my own interpretations of certain conditions and developments, but essentially the events may be recorded succinctly as follows.

Henry Day grew up in a relatively well-settled area, where

economic opportunity still knocked on doors, but less loudly than elsewhere in the nation, and where the making of money had become subject to socially approved expectancies, if not rules. He matured also in a region which was still heavily permeated with religious thought and religious specification of conduct. The uncle in whose house Henry Day lived through his college years could write to his son, "The acquisition of property will not compensate for the neglect of the great interests of eternity." [29] Third, it will be noted that Henry Day was a member of a leading family of Connecticut. Among his uncles, a distinguished lawyer, who was for years the secretary of state for Connecticut, can be added to the president of Yale. On all these counts it is small wonder that Henry Day sought a professional career of some stripe, and decided to settle upon that of the ministry.

There were also idiosyncratic elements in the whole picture. One quite surely was the "poor relation" circumstance in which the lad grew up. Another, hinted at by Professor Wohl, is the interest of Day in the "revival" or more emotional facet of the religious life of his era. His biographer goes further to suggest that the lack of decisiveness in his choice of career implies a measure of instability in Day's character.[30]

Before he left New Haven for the West, his hostages to a circumspect and perhaps circumscribed life had been enhanced by marriage to the daughter of the leading banker. But also one of the supports to his chosen role of religious teacher had been somewhat undercut. A brother of his, Jeremiah, had avoided college and had gone south, where he prospered in the very new but thriving town of Apalachicola. Henry sent small sums to his brother to commit to southern speculations, profits accrued excellently, but the young man was so eager for financial success that even his brother, located in a bubbling community, felt moved to write him, "You are a little too hasty to get rich."[31]

Then Henry moved to what was essentially frontier. Numerous observers have remarked on the tendency of such regions to loosen the social bonds that invisibly but effectively tie men to patterns of moral behavior approved in their older areas of residence. There is likely to be more of heavy drinking, cheating, homicides in frontier communities, at least until law and order have again been restored. Quite surely social roles of less violent character might be modified in such regions. Henry Day did alter his ways. He had not been in Hudson more than a couple of years when, although sitting in a chair of "sacred rhetoric" at the theological seminary, he projected himself into a world of different nature, that of newspaper publishing. Soon he had allowed himself to be carried even further — into railroad promotion, the building of warehouses and commercial structures, the setting-up of businesses such as a general store and a drug-store, and the borrowing of monies wherever he could find investors.

A technical factor in Henry Day's entrepreneurial performance — and we are interested in the how as well as the why of such activity — was something that Day seems to have picked up from President Pierce of Western Reserve University. The institution was young; there were other, competing theological schools in the neighborhood; and anyway funds for the support of higher education were hard to find in that region in the 1840's. Accordingly, the president did not hesitate to budget a deficit, or utilize such credit as he could discover, and hope to come out "in the black" at the end of the fiscal year. Of course, Western Reserve was not the only institution, and probably not the only educational institution, in the Middle West of that period that made use of credit or lived from year to year "on a shoestring." Nor was it the last such in more parts of the country than Ohio! However, this example of "risk-bearing" right under his nose, as it were, and on the part of a respectable institution may well have had a direct and potent effect on Henry Day's concept of the entrepreneurial role.

By a most happy chance, we are able to apprehend how Henry Day justified to himself the changes that he had introduced into his roles. In 1850, before the crash of his hopes, he preached a sermon, the text of which has been preserved. Building from the base out of Daniel, "In the night I saw visions," he evolved the thesis in substance that, from the nature of the extensive country, the character of its political institutions, and the endowments of its people, there was clearly to be seen the handiwork of God; economic development was obviously a directive upon Americans. Day found an "expression of our national life" to lie "in our industry and in our arts."

The characteristics which Christianity at its present stage seems to require are chiefly vigor of invention, skill in execution and subscribing to the true trend of industrial arts — utility. In the activity and vigor of inventive talent and in the general success of mechanical enterprise, the docility with which foreign arts are studied and apprehended, and the restless ambition to press on from present achievements to higher stages of perfection give our countrymen advantages over those countries in which a narrow conservatism veils existing defects and indisposes to further improvements . . .

We must despise all nature's influence, if we be not . . . a united, self-relying, powerful, enterprising and magnanimous people — such a people as the advance of Christianity now calls to its service, such a people, in these respects, as a millennial sun will not blush to look upon.[32]

Professor Thomas N. Carver in his *Religion Worth Having* seventy-five years later could hardly do better. Obviously, it was a Christian's obligation to be productive economically

— and how better than in the promotion of railroads and the reorganization of the local economy?

As a final note to this whole episode, it may be observed that one feature of the disturbing influence was its "foreign" character: the railroad was not a community affair. Perhaps Henry Day would not have been led into so much error if he had limited himself to publishing the local newspaper, even to attempting to erect local stores of various sorts. With the external, regional, even national phenomenon, major uncertainties flowing from "misinformation, conflicts of information and lack of information" entered the picture. Sometimes surely this sort of error — as well as the "constructive" error of which Professor Sawyer has spoken — derived from this transition from community-bound to industry- or nation-bound activity.

Section 3 ·

ENTREPRENEURSHIP AND
TECHNOLOGICAL CHANGE

VIGNETTE 7: "LINES OF FORCE" IN TECHNOLOGICAL DIFFUSION

Almost from time immemorial, the man who chanced to possess a special handicraft skill could set himself up as a small-scale entrepreneur. Sometimes he possessed a unique talent, or desired to establish a personal monopoly, as it were, such as the father and son who produced the glass flowers now in the Agassiz Museum at Harvard. Customarily they trained successors, often became units in an organized system, and under guild rules or more modern apprenticeship arrangements exercised and taught their skills. With the breakup of the guild form of entrepreneurial order, the mode of transmission of technological knowledge became irregular. This was especially true of the geographical transmission of such knowledge in a growing country like the United States. Undoubtedly, thousands of small businesses in this country, from the grist mills of Colonial days to the automobile repair shops of the twentieth century, have been founded on, and have flourished by reason of, technological competence on the part of the proprietors.

In most such cases the trails of movement have been lost, and imitation appears automatic in quality. In a few in-

171

stances the data have chanced to be preserved or have been put together by students. When I was working on the American wool manufacture thirty years ago, I stumbled upon an episode that involved a family.[33] John and Arthur Scholfield came from Yorkshire in 1793. These brothers landed in Boston, accompanied by John's wife and six children, and by a certain John Shaw, a spinner and weaver. They brought with them knowledge of the carding and spinning devices that had come into use in the north of England.

The spread of such information began with the connection made by the brothers in 1793 with the Newbury-Port Woolen Manufactory. Shortly — as I wrote in the 1920's — "John Scholfield, in one of his wool-purchasing trips for the Byfield ["Newbury-Port"] factory, became interested in a water-power site at Montville, Connecticut; and there the Scholfields went in 1799, after selling out their interest in the Byfield concern. In 1801 Arthur parted from his brother and moved to Pittsfield, Massachusetts; while John, after staying in Montville until 1806, sold out and purchased a mill-site at Stonington, Connecticut. Subsequently (1814), John set up another plant at Waterford, near New London, which he placed in charge of his son Thomas. Meanwhile, John's oldest son, John Scholfield, Jr., after being in Colchester, Connecticut, for a time, in 1804 or 1805 set up a wool-carding shop in Jewett City, then a part of Preston, Connecticut. This business seems to have grown into a regular woolen mill, and by 1816 contained a full complement of machinery. Another son, Joseph, became interested in the Merino Woolen Factory at Dudley, Massachusetts, in 1817.

In yet another direction the influence of the family was felt. A third brother, James Scholfield, who had been called from England as soon as John and Arthur had made a place for themselves, in 1802 bought a mill privilege and fulling mill at North Andover, with the financial assistance of Arthur. Here for ten

172

years he carded wool for customers, adding in time the manufacture of broadcloth. For this purpose he used machinery, spinning jennies and looms, operated by hand, which he placed in his house. In 1812 he sold out this business, becoming thereafter superintendent in Mr. Nathaniel Stevens's mill, which was erected the following year.

Finally, of yet greater influence, it seems — though of course one cannot estimate the stimulus given by force of example in the cases above mentioned, — was the activity of Arthur Scholfield, who left his brother John in 1801 (apparently because the latter did not like Arthur's newly wedded wife) and went to Pittsfield, Massachusetts. Upon his arrival, Mr. Scholfield, joined soon by his nephew Isaac, also set up a carding machine and for a few years did carding for customers, until in 1804 he began the manufacture of broadcloth on a small scale. But his main contribution was in another line: the manufacture of carding machines. He seems to have built a few almost from the beginning of his residence in Pittsfield. The first advertisement of machines for sale appeared in the *Pittsfield Sun* of September 12, 1803; and in the next year (May 14, 1804) he informed the public that besides having machines to sell, "built under his immediate inspection," he "will give drafts and other instructions to those who wish to build themselves." The terms of these services are not stated; nor is the reason clear, although reading between the lines suggests the competition which was already developing. He gives warning against imposition "by uninformed, speculating companies, who demand more than twice as much for their machines as they are really worth." However, by 1806 the demand for his products was so great that he sold out his carding business and devoted himself solely to the manufacture of machines for sale. Then, and indeed in after years, no more frequent recommendation of a carding machine was made than that it came from Arthur Scholfield's workshop, and evidently it was believed that none higher could be made.

Incidentally it may be noted that Arthur Scholfield's activities were not confined to carding machines. In 1806 he was manufacturing picking machines, — machines for loosening the matted locks of wool in preparation for carding, and used then in conjunction with the carding machine at the mill of the custom-carder; and by 1809 he was constructing spinning jennies. Finally he was concerned with the manufacture of cloth during the embargo and war periods, for a time by himself, but in 1814 as next to the largest subscriber to the Pittsfield Woolen and Cotton Factory, launched in that year. Like others he suffered from the revulsion and depression that followed the advent of peace, for a while went back to wool-carding, and later acted as superintendent in one of the surviving mills. He died in 1827, apparently little richer than when he came to Pittsfield a quarter of a century before.

When it is recalled that good carding of wool is fundamental to good wool-cloth construction, and that in this country the combined carding-fulling mills frequently became the nuclei of wool-cloth factories, it will be recognized that the contribution of the Scholfield family to technological change — and such change on an entrepreneurial level — was highly important.

Somewhat similar cases can be cited out of other industries. In textile-machinery construction, Samuel Slater's brother-in-law, David Wilkinson (not Slater himself) is noteworthy. Wilkinson's shop "became the training school for many machinists who later were important figures in the history of machine-building in America. With one or two notable exceptions, all the textile-machine companies . . . owe their origin in some measure to the skill imparted by David Wilkinson." [34]

Dr. Redlich presents a somewhat comparable situation relative to the spread of steam-engine construction in Germany. There were a half-dozen pioneers, many of whom had English connections, such as Dinnendahl, Jacobi, and Harkort in the western part of the country, and Freund and Egells in the eastern part. Then of the next generation, three of the most important — Borsig, Wöhlert, and Hoppe — had received training in Egell's plant, Paucksch had worked in Freund's, and so on; and the connections can be carried down into the third generations. In fact, Dr. Redlich exhibits the "lines of descent," as it were, in diagrammatic form.[35]

Correspondingly, Thomas Scott, president of the Pennsylvania Railroad, is given credit for training a number of young railroad managers in the 1850–1875 period, men who later headed other railway lines in the expanding American network; Westinghouse is supposed to have trained men in the electrical-apparatus manufacture, et cetera. In short, one may well contend that in the intermediate period between the reign of individual inventors and the dominance of schools of technology, there was a period when temporary and informal organizations had appreciable influence. Evolution was not random nor wholly unstructured. Entrepreneurs arose who helped to inspire other entrepreneurs, and the direction and rapidity of change were surely affected by the character of these trainers of men.

VIGNETTE 8: THE PARTNERSHIP OF INVENTOR AND
BUSINESSMAN

If local environments are conditioning forces in early technological development and adoption, there comes a time when the introduction of technological improvements requires a wider entrepreneurial perspective, at first perhaps a whole industry and later the markets of various industries in a whole nation. The first of these two stages was signaled when textile-machine building moved out of the textile mills and became a separate industry. And the same was later true in the locomotive-building in this country; it moved out of a variety of temporary homes and established itself as a separate manufacture purveying to the whole industry of railroad transportation.

When an inventor could look to sales over a whole industry, and perhaps an industry scattered geographically over a goodly part of the industrial East, he seems often to have been fortunate if he had a businessman to aid him in

the adaptation of his device to actual manufacturing operations, in providing finance over such a trial period, and in
"making a market" for the apparatus, perhaps in a field which
was already reasonably well satisfied with what it already
possessed. To be sure, there have been a really surprising
number of inventors of important apparatus who have proven
good also at entrepreneurial performance, men like Cyrus
McCormick or Erastus B. Bigelow or Henry Ford. But there
were others not so well endowed — probably thousands if we
could make a count of the failures which never overpassed
the threshold of historical record. One such case has already
been noted above: the failure of the Stanley steam-driven
automobile to succeed in the early competition with the
gasoline-driven type.[36]

The partnership of Edward D. Libbey and Michael J.
Owens was romantic, improbable, stormy, and yet very
profitable.[37] Its history throws into sharp relief a phase of innovation that is often overlooked: that novelties of apparatus,
processes, or products are likely to be successfully introduced
into an economy only if their introduction takes place on
the basis of a firm operating foundation. In this particular
case, the "firm foundation" was supplied by the two elements,
Mr. Libbey's personal character and the enterprise with
which he was first associated. Let me tell the story briefly.
Professor Warren C. Scoville made a splendid presentation
himself in his *Revolution in Glassmaking*.

Libbey, born in Massachusetts in 1854, had inherited from
his father in 1883 ownership of a small glass manufactory
which had ceased to be promising of financial returns, and
indeed was on the brink of bankruptcy. Just before his father's
death, young Libbey had been able to save the enterprise
only by a bold marketing stroke. With a promissory note due
shortly, he took to the famous Tiffany Company — which
had in fact been one of the concern's best customers — a

sample case full of some peculiarly colored tableware which had been put aside as unmarketable and which only chanced to have been preserved. Libbey thought up the new name of "amberina," was able to impress the Tiffany buyer with the virtues of this new color, and did enough business in this novel line to pull the company around the financial corner.

Within a few years, however, the demands of the skilled glassblowers for higher wages threatened to make thoroughly impossible the continuance of the New England Glass Company in a region which had already lost most of the competitive advantages that it had ever possessed. Libbey again was bold. He picked up his enterprise, shepherded such workers as would accompany him, and moved his business to Toledo, Ohio, where he would secure the advantage of low fuel costs (from the natural gas resources of that region) for a branch of manufacture in which fuel costs always counted for much in total manufacturing costs. Curiously enough, one of the representatives of the American Flint Glass Workers' Union who went to Boston to try to strengthen the resistance of the strikers against Libbey and his company was Michael J. Owens, at the time a worker in a glass house in Wheeling, West Virginia. From 1888, when the move was effected, the Libbey Glass Company, as the new enterprise was named, enjoyed financial success. The glass industry was expanding, in part because of rising American standards of living and in part because of the increased use of glass containers for foods. Factories in Ohio probably enjoyed differential advantages in costs, and the Toledo company was enterprising enough to purchase or develop glass-manipulating apparatus, the products from which were required by the electrical industry, which was also expanding at that time.

And a third bold stroke of Libbey's should be mentioned. Despite objections from most of his associates, he set up a sizable exhibit of glass blowing at the Columbian Exposition in Chicago in 1893, only five years after he had established his plant in Toledo. (By this time, incidentally, Owens had become superintendent of Libbey's factory, and supervised this exhibition at the fair.) The experiment was a conspicuous success, attracting thousands of the visitors to the exposition, and doubtless resulted in giving the Libbey company a position of some prominence in the minds of consumers, again a differential advantage which would make for financial soundness.[38]

Owens was distinctly improbable as a great inventor. Son of an immigrant coal miner of West Virginia, and under the necessity of going to work at the age of ten, he always labored under handicaps: it was near to the end of his life that he mastered the use of decimals, and he seems never to have learned to read mechanical drawings. The basis of his inventions appears to have been mainly a sense or uncommunicable impression of what molten glass may be made to do, and what not. He was a difficult man in his interpersonal relations, at least relations with his business associates but he did "get on well" with workingmen, although he never returned emotionally to the point where he could support labor organizations. And he was improvident, and jealous of those, like Libbey, who were provident. At a time when the latter was collecting paintings for his private art gallery and enjoying the pleasures of a California ranch, special arrangements had to be made whereby Owens was compensated for an action that had happened twenty years earlier, and provision established for a royalty payment on his bottle-blowing apparatus, that had not been contemplated when the invention was turned over to the "partnership."

Yet Owens had a flair for handling hot glass, a quasi-passion for the improvement of technological procedures, and an inner compulsion for accomplishment that Libbey recognized as extraordinary among men. He supported

178

Owens' experiments with his own money or saw to it that funds were forthcoming from some source; he went to considerable lengths to avoid personal disputes with his quick-tempered, frequently stubborn associate; and he gave Owens his loyal endorsement on many occasions even against the other men in the Toledo group, who were inclined generally to think and feel as did calm, suave, cultured, men of substance. The patience and the loyalty which Libbey displayed may be regarded as a special sort of foundation on which Owens could erect the devices of his imaginings. They were fit and fruitful complements to the pecuniary support that Libbey derived from the glass-working enterprise, the Libbey Glass Company, itself founded upon sound economic rocks and favored by potent economic trends.

The joint endeavors of Libbey and Owens in inventing labor-saving devices for glass-working, and introducing them into general use, began almost immediately after the successful display of processes at the World's Fair at Chicago. In almost a torrent, inventions to make semiautomatically or wholly automatically such items as electric light bulbs, lamp chimneys, tumblers, bottles, and the like flowed from Owens' laboratory or workshop, or he was improving the inventions of others, as in the case of the Colburn sheet-glass machine. A modern touch was given to the mode of capitalizing on these developments by the formation of companies, the function of which was to sell rights to utilize the inventions. This was particularly true of the bottle-machine patents. But in almost all instances the entrepreneurs found themselves drawn sooner or later into actual manufacture of products which were turned out by the use of their patented apparatus. On the whole, this latter phase of their operations seems to have been less profitable than the invention and leasing one, even less profitable — at least relative to the capital involved — than the original Libbey Glass Company.

Libbey appears to have been too much preoccupied with too many ventures to take continuing charge of these manufacturing enterprises; and Owens was not a good executive. He would probably have wound up in a bankruptcy court if he had tried to operate the concerns by himself. He never had operating charge of the Libbey company, and seems to have been kept at arm's length by those who did take charge of it in the middle 1890's, when Owens turned his attention to full-time invention.

The cooperation of the two principal characters occurred within the structures of business corporations. Always they were the principal figures, but they did have support from some individuals, some men with good judgment and some with willingness to carry routine administrative tasks; and these latter contributed to the total success. As Professor Scoville suggests, there was something of a fairly effective entrepreneurial team, with Libbey and Owens the provocative leaders, and not always leading in the same direction! Yet the aggregate result was startling. Libbey had come to Toledo with something like $100,000, and Owens with practically nothing. By 1920 both were millionaires, although one cannot be more precise. We do know that the enterprises over which they then exercised control possessed a value in excess of $50 million, and this had been accomplished in something like twenty-five years. Joint inventor-businessman entrepreneurship paid handsomely under some conditions.

VIGNETTE 9: VARIETY IN PATTERN

Thanks to the extraordinary path-breaking contributions of Professor Schumpeter, entrepreneurship has tended to be made synonymous with the introduction of technological innovations, especially innovations of a momentous character. I believe this identification to be an error, and that Schumpeter came in his latter years to take a broader view.

In his *History of Economic Analysis,* he stated that entrepreneurial gains emerge each time that "an entrepreneur's decision in conditions of uncertainty proves successful and have no definite relation to the size of the capital employed." [39] At another point he seemed to assert that he had placed himself beside Maurice Dobb in defining entrepreneurs as "the people 'who take the ruling decisions' of economic life." [40]

The research which Dr. Harold C. Passer carried through on the evolution of the American electrical manufacturing industry serves to illustrate the variety of performances that fall clearly within the borders of entrepreneurial activity.[41] Among the men who come under his analysis are four that I venture to label the calculating inventor, the inspirational innovator, the overoptimistic promoter, and the builder of a strong enterprise. All four types — and others — can be found in industry, probably in any old industrial country.

Edison was the calculating inventor. There had been arc lighting before he began experimenting with incandescent lights, but he deduced from his study of the former, and deduced rightly, that it could not reach the big market, that of the individual home. Then, having settled on incandescent lighting, he reflected on the existing situation and decided that he should try to "effect exact imitation of all done by gas so as to replace lighting by gas by lighting by electricity." He recognized that gas lighting had secured consumer acceptance as to devices, methods, and practices; and saw an advantage in capitalizing on that fact. His technical problem, then, was to develop a superior and more desirable light which should be delivered to the consumer in much the same manner as gas. His business problem was to be able to deliver that better light at no more than the consumer was already paying for his gas. Such ends became his goal, and such were in fact his achievements. Not the least of his intermediate accomplishments was the invention of a meter by means of which electricity consumption could be measured just as well as a gas meter measured gas consumption.

To be sure, perhaps, cautious calculation exacts its penalty — or the personality that operates in the manner of careful planning will let matters once decided stay decided. At all events, Edison pioneered with a direct-current system, a technique that entailed scattered power stations with short transmission lines. Such installations were set up in lower New York City — and, incidentally, are still there. Not long thereafter Westinghouse came along with an alternating-current system, one which permitted safe transmission at considerable distances. But Edison did not — or could not — change.

Again, Edison had framed his original conception around the notion of household use, imitating the gas utilization in residences. Having achieved a workable system for that purpose, which was, of course, a tremendous accomplishment, he seems to have retired from the field. The development of motors for industrial uses — indeed, the whole exploitation of electricity for power — was left for others to carry through.

The innovator who seems to have been able to rely much on inspiration was Frank Julian Sprague (1857–1934), who may be credited with the adaptation of electrical power to urban transportation. The crucial test came at Richmond, Virginia, in 1887–88. In May, 1887, Sprague entered into a contract to install an electric railroad, at a time when he had had no experience in the field, and when, as he said later, he "had only a blueprint of a machine, and some rough experimental apparatus." Yet by the fall of 1888, despite an intervening bout with typhoid fever that laid Sprague up for more than two months, the railroad was running satisfactorily; and this demonstration of the practicality of electric traction launched a new industry which at its height ranked with the largest in the country in size and in social effects.

To be sure, Sprague had had scientific training at Annapolis and he had pursued some experiments on his own after graduation. Resigning his commission in 1883, he worked for a year or two with Edison; he designed and sold industrial motors; and in 1885-86 he had conducted experiments in New York City, looking toward the replacement of steam trains on the elevated lines with electrically driven ones. (A minor accident may have moved the locus of Sprague's initial triumph from New York to Richmond. Jay Gould had financial control of the Manhattan Elevated Railroad Company, which in turn controlled four leading lines. He chanced to be riding on one of Sprague's experimental cars when a fuse blew out with a frightening detonation. Gould was prevented from jumping off the moving car; but he lost interest in electric traction!)

Actually Sprague took on major technical as well as financial risks at Richmond. He was supposed to produce a forty-car system, with thirty cars to operate at any one time, when the largest existing railway had no more than ten cars all told. And his cars were to surmount grades of 8 per cent, which were considered too great for horses or mules! It is true that Sprague could not meet the original completion date, and true that he lost heavily in unanticipated costs. But his system proved successful without much delay, and with that success his financial future was well assured. His services were much in demand.

One subsequent occasion for his services involved an episode almost identical with the foregoing. It concerned the electric railways of Chicago, and the multiple-unit system of control: a system whereby each car in a train was to be equipped with a motor adequate to start and move it, not have all the power generated or applied in a front-running locomotive.

Sprague sought a contract, and secured it in April, 1897 — as Dr. Passer says, "by agreeing to take upon himself all risk that his plan might fail . . . and the railway company, for its protection, required him to furnish a $100,000 bond for penalties in case he did not fulfill the terms. He agreed to have six cars completely equipped and ready for test on or before July 15 on a standard track, at least one mile long, to be supplied by him at his own expense." Yet, at this time his scheme "existed only on paper"! Actually, Sprague left shortly for London to see about a large contract there, and did not reach New York again until June. He was ten days late in putting on his six-car demonstration, but by that time he had so simplified the apparatus that he allowed his ten-year-old son to handle the controls! And the major installation on the whole South Side system gave efficient and safe service at reduced cost. Net earnings of the line increased nearly fourfold.

The third type mentioned above, that of the overoptimistic promoter, was E. H. Goff. He differs from Edison and Sprague in entering the industry from the sales end, being, in fact, one of the few early figures in the industry who lacked an engineering or scientific background. He differs also in being financially unsuccessful. He appears first in 1881 as sales agent for arc-lighting apparatus of an early concern, the American Electric Company, and by mid-1887, he had lost control of the company which he had set up, but which shortly closed its doors.

Goff's difficulties appear to have derived from the haste with which he pushed an essentially sound scheme. Other early sellers of arc-light equipment had followed the practice of organizing the citizens of a community into a company

184

which then bought the apparatus, ran it as best they could, and hoped to make a profit in the process. Goff chose to set up his own companies in communities which he believed to have need of arc lighting, to get the equipment going properly and giving satisfaction — and profits — and then to sell the concern to the local citizenry.

While this procedure would seem to be one that should have gained him much business in the end, unhappily it did call for the temporary commitment of considerable capital, and apparently the industry was too young to gain the nod of commercial banks. The first successful installation of arc lighting having been made only in 1879, Goff's sole source of funds was the sale of stock in his enterprise; and to sell stock he had to pay generous dividends. He did resort to publicity in his stock-selling endeavors — from a display of lighting on Tremont Street, Boston, to the donation of equipment to illuminate the Statue of Liberty. But cash failed to come in fast enough, and some that did come in was drained out by needs of the manufacturing establishment that he had erected. A couple of adverse patent decisions in the courts came just when the enterprise was shaking, and they precipitated the wreck. Goff was finished — and actually was dead by 1891.

Charles A. Coffin, who had been a top salesman for a Lynn shoe manufacturer, was the first all-round company-builder in the industry. His introduction to the manufacture had been almost casual, since in 1881 he was appointed a member of a committee set up in Lynn, Massachusetts, to select arc-lighting apparatus for the local Grand Army Hall. Coffin chanced also to have encountered the equipment produced under Thomson-Houston patents.

From that point, however, Coffin was on his own. He was impressed by the apparatus; perhaps he was moved by the fact that both Thomson and Houston had scientific backgrounds. At all events, he raised money in Lynn to buy up the enterprise with which the two men were associated, the American Electric Company, renamed it the Thomson-Houston Company, and moved it to Lynn.

With scientists in charge of experiments and research, and with good present apparatus to sell, Coffin could give his attention to the financial, production, and marketing aspects of the concern. Perhaps he would qualify as one of the earliest professional managers in manufacturing industry, although of course he had some financial stake in the company from the outset.

No detailed account of his stewardship should be attempted here. Suffice it to say that he avoided Goff's mistake. Coffin followed the more general practice of encouraging the formation of local companies to buy equipment. His enterprise did accept securities sometimes in part payment, but he was able in effect to pass them along through the formation of "trusts," which held stocks and bonds of several local companies, and which attracted investors. He also rationalized the manufacturing side of the business, being one of the first to organize operations on a functional base. About 1885 he established separate departments of purchasing, production, accounting, et cetera, and with his own skills in marketing, he succeeded in providing all-round competence for the enterprise. Dr. Passer calls him "the leader of the industry by 1890."

Section 4 ·

ENTREPRENEURSHIP
AND BUSINESS ORGANIZATION

In analyzing the economic and social activities of the
merchant in the seaboard towns of the American colonies
and early post-Revolutionary decades, one is in reality dealing with a species of an extensive genus. Professor Stuart W.
Bruchey makes a nice point when, in summarizing the career
of the Baltimore merchant Robert Oliver, who was active
from 1783 to 1819, he draws a comparison with that of
Andrea Barbarigo, Venetian merchant of the fifteenth century.[42] The latter's activities reach back toward the beginnings of the era of "commercial capitalism" or dominating
commercial entrepreneurship, and yet Professor Bruchey
points out how similarly the two merchants acted. Barbarigo
would have almost immediately understood Oliver's form of
organization and his methods of managing men, records, and
investments. In looking at the early American merchant,
then, one is in a sense examining the entrepreneurial figure
that dominated urban life in the Western world for something like five hundred years.

In a broad frame, the social function of the entrepreneur

187

generally is to provide goods or services to his community or market in such a manner as satisfies its moral sense, at least does not violate that sense too blatantly. In other words, there is a technical or economico-business aspect, and there is a moral one. It seems valid to hold that the American merchant of early decades performed the first function rather poorly, but he sustained the moral relationship very well. Let us look at both, with special reference to the case of Robert Oliver, since only in connection with him has a biographer pursued certain important inquiries.

The operations of Oliver and his predecessors and contemporaries in mercantile life must be considered as wholes, including both export and import activities. In terms of a merchant's relation to his community, either from the point of view of business or morals, his import activities may seem more significant, yet exports were necessary to sustain imports, and the exportation of goods had to be carried out in a manner that was reasonably satisfactory to the communities or markets to which goods were sent. Two elements were important in the performance of these tasks: the acquisition of information about wants, and the expeditious satisfaction of those wants. In both these features the early merchant encountered difficulties.

Beyond the merchant himself the key figures in the operations were his correspondents in the foreign ports, and the supercargo (or the captain of the ship carrying the goods, acting as supercargo). Problems arose almost inevitably with respect to both parties. Correspondents of reliable character had to be located; then they went out of business, or they turned unreliable, and I suspect that those in the smaller ports accumulated conflicting loyalties. Some American merchants sought partial relief from such difficulties by encouraging relatives to settle in foreign commercial centers, at least for a while, or by making good use of those who did live abroad. The Hutchinson family, centered in Boston, had a very good organization in the late seventeenth century. One brother was a prosperous London merchant, two brothers and two nephews carried on trade in the thriving New England port, another nephew — and so a cousin of the Boston nephews — resided in Portsmouth, Rhode Island, where he traded as far west as Hartford, Connecticut, and from which he pushed a considerable commerce with the West Indies, and two brothers of his carried on the latter business from Barbados.[43] Robert Oliver enjoyed communications from his brothers, John and Thomas, one or the other of whom was visiting in Europe almost continuously from 1796 to about 1803. He also had a valuable ally in Philadelphia, a brother-in-law who was a prominent merchant there. However, relatives surely did not suffice to cover even the most important foreign spots for most merchants; and the complaints about correspondents in general, sometimes relatives also, lead one to conclude that the actions of the agent were quite often indifferent reflections of the desires of the principal.

Time and uncertainties of communication were factors in the situation. A voyage to the West Indies required three or four weeks each way around the turn of the eighteenth century, and might take nearly twice that time under unfavorable weather conditions. A voyage to London or Hamburg demanded five or six weeks each way, while one to the Far East could consume four or five months in either direction, often longer. During such periods of transit the conditions in the market of destination could well change as compared with the merchant's anticipations, and the home market for which he had planned purchases in the foreign ports might well move contrary to his expectations. All the time his ship's captain, his supercargo, and his foreign correspondents were really at arm's length from him, subject to the vagaries of unorganized, informal transmission of letters.

Writing about the New England merchants of approximately the same period, Professor Kenneth W. Porter had some rather unpleasant things to say about this mail service, some merchants accommodating other merchants. Ships' captains would accept letters but be curiously tardy in delivering them; they would insist on the letters being given over unsealed, or would not hesitate to open them surreptitiously. Sometimes they refused to take letters of competing merchants. And, of course, sometimes vessels were lost or they changed their course while at sea.

In a recent study of "Merchant Shipping in the [English] Economy of the Late Seventeenth Century," Mr. Ralph Davis states that the charter parties covering voyages to Portugal or the Canary Islands made allowance for forty to forty-five working days for loading in port, while those covering voyages to Virginia allowed for a hundred working days for such loading in port.[44] Butel-Dumont, in describing the conditions in the American tobacco trade of the mid-eighteenth century, talks of ships staying "three or four months, often six months" in Chesapeake Bay collecting a load, while an unusually large vessel might have to spend a whole winter there.[45] Professor James B. Hedges of Brown, who has studied the shipping experience of the Brown family of Providence in the latter Colonial and early national periods, writes me that turn-around in Providence for the Brown ships would average around three months, but this time could on occasion be shortened if news of conditions in a foreign port — for example, a shortage of flour in Surinam — could be sent ahead by another ship. A return cargo might be made ready.[46] However, all these data point to a slow pace of commercial interchange. I wonder how well, indeed, the individual merchant of pre-steamship, pre-cable days could rationally adjust his activities to the needs of his community. I am even tempted to draw inferences from the language in which "sedentary" merchants in Boston or other Atlantic ports were likely to couch their advertising in the daily or weekly newspaper: "J. and H. Perkins announce that they have received a shipment of linens." Did Boston (or the other subject ports) *lack* linens until Messrs. Perkins received their supply?

Finally, it may be noted that purchases had often to be left largely to the discretion of the agent, correspondent, or supercargo. Orders from the principal had to be couched in terms that carried the qualifications: "if prices are not too high," "if the quality is good," "if not too many other ships have loaded up with the item." And, as I have implied already, once the ship had left Baltimore or Salem or Charleston, there was small chance of changing the statement of desires. The lengthening of the lanes of American commerce after 1790, especially the evolution of the trade with the Far East, promoted an alteration in organization. Now the importance of the non-American offices grew. Young Forbeses and the sons in other merchant families served their apprenticeships in Hong Kong or Manila; until, at a still later date, the principal offices of houses, English as well as American, came to be located in the Far Eastern areas. (The English and other East India companies had encountered a similar administrative or control problem earlier.)

A modern observer looking back from days of almost universal airmail, radiograms, and often overseas telephonic communication, and from days when supervision of correspondents or wholly-owned agencies is relatively easy, may perhaps be pardoned for conceiving the older mercantile system as hardly better than a vehicle that wobbled and creaked as it slowly got over the ground. We should probably marvel that, technically, it did as well as it did.

On the other hand, the moral relationship appears to have been quite satisfactorily maintained. I am disposed, with Professor Porter, to relate business ethics to no transcendental criteria. "Ethics, like international law," says Porter, "is a matter of precedent, and the individual who conforms to the standards of his group [of his day and generation] has done all that his biographer [and presumably any other appraiser] can reasonably expect from him." [47] Dr. Redlich would complain — and rightly — that this definition fails to cover the possibility of variant standards of action as between dealings with members of the merchant's "in-group," and those with other members of the whole society.

This situation did occur in the early days of Massachusetts Bay, and may have become briefly manifest in certain other colonies, such as Pennsylvania or Georgia. In the first case, considerable evidence has come down to us, especially the 158-page will of Robert Keayne, a merchant of London. Keayne came to Boston in 1635, and three years later was in trouble with church and state "for selling his wares at excessive Rates, to the Dishonor of Gods name, the Offence of the Generall Cort, and the Publique scandall of the Cuntry." Fourteen years later still, he drew up a will as a "demand that justice be done him even if only in memory." He died in 1657.[48]

With the subsidence of religious controversies, a condition of relative calm seems to have evolved in the colonies, at least as far as the merchants' actions as merchants were concerned. To be sure there were divisions among the merchants, at least in Massachusetts, as Professor Bailyn has shown.[49] These disputes involved matters of public policy and preferments among their own group, and these controversies continued into the Revolutionary period. But the activities of merchants in their business roles did not provoke controversy. Even those who took a larger or smaller share in the slave trade, in smuggling, or in privateering appear to have done so with the acquiescence of their fellow citizens. Nor is this situation surprising. The urban communities were still small enough for communication among the dominant members to be relatively effective. The merchants had not developed a zest for business that made it plausibly a self-sufficient calling; and, despite the decline in the Massachusetts theocracy, the colonies were dominated by unity in a Christian philosophy. Merchants were responsible members of the closely knit Christian societies; there was every reason why they and their communities should think alike; and there was no sufficient reason why the mercantile segment should not *act* in a manner that would receive the approval of their fellow citizens as far as their role performance as merchants was concerned.

VIGNETTE 11: THE "GENERAL ENTREPRENEUR"

A historical view of entrepreneurship is bound to be closely concerned with business forms and their evolution through time. As already indicated, one must have regard for the process or manner of entrepreneurial action as well as its motivation and conditioning. The "regulated company," the joint-stock limited-liability form of enterprise, the partnership, the "public" company — all of these have importance in our field insofar as they have contributed to shaping the economic and social aspects of entrepreneurial performance.

It is to Professor Cochran that we owe the discovery and delineation of the "general entrepreneur." [50] He describes the phenomenon only in relation to the railroad industry, but he recognizes that this type of entrepreneurial actor, at least, had occurred somewhat more widely.

By the term "general entrepreneur," Professor Cochran seeks to differentiate the financier of the mid-nineteenth century in this country who had effective, if not absolute, financial control over several business concerns usually in a single industry, did not typically attempt actually to manage any of them, and yet, by reason of his financial position, did possess final power over the formulation and change of general corporate policy. In historical sequence he represents a business form lying between the individual proprietorship or partnership of the earlier decades of the nineteenth century and the investment bankers of the last decades.

John Murray Forbes's career did not differ markedly from that of men like Israel Thorndike, Nathan Appleton, Erastus Corning, or Nathaniel Thayer, all of whom could be catalogued as general entrepreneurs, at least in the essential element of having made money in mercantile operations — incidentally as had Forbes. They all chose to dominate manufacturing or transportation enterprises through the direct or indirect influence of their possession of wealth. Forbes himself was born in 1813, started apprenticeship in trade at the age of fifteen, went to China at seventeen to serve with his uncles' enterprise of Russell and Company, made the lasting friendship of a wealthy merchant of that country, and, returning to Boston, carried on commercial activities there for the decade 1836–1846. Then with his own money, with that of his friend Houqua, and later with funds secured from family and friends, he began to invest in western railroads: the Michigan Central, the Chicago, Burlington & Quincy, the Hannibal & St. Joseph. He did serve as president of the Michigan Central for the years 1846–1855, and of the Chicago, Burlington & Quincy for the briefer period, 1878–1881, but he did not attempt to manage the properties. That is the important characteristic of the general entrepreneur. Nathan Appleton might have large or controlling financial interests in certain cotton mills, but he did not pretend to operate them. So likewise with Forbes or Thayer or others concerned with railroad lines. The latter

194

men remained typically in the East and constituted the court of last resort relative to decisions on western railroads that contained a significant financial aspect. And it need hardly be asserted that the combination of such discriminating purveyors of funds with the technically trained, carefully selected managers of the enterprises contributed much to the economic development of the country beyond the Appalachians. Here a business form, not determined by, or necessary in, contemporary social, political, or economic conditions, had an important economic effect.

Professor Cochran makes the point that the role of general entrepreneur in such a case as that of Forbes was perfectly consonant with the social concepts of the era. Not only was property protected at law and unquestioningly respected in the public view, but the possession of much property — wealth — had itself a power of command. The boards of directors of the companies should, of course, be made up of representatives of investment groups; the operating heads of the lines in the West should naturally turn to Forbes and his ilk for policy decisions, since hardly any of the latter failed to have a financial feature.

One element in the structuring of this role is a sort of residue from earlier days. Men like Forbes "wanted to live in east-coast civilization," [51] and they were willing to assume executive posts only when their sense of obligation to their fellow investors overcame their disinclination to leave Boston or other eastern cities. Merchants of the Colonial period had retired in middle life to give themselves over to community and family life. Even in the 1840's and 1850's it was not essential, in order to command the favorable regard of their peers and social censors, that they put first and always the making of money, of arranging their lives to that end.

Another element in the role manifests its intermediate character. At an early time proposals for the formation of companies were not uncommonly posted in coffeehouses or similar public places, with blank space below the terms of the proposal, on which the names of interested parties, together with the number of shares which they desired to secure, could be "underwritten." Capital, like other components of entrepreneurship, was at this period community-bound in large measure.

When projects requiring larger amounts of capital — for example, railroads — began to be launched, promoters frequently made journeys about the various centers of potential investors and personally solicited subscriptions. Forbes and his type acted in much this fashion, except that now — at least more than ever before — they spontaneously conceived a responsibility to their friends and neighbors and other investors for the safety of the monies invested in projects of their promotion. There is a particularistic feature and a public-responsibility one. And, when subsequently the particularistic element of soliciting subscription from among friends, family, and social acquaintances pretty much ceased with the rise of investment-banking firms, the latter still retained in some measure the responsibility aspect. The better investment houses "stood behind" the issues of stock that they sponsored, indeed, frequently sought membership on boards of directors of railroad or other enterprises in order that they might "carry through" on the obligation implied by their issuance of the securities of such business units.

Obviously, the roles of general entrepreneur and operating manager were mutually complementary; they each supplied functions necessary to the "initiation, maintenance, and aggrandizement" of the enterprise which the other could not supply, or could have supplied much less effectively. It was a form of the division of labor. There were, to be sure, limitations to the "separation of powers." One was the fact that a general entrepreneur was not always available when he was needed or had other affairs in hand that distracted him from the prompt performance of his duties in his chosen role. For example, Forbes was in Europe when the important Burlington strike broke out in 1879, and Charles E. Perkins, the president, had to make the decisions. At another point, Forbes wrote to his operating president that he could not "attend systematically to the business of the road," that the best that he could do was "perhaps at midnight as now . . . to write a private letter with such hasty suggestions as occur to me." [52]

There seems also to have been some change in the degree of complementary activity over time. For one thing, as the railroad grew longer and its relationships became more complex and numerous, it grew more and more necessary, and common, for subordinates in the growing hierarchy to make important decisions and then turn to their superiors, to the board of directors, and to the general entrepreneur for confirmation. And the operating heads of railroad lines came increasingly to take more and more initiative in at least the framing of alternatives in decisions. Again, the rise in the post-Civil War era of investment-banking enterprises meant inevitably a weakening of the business requirements of the general entrepreneur and his functions. The managers of railroads could surely perform their functions and could maintain and expand their companies much more readily without dependence upon such men as Forbes than they could have in earlier decades.

The complemental quality just mentioned stemmed in part from the intellectual, social, and economic conditions of the period. One way of phrasing the matter is to say that the industry was gaining importance relative to the community. The railroad was a particularly effective instrument in this separation because of its geographical extension. However, it also required an expertness of management that could not be found as a normal element in community life. As early as 1856 William Osborn, president of the Illinois Central, complained of his directors, "I do not think any of them are aware of what an immense machine this is to handle." [53] Education for administrative duties was possible only through apprenticeship; and, given the state of conceptualization regarding management and given the state of railroad literature, it would have been impossible for a general entrepreneur to have learned the "railroad game" except through such a schooling. Those who had grown up in mercantile pursuits would have had to study long to have equipped themselves for railroad management in its totality.

On the other hand, there existed at this period special demands and special opportunities for those who had wealth or had contacts with potential investors, particularly in the railroad world. One peculiar feature of that world was the need of chunks of capital, sizable chunks. As the canal builders had learned earlier, a transportation facility aimed to link two places was not of much value monetarily until the two places *had* been linked. A canal halfway to a coal mine was not really worth much; and, by the same token, neither was a railroad halfway from New York to Buffalo. Given the rather common entrepreneurial (and engineering) tendencies to minimize anticipated costs of construction and to inflate potential earning powers of any such facility,[54] it was just as well if the person taking responsibility for a railroad had a long money pocket, and those possessing contacts with potential investors had relations with a considerable elastic supply of funds.

The last consideration is connected with a more general phenomenon that should not only be specified as a peculiar feature of the experiences now under view but as an integral element in entrepreneurship. I have in mind the apparent capacity of a business unit to take on a life of its own —

really, of course, that of the human individuals that from time to time make up its directing personnel — and to grow in various ways differently from the way its projectors had envisaged. Mr. Charles Wilson presents cases in the West African trading and nut-collecting institutions that Lord Leverhulme set up to provide a dependable source of raw materials for his expanding soap and margarine empire. Soon the trading companies had lands of their own, possessed steamships, were looking around for freight to fill these vessels on their return voyages, became involved in quasi-political relations with the local tribes, and so on.[55]

The general entrepreneurs and the railroad industry went through quite as extensive an evolution. Beyond the formation of the transportation enterprise, there was the development of the construction company, after a time the appearance of a conflict between the objectives of the two institutions, and, as Professor Cochran points out, an alteration in the role structure of the railroad executive in the degree that he must put the interests of his company unmistakably first. There were chances to participate in city real-estate dealings and in the erection of commercial buildings. There was the particularly important development of new extension of track to be considered, the building of strategic lines ahead of economic need in order to forestall competitors; and there was the evolution of community and political relationships until the original enterprise was to be seen in the midst of a network of connections, rights, duties, and opportunities, a situation far removed from the simple pair of rails from one city to another with which it might often have begun in men's minds.

Professor Cochran seems wholly justified in paying as much attention as he does to the railroad general entrepreneur in the economic and social setting of the 1845–1890 period. In this kind of entrepreneurial situation, the problems of communication and control that are to be observed in the operations of the Colonial merchants (and their post-Revolutionary successors) became intensified by the change in the time-horizons relative to most managerial operations in variant industries. If the Colonial mercantile system could be said to be like a poorly constructed carriage that wobbled a good deal as it went along, the railroad enterprise was at least a well-turned vehicle, if still horse-drawn and not quite so responsive to external forces as the twentieth-century equivalent. The railroad-plus-general-entrepreneur combination was also noteworthy as one of the first business situations that was, as it were, open-ended [56] and thus capable of promoting company growth. It was, likewise, notable as presenting cases of the separation of ownership and management long before the dawn of the twentieth century. The combination offers in a way a transitional form between the earlier world of proprietary and that of the more modern corporate entrepreneurship.

VIGNETTE 12: THE CORPORATE EXECUTIVE

The members of a corporate executive team would form a multiple entrepreneur, according to the contentions presented above. It appears to me, however, that the members of an executive committee comprise even more clearly a multiple entrepreneur. However, the fact must be faced that the president of a corporation or the chairman of the board of directors, or both, will usually be found to possess somewhat more influence than other members of the whole "top management" or the other members of an executive committee. In some cases, as in that of Mr. Sewell Avery of Montgomery Ward, the differential may be so great that the president or chairman seems closely akin to the traditional entrepreneur. But these cases have now become exceptional among large American companies.

Still the normal differential is adequate to validate the preparation of a brief sketch of the career of Mr. Frank W. Abrams as a typical leader in an entrepreneurial group. The honors which Mr. Abrams has received both within "his" enterprise and outside it lead one to think that he may in quality lie in the top stratum of his category, but an excellent ballplayer is still a ballplayer!

Information about Mr. Abrams after he became an executive is meager — which is just what one should expect: he had been made a member of a team, and only the action of the group was recorded. However, one can learn something.

Let us first look at his initiation. From a home in Rockville Center, Long Island, he went to Syracuse University, and received a civil engineering degree in 1912. He began work with a subsidiary of the Standard Oil Company (New Jersey) almost at once, and almost at the bottom, namely as draftsman in the Eagle Works in Jersey City. By 1917 he was assistant superintendent and by 1922 manager. And at this period he distinguished himself, with the company and ultimately with the industry, by a notable feat of organizational placation which, in a sense, laid the foundation of his subsequent career. This was the period when university-trained engineers like himself were coming into the employ of the company. They found themselves working beside men who had learned their skills merely from experience, and it was Mr. Abrams's task not only to keep the peace, but to preserve the preexisting relationships, intangible but important, of an operating team. He manifested an ability to work with men, but also an interest in trying to make men want to work together.

At about the same time, according to his own admission, a session of self-appraisal convinced him that he possessed no special talent in engineering or executive experience which would give him any peculiar value in the eyes of company officials, and decided that his only chance of advancement lay in making people like him. I suspect that a psychiatrist would readily explain this decision as merely a revelation that Mr. Abrams himself liked people and sought to understand them as brother human beings.

However, the course of Mr. Abrams's career with the enterprise was not immediately altered. In the mid-1920's he performed his stint of foreign service (which is common with "Jersey" for rising young executives) by supervising the construction of a large refinery in Sumatra. Returning to this country in 1926, he was placed in charge of all the refining carried on in the New Jersey area. But by that time Mr. Abrams had apparently served his apprenticeship; indeed, he had almost completed all the administrative work that would be required of him. He had shown that he could think new thoughts, and that he could direct groups of men in several types of operations. Thereafter his posts became more specifically consultative.

In 1927 he was elected to the board, presumably an administrative board, of what is now the Esso Standard Company; in 1933 he was made its president; seven years later he had moved to the top administrative unit, the Standard Oil Company (New Jersey), at first as one of the directors, in 1944 as a vice-president, and the next year as chairman of the board. He remained in the last office until his retirement from the company in 1954.

This is a thoroughly typical bureaucratic career, such as William Miller traced among the top executives whom he studied in his research.[57] Probably the period of operating work, only fifteen years, was on the short side, but the period which he enjoyed in the topmost place, a decade or so, is not far from normal.

Within the administrative groups, Mr. Abrams's personal

qualities seem to have counted heavily in his further advancement because of their correlation with the trend of the times in social relations. According to reports he was what the Spanish call "simpático," an informal man who preferred to persuade and suggest, rather than to criticize harshly, let alone issue orders. His strength derived from his reservoirs of patience and from his social philosophy. The former lack formal recording but are remembered by those who worked with him. His philosophy is exhibited in an article published in 1951 in the *Harvard Business Review*.[58] Briefly, it is founded on the belief that, as a result of the machine age, men are brought ever nearer to one another, and so must learn to get along together — to which Mr. Abrams adds merely the specialized conclusion: that it is the duty of business management to facilitate the process.

It has become more important for us to live in harmony in a new kind of world. People are now more concerned with each other and much less with the mastery of their physical environment. The importance of faith in our fellow men, and understanding among men is thereby made the greater.[59]

The job of professional management, as I see it, is to conduct the affairs of the enterprise in its charge in such a way as to maintain an equitable and workable balance among the claims of the various directly interested groups. Business firms are manmade instruments of society. They can be made to achieve their greatest social usefulness — and thus their future can be best assured — when management succeeds in finding a harmonious balance among the claims of the various interested groups: the stockholders, employees, customers, and the public at large. But management's responsibility, in the broadest sense, extends beyond the search for a balance among respective claims. Management, as a good citizen, and because it cannot properly function in an acrimonious and contentious atmosphere, has the positive duty to work for peaceful relations and understanding among men — for a restoration of faith of men in each other in all walks of life.[60]

203

The citation which New York University prepared when it was conferring upon him an honorary degree in 1950 gives the right flavor:

For his significant achievements as engineer and administrator, for the part he has played in the evolution of oil refining from a limited mechanical method to the chemically precise process it has become today, for his sincere interest in the welfare of employees and his many benefactions on their behalf, for his forthright assumption of industry's responsibilities to the community and the nation, for his inspired crusading as a champion of institutions of learning, for his personification of the conscience of American business, we bestow upon him with esteem and admiration the degree of Doctor of Commercial Science, *honoris causa.*

Mr. Abrams has gone on to public service of various sorts — as trustee of Syracuse University, as member of the National Planning Association, as a member of Mr. Hoover's task force, as advisor (and sometimes administrator) with the Ford Foundation, the Alfred P. Sloan Foundation, and the Industrial Relations Counselors, among others. He has been a man much sought after by institutions of such character. Perhaps most noteworthy and characteristic of Mr. Abrams' later activities — even before he retired from office with the Standard Oil Company — with his sponsorship and support of the Council for Financial Aid to Education, through which corporations may contribute funds for the maintenance of schools and colleges. He even helped to secure a judicial decision on the legality of such gifts by corporations. (Incidentally, he has had the cooperation of many American businessmen in this project, including such leaders as Mr. Irving S. Olds of the United States Steel Corporation and Mr. Alfred P. Sloan of General Motors.)

For entrepreneurship, however, it is evident that, in sociological terms, Mr. Abrams constituted a deviant whose modification of the role of major entrepreneur proved congruent with the emergent ideas of his peers and with those of public censors. As a result, the alteration in the role may be regarded as incorporated into the total behavior pattern, at least for the current era.

Mr. Abrams's experience is noteworthy in yet another regard, significant at least for American entrepreneurial life. Not alone did his views correlate with the contemporary trend in social thought, but the record of his speeches and actions makes manifest that he was a force himself in accelerating these trends. This is as it should be: a business institution as powerful and extensive as the Standard Oil Company (New Jersey) should be conversant with and conscious of the emergent tendencies in national thought, should select top executives with knowledge of their competence in such expanding fields, and should encourage these executives to seek leadership in the new movements. It was in this correlation of actions that Mr. Abrams himself asserted in substance that what was good for the country should be made good for "Jersey."

Section 5 ·

ENTREPRENEURSHIP AND THE STATE

Economic development, so universally desired in the Western world, at least since the Renaissance, has been propelled along divers paths according to the various combinations of economic, political, and personal factors that chanced at the divers times to obtain. It might occur through the action of a monarch. Such was the contribution of Gustavus Adolphus (1523–1560), whom Professor Eli F. Heckscher describes as "a great business manager in control of the Swedish economy." He was particularly important for launching the Swedish iron industry on its long career, and his endeavors in all directions resulted in "a remarkable increase in the prosperity of the Swedish people." [61] It might take place through the self-inspired efforts of forceful statesmen — Colbert or Hamilton or Peel, Julius Vogel of New Zealand, or Macdonald of Canada.

Not infrequently entrepreneurs have been involved as the instruments through which a monarch or an economic statesman or even a democratic state may choose to act. The East India companies of England or Holland, perhaps the land-grant railroads of the United States, or the "chosen instrument" airlines in various modern states may be suggested as typical cases from a large population.

Two representative cases are worth presentation in some detail, to illustrate how the collaboration of state and entrepreneur rises, and how it develops in different situations. One case pertains to eighteenth-century France and becomes available through the research of Professor Paul W. Bamford; and the other relates to nineteenth-century Belgium and derives from investigations of Richard M. Westebbe, erstwhile a research fellow attached to the Center in Entrepreneurial History at Harvard.[62]

Professor Frederic C. Lane once gave a paper to the entrepreneurial history group at Harvard of which the main thesis, based on his research in early modern commerce, was to the effect that in times of uncertainty the businessman sought the protection of the state. Such seems to have been a principal ambition of Pierre Babaud, later Pierre Babaud de la Chaussade, whose career in eighteenth-century France interested Professor Bamford as a particularly neat case illustrating the problems of the French navy vis-à-vis the whole economic and political situation of the *ancien régime.*

Actually, it is almost impossible to digest Babaud's career beyond the point which Professor Bamford squeezed the data in his essay in *Explorations in Entrepreneurial History,* since there are so many special circumstances of the government or the society or the period which conditioned the performance of this entrepreneur. Thus the *contrôleur général* to the Duke of Lorraine could be a secret partner in Babaud's exploitation of the Duke's forests for nearly a decade without knowledge of the latter — and so there might have been other deficiencies of communication; Pierre could purchase the post of *Secrétaire du Roy* and thereby secure privileges and exemptions not available to competitors; and, since most of his workers in the iron as well as in the lumbering business lived on land which he owned, they were, in a sense, dependent upon his political authority as they were upon his economic. By reason of these latter elements, Professor Bamford says that "Chaussade can rightly be called an industrial lord, or feudal industrialist."

Chaussade chose to link his fortunes with those of the French navy by contracting to supply anchors and other iron parts for ships. Not every aspect of this relationship proved fortunate. He had difficulties in securing payment; shipments of products across certain territories were subject to tolls which individuals more privileged than he kept collecting; and the business was hardly steady in volume — in part because France at this period had only a second-class navy, and therefore had poor success against England's first-class service. As a result it was condemned to further second-class treatment by the French government.

However, Chaussade's activity on government contracts did yield numerous advantages. For example, other landowners of the nearby provinces were obliged to transport coal and wool for him at fixed prices; navy inspectors resident at his plants became partisans with him in his efforts to gain even greater privileges and exemptions; while the nature of his work enabled him in effect to put his employees into slavery: if any left his establishments, they could be forcibly returned.

The balance between such advantages and the foregoing disadvantages is indicated perhaps by two circumstances: when in his later decades he tried to sell his products to civilian ship-builders or ship-owners, he found that he could not begin to compete with English ship-iron brought in over the existing tariff duties. According to Bamford, Chaussade wound up as "one of the richest industrialists in France."

But Chaussade was more than a mere governmental dependent. Like all true entrepreneurial actors, he had to be concerned with managing the flow of goods and managing costs. In furtherance of the flow, he tried to assure himself of adequate capital. Relative to working capital, he seems to have gone to quite considerable trouble to convince leaders that he was always liquid. At least there appears to be no other explanation of his persistent borrowing from one person to pay his debt to another. He also kept his hands on his accumulated wealth in part by arranging to turn over dowries for his daughters only at his death, and meanwhile paying his sons-in-law interest on the promised amount!

More importantly, he did introduce technological improvements in the treatment of iron, such as the use of reverberatory furnaces fired with mineral fuel. He built nearby housing for his workers, with at least one building equipped with a clock, since, as he said, it was "extremely desirable that all be on hand to receive quickly the orders of the directors of the forges." In addition, he devised at least two procedures appropriate to large-scale operations anywhere at any time: he delegated the actual management of his numerous and geographically scattered enterprises to such supervisors as the "directors of the forges," reserving to himself the policy decisions; and he "contracted out" the maintenance of his buildings, and again the maintenance in repair of his industrial equipment, to individuals who received annual fees.

Babaud de la Chaussade is really a most interesting figure, and none the less so because Professor Bamford puts him forward as a not-untypical specimen of the eighteenth-century French entrepreneurship. In character Babaud would seem a worthy predecessor of the St. Simonists under the Second Republic and Empire. In method he appears to manifest the pliancy of entrepreneurs elsewhere and at other periods to take advantage of conjunctures, even decadent governmental conditions. Professor Bamford is quite sure that Babaud did not purchase his royal secretaryship solely or principally for the distinction that it gave him; Babaud was intent on using the privileges of nobility to compete in an economy which was shot through with noble privileges. The status was for him a tool, not an end in itself. A way could be found through the tangle of privileges and exemptions — a person with some funds could "buy into" the show!

The case of John Cockerill, like that of Babaud, concerns, at least in part, the development of the iron industry in what eventually became Belgium. Actually, the Cockerills had begun smelting iron ore with charcoal, as had the Frenchman earlier.

The Cockerills are akin to the Scholfields considered above.[63] They were mechanics, familiar with the front-running English technology, who migrated to underdeveloped countries with the purpose of capitalizing on their advanced knowledge. They were the bearers of technological change, the agents of technological diffusion.

William Cockerill, the father, had left England in 1797, a year of business depression in that country, and some time between 1798 and 1800 had settled with his family at Verviers on the Continent. The family contained three sons, of whom John was the youngest. William, like the Scholfields, became a figure in the wool manufacture. He manufactured textile machinery at Verviers, and is credited with reforming the production methods in the Belgian wool manufacture.

Before the close of the Napoleonic period, the three sons had all grown to manhood, and had enlarged the family operations. The Peace of Vienna found them producing steam engines and hydraulic presses at Liège. In the new organization of Europe, what is now Belgium, the Netherlands, and Luxemburg were united, with Willem I as king, but the area was largely shut off — through high customs duties — from the market of almost the whole Continent, for which it had been producing before 1815. There was need for a positive developmental policy, and Willem embraced a program of that character. Support of the entrepreneurial ambitions of John Cockerill came to form an important part of that program.

From the point of view of the King and the nation, there seem to have been several purposes in the support of Cockerill. Initially, the Belgian machine-building should be brought up to the level of the British industry; and obviously the ex-Britishers were well circumstanced to do that. Again, the country should not be dependent upon foreign makers for certain types of machines, especially marine engines for both the new navy and the contemplated fleet of steamships for the Rhine traffic. Third, it appears that the national policy contemplated Belgium's becoming a builder of steam engines and machinery for much of Europe. The country could build on the foundations laid by the Cockerills over the 1800–1815 period.

The part in the drama played by John Cockerill is more difficult to assess. Westebbe portrays him as an indifferent financier, perhaps an indifferent technician, and not a very good manager. Surely he was continually in financial hot water and surely he underestimated the difficulties of constructing marine engines. Westebbe thinks that Cockerill did not appreciate "the real problems of dealing with an unskilled labor force, underdeveloped markets, and large-scale concentrated output." Even a government report not long before the Revolution of 1830 advocated a more aggressive sales policy.

However, the events of the years 1815–1830 are subject to a rather different interpretation. Here are the more striking ones: Cockerill made the first move in attaching himself to the King, when in 1816 he sought to acquire control of a sizable royal estate at Seraing, to be used for industrial purposes. He is alleged to have been persuasive in conversation or argument inducing the government to take half the stock in his enterprise. (Cockerill was always "needing" more money, and getting it — more or less fully — from the government, but he seems to have remained wealthy.) At one time he tried to get the government to take more than 50 per cent control of the establishment; the only other prominent entrepreneur of the young nation threatened to leave the country unless he could have his way with government policy. When Cockerill determined to set up cotton manufacturing, and asked governmental support, his petition was turned down, but he went right ahead anyhow, and soon the government was making a contribution.

The whole sequence need not have been contrived, but I am reminded of a Harvard student who one June told me that he was leaving that day for New York to "sell a monopoly" — namely, his services. Westebbe intimates that entrepreneurial talent was scarce in the Low Countries at this period. Quite obviously Cockerill, as a result of his family's and his own endeavors, enjoyed a differential advantage over the others. And seemingly he understood, and acted consciously or unconsciously to take advantage of a conjuncture. A state policy of economic development can sometimes be made to yield private returns. In this particular case returns appear to have been put to good use: the *Société Anonyme John Cockerill* survives to this day.

VIGNETTE 14: THE STATE TAKES OVER

The notion that entrepreneurship (or private enterprise) formed the all-prevailing element in the economic development of the United States before 1860, that those decades can be accurately labeled a laissez-faire period, has been pretty severely mauled by the series of studies promoted since 1940 by the Committee on Research in Economic History, and is in process of complete demolition at the hands of Professor Carter Goodrich of Columbia.[64] In the period with which we are chiefly concerned, however, 1818–1841, no clear decision had been reached as to whether private or public auspices should prevail in the construction and operation of public works: highways, canals, and railroads. Common roads and town streets were government affairs; turnpikes private; bridges divided, but chiefly public; canals, earlier private and not very successful, more recently public; and railroads private but with some indirect aid. In 1818 the principal item of interest was the successful launching of the Erie Canal, to run more than 350 miles across New York State, with the planning and carrying through in state hands, and the construction scheduled for the same auspices. With the stirrings in Pennsylvania, Massachusetts, and elsewhere along the Atlantic Coast for potentially competing facilities, quite surely at government expense, and with the Cumberland Road authorized by the federal government, there seemed the prospect of a swing toward greater participation of the state in transportation affairs.

It was at the close of the summer of 1818 that William H. Merritt made a survey with such instruments as he found available in the locality, and it was on October 14 of that year that he made the first public presentation of the scheme which later blossomed into the Welland Canal.[65] These events were critical for determining the auspices under which this new enterprise should be initiated, and they reveal aspects peculiarly interesting to the study of entrepreneurship and of economic change.

There was the circumstance that Merritt had connections

south of the border. His father had been a Loyalist at the time of the American Revolution, and had moved from Connecticut to the Niagara peninsula, which was in fact a haven for numerous men of similar sentiments. William Merritt had volunteered for the war that broke out in 1812, had been captured in the battle of Lundy's Lane, and had spent an appreciable period in a prisoners' camp in Massachusetts. He could have learned there of the Middlesex Canal, while, with the proposed terminus of the Erie Canal at Buffalo, it is highly probable that he knew of that project as well.

The original objective of Merritt and his immediate associates was merely a minor addition to activities in which they, and especially Merritt, were engaged already. Merritt was, if you will, acting in a manner typical of a frontier-type entrepreneur. Building on the start which his father had achieved at St. Catharines, William Merritt had successively established a flour mill, a sawmill, a potashery, a distillery, a cooper's shop, and a smithy. The success of these enterprises was in considerable part dependent upon a steady year-round flow of water; but the lumbering of the peninsula — to produce building materials for the growing population of the region — had rendered uncertain the water supply in the local Twelve Mile Creek, especially in the summer months. Merritt's surveying excursion was in search of a means to improve that water flow, just as Nicholas and Moses Brown might help to found the Bank of Providence the better to finance their enterprises of that region. Merritt found no supplemental source short of Lake Erie; but, with the difference in the height of water in Lakes Erie and Ontario spectacularly illustrated by the falls at Niagara, it was easy for Merritt to conceive of a ditch between the two lakes, a mere twenty-eight miles, which could indeed give a steady water flow to his creek. To be sure, a ridge or escarpment stood in the way, but Merritt estimated the ridge to be only thirty feet high.

Here in the study comes an instance of the "locally-oriented" or limited enterprise, of which I have spoken above.[66] The surveying instruments that the locality boasted were in fact defective. The aforesaid ridge was sixty feet high, not thirty; and Professor Aitken speculates that quite conceivably Merritt would not have had the temerity himself to proceed further, and he would not have succeeded in persuading his neighbors to join with him, if he had gotten a true measure of the physical difficulties that confronted construction gangs. Probably Professor John E. Sawyer would classify this episode as a case of constructive error.[67]

The meeting on October 14 reveals finally the elaboration of plans through which an originally simple scheme may go when application succeeds upon initial conception. Now the ditch for the conveyance of water had become a "canal" for the transportation of boats; the advantage which a few mill owners on Twelve Mile Creek might secure had expanded to "the great benefits [that] these provinces will derive"; and the provision of a steady supply of water to a few mills had given way to the capability of this new canal to "counteract" the possible influence of the projected Erie Canal, especially being able to "take down the whole of the produce of the western country." [68] One is led to think of Professor Daniel R. Fusfeld's "Heterogony of Entrepreneurial Goals," [69] to wonder whether this is not a case of the same genus as those which have begun to interest Professor Diamond, where the implementation or carrying-into-effect of a concept has inevitably brought with it a reorganization and redirection of the program.[70]

Many years ago, Charles W. Moulton analyzed several well-known plays of Shakespeare in terms of inevitableness

215

of the subsequent action given the situation exposed by the dramatist in his early scenes: Caesar, Othello, King Lear, et cetera, were, as it were, doomed from the start.[71] Similarly, the subsequent experience of Merritt and the Welland Canal Company were largely contained in the circumstances of its origination. Surely the element that became ever more crucial, the difficulty of securing capital, might be deduced from the location of the project on a frontier of civilization. On the other hand, a reason for governmental interest existed in 1818 but was not specifically mentioned by the petition to the legislature which was drawn up by the meeting of October 14 of that year. I have in mind the military argument. In the war just concluded, the Canadian government had found it necessary to maintain two fleets with no communication between them, one on Lake Erie and one on Lake Ontario. There was continuing danger of attack from the wild men below the border, and thus a sizable canal between the two lakes would be very welcome by those charged with the defense of Canada. (Actually the government went forward with the survey for the construction of the Rideau Canal, which had almost exclusively a military objective.)

The barest facts of this subsequent development are as follows: the company was chartered in January, 1824; it had the outward aspects of a wholly private enterprise, although it did have the right to seize land for its proper purposes (but paying indemnity), and the government had the right of purchase after a thirty-year period (but that was common practice in charters pertaining to enterprise with monopolistic power).[72] Capital proved persistently difficult to secure, although one John B. Yates, who, in today's parlance might be called the "king" of the contemporary American lotteries, was induced to make substantial investment in the stock of the Company. Planning of construction and the execution of plans, the search for capital, and relations with the Canadian legislature came almost exclusively into the hands of William Merritt, largely because he wished it that way, but partly because of the lack in Upper Canada at that time of competent assistants. The administration was not efficient; public money became ever more essential to maintain construction; to some extent the project became a football of politics in a Canadian domestic "revolution" which seems to have had some of the character of Jefferson's struggle with the Federalists around 1800 in the United States. Financial conditions in England and the United States after 1836 added to the pressure, and the canal was forcibly purchased by the government in 1841. The relative stakes of government and private enterprise at a fairly mature date are indicated by a record of stock ownership as of December, 1836:

	Number	Percentage
Government of Upper Canada	8,600	43.0
Government of Lower Canada	2,000	10.0
Individuals in Upper Canada	297	1.5
Individuals in Lower Canada	1,106	5.5
Individuals in New Brunswick	40	0.2
Individuals in New York	5,570	27.8
Individuals in England	2,411	12.0
Total	20,024	100.0

At this time, William Merritt himself owned 38 shares, or less than 0.2 per cent of the total number outstanding.

Professor Aitken gives the mature situation among the interested parties in terms that are somewhat reminiscent of Wellington's illuminating treatment of sectional issues in the United States in the 1828–1842 period: cheap public lands, the protective tariff, and public improvements at governmental expense.[73] Here one might differentiate three principal parties. First, and ultimately the most powerful, was the government. (One should perhaps distinguish two governments: the English and the Canadian. At one stage it seemed possible that the English government might take a larger share of responsibility than it actually did. At all events, the interests of the two governments were parallel in most regards.) The Canadian government did take an increasingly positive view of the canal as a public utility, a means of improving its military defense, and one of challenging the waxing economic power of the United States, while at the same time benefiting its citizens. It manifested, on the whole, less of the desire for rapid completion of the scheme than did the other two chief participants; and surely it welcomed any opportunity to economize on the investment of its own scarce funds.

The attitudes of these other parties, Merritt and Yates, who seem to have carried the entrepreneurial responsibilities, are skillfully sketched by Professor Aitken.

Merritt had taken the lead in the launching of the enterprise primarily as a means of increasing the value of his properties, but gradually, perhaps as a result of the financial and technical difficulties of getting the work completed, he became more and more concerned merely in bringing the job to completion at almost any cost.

Yates began and ended a financial man. He had been involved in the lottery business in New York State, at that period a large-scale affair, and had become interested in the canal as an investment or, perhaps better, a speculation. He was also eager that the waterway be completed, but not as a means for the aggrandizement of St. Catharines, or indeed, the whole of Canada, but as a source of profits which in turn would make marketable — hopefully at a profit also

218

— the shares of the canal company in which he had placed his money.

The paths of the two men diverged when, viewing the advancing activity of the Canadian government, they saw their respective primary objectives promoted or submerged. Professor Aitken puts the situation thus:

Merritt regarded with equanimity, and indeed welcomed, each successive government grant and subscription. He saw no threat either to his own interests or to those of the Company in dependence on the legislature as a source of capital. The prospect of eventual government purchase he found by no means unattractive. After all, what did "the government" mean to him, if not the Executive Council, composed largely of his friends and fellow directors, the Legislative Council, dominated by the same group, and the Assembly, which might indeed prove bothersome on occasion but which could generally be counted on to grant what was requested? "The government" to Merritt was not an institution existing over and against the Company, but rather an instrument which the Company might use for its own purposes. Just as in his speeches and public papers he portrayed himself and his colleagues as acting *for* the province, so he expected the political leaders of the province to act *for* the Company. And until Mackenzie demonstrated that "the government" could be used as an instrument to destroy the Company as effectively as it formerly had given support, his expectations were not disappointed.

John B. Yates seems to have found this attitude hard to understand and harder still to accept. As a major stockholder, he was by no means content to let the government have the canal, even with repayment of principal and interest, unless complete and final bankruptcy were the only alternative. It was in the expectation of profits — large profits — that he had bought the stock, and that these profits, given time, would be realized he never doubted. To be sure, in the early years he had been as anxious as Merritt that the government should take an interest in the canal and demonstrate that interest by financial aid. But the successive encroachments of the legislature upon the Company's freedom of action he resented and feared. Earlier than any of the directors he recognized the danger implicit in Mackenzie's appointment to the board, suspecting (correctly, as it turned out) the imminence of the kind of organized political attack which he had learned to dread and respect in the lottery business. "The Government" for him was not *his* government; with the office-holders and Councillors whom Merritt admired and attempted to emulate he coöperated because there was no alternative. But he had little confidence in their ability and less in their willingness to put the interests of the stockholders first and their own careers and reputations second.[74]

Economic circumstances in Upper Canada in the 1818–1841 period did not permit the efflorescence of the sort of single-headed, innovating entrepreneurship with which Merritt launched the Welland Canal enterprise, and of which he seems to have been both desirous and capable. Conditions were also unfavorable for the sort of high-profit, quick-return operation which to Yates seemed the only worthwhile form of entrepreneurial performance. Merritt appears to have accommodated himself rather readily to the changes in fortunes. The achievement of construction — construction under almost any circumstances — came to supersede any ideas of the better and worse means of effecting that achievement. The circumstances surrounding the enterprise — economic, political, and to some extent personal — all favored the ultimate eventuality that the state should "take over."

VIGNETTE 15: LONG-TERM SUPPORT OF ENTREPRENEURSHIP

The promotion of industrialization is, of course, an old story, even if it has acquired a new name. The English from Tudor times on, the French under Colbert, the United States under Hamilton, Carey, Clay, and others, the Germans, the Russians — almost every nation has sought to encourage the introduction or expansion of young industries by protection. Economists realize that such state aid may be dangerous. It can become infectious. Manufacturers other than the original ones may be tempted to apply — and have at least a precedent in their favor — and farmers, miners, even organized labor may seek corresponding protection. However, there is often, if not usually, trouble even in the best cases. The "young" industries never grow up. Part of the explanation may be in the variant moods of entrepreneurship, and here we can draw data from a study of Brazilian experience with the cotton manufacture over a century of trial, a study made in large part on the ground by Professor Stanley J. Stein.[75]

The employment of this particular case to illustrate general points may not be appropriate. Possibly Brazil is not a propitious country for the development of industries. Surely Professor Stein shares the view of observers in a number of South American countries, that the market is inelastic; "the problem of cotton textile entrepreneurs was indissolubly linked with the national economy; a sound cotton manufacture could not exist alongside a sick rural economy." This seems to be the situation elsewhere on the continent. As Professor Henry G. Aubrey once put it, unlike the North American industrialist, a South American one does not presume that a reduction in the price of his product will increase the volume of his sales.[76] And a report of the United Nations on economic development in Latin America spoke mainly of overcoming the uncertainties of export volumes.[77]

Perhaps there is something odd about entrepreneurship in Latin America, at least something destructive enough to make unwarranted deductions based on North American data. More than one observer, surely, has commented on the greater measure of fatalism evident among Latin Americans in general. They seem to think that if the good Lord gives wealth, that is fine; if he does not, that is all right too — after all, life is short and not very important. Perhaps financial success, even accomplishment of any sort, counts for less than it does north of the Rio Grande.

There is also a question whether the position of industrialist, even large-scale or successful industrialist, carries the prestige that it does farther north. Professor Stein finds "a landholding aristocracy and a merchant oligarchy" to have constituted the elite group in Brazilian society at least through 1914, and that even now politically "a rural oligarchy and an impoverished rural electorate" are dominant. It is possible that the industrialist's prestige varies among the regions of the very large country, is high in such an industrialized area as São Paulo and lower elsewhere. Brazil was after all, predominantly an agricultural country until World War I, and is still largely so.

At all events, the cotton manufacture in Brazil made slow, although persistent, progress through the second half of the nineteenth century. During this period production was limited pretty much to coarse fabrics for rural consumption — and this despite a rising degree of tariff protection. The industry had attracted the support of well-heeled and influential Portuguese importers in the 1880's. They contributed capital, marketing skill, and presumably political connections. At any rate, the manufacture had reached a reasonable state of maturity around 1890, and secured a tariff wall that was held constant — and rather high — for forty years. Thereafter, administrative measures taken to combat the depression, or the conditions of World War II, made tariff protection less important.

Two developments occurred; one that is rather common under protectionism — although apparently not recognized by so eminent a writer on tariff matters as Taussig — and the other perhaps more noteworthy in Brazil than elsewhere. The first phenomenon is the tendency of entrepreneurs behind tariff walls or their equivalent to "edge up" on the quality of their productions. The Brazilian manufacturers did so before 1934 in a modest degree, and more extensively in the period of World War II. There is a competitive advantage in pressing costs down, and raising the quality of the output. There is probably some "psychic income" also; one has risen a bit in the scale of things, become more akin to the superior foreign producer. At all events, the point which I wish to make is that by reason of this propensity "infant industries" in a sense never grow up; the elevation in quality of output means that there is always some portion of the industry on "the margin," as it were, still as dependent on the same amount of protection as the portion originally sheltered — at least until all qualities of all varieties of the product which can be sold in the domestic market come to be manufactured in domestic mills more cheaply than they can be produced in any other competing country.

The second feature, not peculiar to Brazilian cotton manufactures, but seemingly more noteworthy in their case than in other somewhat comparable affairs, is the persistent and varied reliance on government for aid. Industrialists and farmers in the United States, France, Germany, indeed, in many countries, have gone to considerable lengths to keep a protective umbrella over their heads, and some sorts of farmers in more than one country have sought and accepted other forms of financial aid, usually subsidies of some type. In Brazil aid from the state is allegedly a spontaneous first thought of the cotton manufacturers in time of trouble. Not merely tariff increases, but special loans, or prohibition on the erection of additional mills, or restriction on the import of new machinery — all these have been advocated or accepted.

An explanation is offered by Professor Stein after his scholarly survey of the facts:

As early as the 1890's, the leaders of the Brazilian cotton manufacture advocated practices which converted them forty years later into a business oligarchy operating closely with government. The frontier between industrialization in the national interest and legalized favoritism for a minority of cotton industrialists was vague and easily passed. Here the cotton manufacturers merely followed the traditional patterns of planters and merchants who demanded and received from the state both concessions and privileges in the nineteenth and twentieth centuries.

The rise of rival groups "equally vociferous and influential" in the decades after 1930 made the acquisition of special favor more difficult to secure, but even after 1945 the effects of "government intervention in various forms, the absence of effective competition, and a rapidly growing population" were clearly to be seen: they were evident in a failure to maintain technological and managerial advance.

Professor Stein reaches the conclusion, valuable in other situations, that what Brazil has secured after a century of effort is "a developed segment of an underdeveloped economy," and seemingly an entrepreneurial group that appreciates its somewhat unfortunate situation and, for the most part, merely continues to look toward the state for support. Entrepreneurship does not necessarily grow vigorous with age.

PART THREE·
POSTLUDE: PROCESS OF
ENTREPRENEURIAL CHANGE

THE CHARACTER OF KNOWLEDGE or research in entrepreneurial history is evident in the foregoing parts. It represents a commingling of economics and history, sociology and business administration, technology and social psychology; it constitutes an interdisciplinary inquiry. Obviously, it is "behavioristic," has a good deal to do with communication, and comes close to concerning itself with forecasting, because the forces with which it deals are largely slow-acting and slow-changing, since "history" continues up to the present moment. Again, it is a meeting ground of many varieties of history: economic, social, intellectual, institutional, and technological, with a little religious and philosophical history thrown in. It is international in its scope, and cultural in its focus.

Most practically, the study of entrepreneurial phenomena offers economics on a time dimension, and economics stripped of its *mutatis mutandis,* its assumptions, and its caveats. Its pursuit would constitute in part a return to a range of questions and problems that interested economists of earlier generations: matters of progress, improvement of mankind, the trend toward a "stationary state," and the like.

Alfred Marshall was still influenced by such considerations. In his *Principles,* he mentions the problem of the competitive growth of business units, "trees" in his "forest," but he turns to other matters when he observes that the trees do not last forever. Of course, there are three ripostes to such an argument. When he wrote, there were actually in Britain a number of enterprises that could trace back continuous ex-

227

istence a couple of centuries; second, we should have no study of forestry or even botany in general if scientists were discouraged by the mortality of their specimens; and, anyway, nothing much in economics remains valid much longer than an oak, let alone a redwood, not even the whole economic system which Marshall took for granted.[1]

On the other hand, Marshall does recognize specifically that there are long-run considerations that differ from those pertinent to the short run; and he was prepared to admit that "even indirect influences may produce great effects in the course of a generation, if they happen to act cumulatively," and accordingly, "violence is required for keeping broad forces in the pound of *caeteris paribus*" over any such period.

Marshall in his *Principles* seemed to take fright when he looked into the "pound" of long-run forces. "A theoretically perfect long period," he writes, "must give time enough to enable not only the factors of production of the commodity to be adjusted to the demand, but also the factors of production of those factors of production to be adjusted, and so on." This process perturbed him the more since, as he saw it, "when carried to its logical consequences, [it] will be found to involve the supposition of a stationary state of industry, in which the requirements of a future age can be anticipated an indefinite time beforehand." [2] Obviously, this is not the place to argue scientific procedure in economic research, but it should be clear that, if it is logical for some purposes to stop at the stage of the action of one set of productive factors, it is equally logical for other purposes to stop at one stage removed. And, as a matter of record, Marshall attempted a consideration of once-removed forces in the international comparisons contained in his *Industry and Trade*. Here national aptitudes, national experiences, and the like are called upon to explain economic trends.

Studies of population are, for the most part, good examples of long-run economics. They contain everything from the effects of marriage customs today or in Roman times upon the birth rates of the respective eras to the rate of the communication of medical knowledge upon the death rate, now as compared with a century ago. In fact, thoughtful students do not hesitate to carry the analysis "logically" a step further, concerning themselves not merely with what happened, but what the events meant for the thinking of the people to whom the events related! Such is the contribution of Professor Helleiner to the study of the "vital revolution" of the eighteenth century in Europe. As he states it: the disappearance of the black rat should be given its due "not merely in the sense that it helped to eliminate the greatest single agent of mortality [by the spreading of the plague], but in the sense that perhaps only a society freed from the fear as well as from the material and spiritual consequences of sudden death was able to achieve that high rate of intellectual and technical progress without which population growth could never have been sustained." [3]

The evolution of economico-business literature is a further case in point. I have attempted to outline the more important changes that have occurred in the printed materials since Gutenberg, with some effort at examining the changes, in an essay entitled, "Conspectus for a History of Economic and Business Literature." [4]

So also are the efforts to discover periods of broadly running secular change such as that recently elaborated by Professor Herbert Heaton on the basis of changes in standards of living, or the earlier one of Professor Edwin F. Gay relative to degrees of economic freedom and restraint. [5] Such interpreters of history do not hesitate to bring into their arguments anything from religious and political beliefs to the impact of improved education.

Economics on a time scale will always draw heavily from the facts and theories adduced by economic historians. That form of economics would fail to reach its potential, however, if, as one author lately phrased the relationship, economic history should be "based on economic theory." [6] It would seem a mistake also for economic historians to follow too slavishly the admonitions of well-intentioned advisors and use more economic theory in their work — if they were to consider themselves limited by the current body of economic theory.[7]

The point that I am making is an obvious one, really: theory is based on facts, including many historical ones, not facts on theory. Economics on a time dimension may well make use of certain dynamic propositions of current economic theory — such as the Malthusian law (in some form), Gresham's law, and the like — and may wish to employ for its convenience such static notions as noncompeting groups or consumer's surplus. But it may well look to the theorist to provide theories to explain the facts, as indeed they did in the case of business cycles or changing location of industries. Theories important for historical economics need not be the same as those for short-run matters, any more than macro-economics should cover the same topics as micro-economics.

Historical economics would necessarily have a tempo or "time horizon" appropriate to its materials and purposes, just as the tempo of the geologist is different from that of the botanist, and that of the latter different from that of the present-day economist. Yet it does seem important that some branch or section of the social sciences (including analytical history) should pay concentrated and continuous attention to the theoretical explanation, limited though such explanations may be in many cases, of the rise and decline of economies, of the speed in the spread of technical or business knowledge, of the significance of education (of various sorts) upon economic productivity, and — not least — of the consequences upon national income of the changing role, changing proficiency, and changing motivations of entrepreneurs. When economists more generally adopt longer time perspectives, and when they venture to open the "pound" of factors that condition the changing complements of the productive factors, it may well prove convenient — at least for relatively modern Western economies — to make entrepreneurship the central focus. A whole gamut of dynamic flows would be encompassed thereby: relations to the discovery and tapping of new natural resources, relations to the implementation of capital and of labor, relations to the introduction of technological or intellectual innovations, even relations to the circumambient society. It was in the context of economics of this character that, a decade ago, I ventured to speak of "the entrepreneur" as indeed "the central figure." Since doctors should in theory take their own medicine, I venture to elaborate a "model" of the nature of entrepreneurial change.

Entrepreneurial Change

At the outset of an explanation of entrepreneurial change, it will be useful to make manifest what the exposition aims to do, and what it does not attempt. I do think that the analysis should have in mind changes of all sorts, those that seem connected with economic decline of areas or nations as well as those that seem associated with economic development.[8] The explication should perhaps be flexible enough to fit the exigencies of the case of a "moving equilibrium" of entrepreneurial character and performance — a rather improbable situation over any period of time that would be significant for studies other than short-run adjustments.

On the other hand, we are not directly concerned with

the whole subject of economic change. We believe the two to be interrelated, indeed, that the real availability of natural resources, the flow of capital, the improvement in quality of labor, the generation of consumer demand, and the like are much affected by the changing quality of entrepreneurship. Yet the sources and process of economic change are by no means identical with those of entrepreneurial alteration.

"Change" in this whole connection does comprehend the degree to which entrepreneurs take advantage of the total economic situation, but it also comprehends the entrepreneur's interaction with the total cultural situation. The willingness to grasp the possibilities of professional education as well as to accept new and improved machinery must be included. And change is constituted of innovations that alter pre-existing entrepreneurial behavior. The innovation may be largely ceremonial, as when New York bankers ceased to wear cutaway coats to their offices; they may be *fachmässig*, such as the inauguration of a cost-accounting system or — operating in the direction of decreased effectiveness — the acceptance of longer week ends at country houses. And they may be affective (if I may employ this term in the current connection), as when Frederick W. Taylor and his followers promoted the notion of *right* ways of doing things in business, or when businessmen in America took seriously the ideas of natural selection as voiced by Herbert Spencer. At all events, change may be conceived as innovations of thought, procedures, or instruments, initiated at any of several possible points in the entrepreneurial world, and spread among entrepreneurial actors by imitation of one man or institution by others.

The explanation of enterpreneurial change may best be elaborated in three stages: that of entrepreneurial structure, that of motivation, and that of process or course of movement.

The nature of the entrepreneurial world, in terms of structure, has been examined in foregoing chapters.[9] A brief résumé will suffice at this point. I conceive the entrepreneur or entrepreneurial team — those who make, execute, and are responsible for the strategic decisions of a profit-oriented enterprise — as located in the center of a series of concentric circles, or riding a log in the grip of a set of close and distant forces. Nearest to him (or it) is the personnel of the business unit for the "maintenance and aggrandizement" of which the decisions are made. Indeed, I have conceived of this personnel as constituted of two circles or layers, the individuals responsible (with the entrepreneur) for the conduct of the enterprise, and those only indirectly associated, such as the stockholders, bankers, suppliers, and the like.

The latter congeries merges with the next external group, which I have denominated the entrepreneurial stream. Here would be the service institutions, the ancillary units, the purveyors of business information, the schools of business, and the like.

Still further removed, at least in the aggregate, from the decision-making center would be the entrepreneurial world, which I conceive as those facets of the total culture that have relevance for entrepreneurial character and performance; for example, ministers giving their interpretations of proper business conduct, but not the same men calling upon the sick, or an engineering school in its "applied" instruction, but not in its prosecution of basic research. Here would fall the public censors as a whole, the consumers affiliated and potential, the educational system, the governmental organizations, et cetera.

It will become obvious on second thought that while "in the aggregate," as I said immediately above, one circle, or one current in a stream, may be conceived to lie at one or more "removes" from the entrepreneurial center, actually the entrepreneurial actors have in major or minor degree direct interaction with all such circles or currents. These actors read the general literature of their culture, see its motion pictures, and hears its sermons. Similarly, they may well have direct contacts with the theory of games, with Keynesian economics, or other bodies of thought not directly concerned with business administration. And I speak of interaction, since quite obviously businessmen are not passive recipients of social forces; they help to mold those forces.

From time to time in the foregoing exposition I have mentioned various incentives to action on the part of entrepreneurial figures: financial reward, prestige, rise in a business hierarchy, sense of power, sense of public service, and the like. Professor David C. McClelland has coined the general term "need for achievement," [10] although I would be disposed to give the phrase a slight twist, to become the "need for recognition of achievement." There may be some entrepreneurs so "inner-directed" as to gain complete satisfaction in their contemplation of their own work well done; and surely such contemplation constitutes part of most businessmen's flow of psychic income. But achievement is generally a social event; and indeed Professor Drucker has indicated his belief in a report that business executives in America are not so much concerned over the absolute size of their salaries as in the *relationship* of their salaries to those of comparable officers.[11]

I have noted elsewhere that a "need for achievement" or something similar acts as the motive force for the erection of service institutions, and the propagation of a sort of circular action.[12] I would suggest here that the same need operates to galvanize the executives of management advisory enterprises, trade associations, and so on, even deans of business schools or ministers of the gospel, at least in some measure. Before his recent, untimely death, Professor R. Richard Wohl had almost, if not fully, completed a study of the success theme in American life. I believe that it would have carried further the data offered by Professor Irvin G. Wyllie in his book, *The Self-made Man in America*.[13]

A corresponding examination of English, French, Italian, or other experience, and the relevant literary expressions, might reveal a less vigorous growth, but the evidence of the "need for achievement" as well as the social recognition of accomplishment will not be found wholly absent from any of these countries, while the record in Germany and the Netherlands might well rival that of the United States.

It is noteworthy, however, that in entrepreneurial life more than in most other pursuits of achievement, the business unit counts for much, more than in most other social institutions; chambers of commerce, scientific associations, even political parties and most churches. The entrepreneurial actors find themselves compelled to share responsibilities with others; and the instillation of company loyalty forms a protection against too great inefficiency. Competition among business units, where alone the action is alleged sometimes to be "cutthroat," helps to increase the feeling of loyalty, by virtue of the need for individual security. So also does the endeavor of the individual actor in large business organizations to rise in the hierarchy. But surely not least is the entrepreneur's acceptance of the measure, even the reality of his achievement in the aggrandizement of the business unit with which he is affiliated.

Thus, the development of business enterprises comes to support the incentive of personal need for achievement, at least in most cases. The latter qualification is necessary because of the possibility, deriving from features of corporate finance, that a Jay Gould or his ilk may "achieve" the financial wreckage of the enterprise for which he is the effective entrepreneur, in order that through short selling of its stock in the public market, he may secure personal profit. Fortunately for society, most entrepreneurial actors envisage achievement in the shape of company expansion and institutional growth.

Beyond incentive to entrepreneurial change, there must be opportunity. The latter arises chiefly in the circumstance noted by Professor Cochran in *Change and the Entrepreneur,* that the entrepreneurial role is not closely defined. (Professor Cochran was writing about the United States, but his assertion would seem to be true in other Western countries.) Within the individual enterprise, there are in some measure "natural" contenders — the selling versus the production divisions, the stockholders versus the labor unions — each endeavoring to push the entrepreneurial actors in one direction or another.[14] Outside these institutions, in the entrepreneurial stream, lies also the potentiality of contending pressures. The organizations themselves — trade associations, management counselors, public accountants, and the like — may each represent a pull or push in a given direction, the stronger because of the very organization itself (with personnel also concerned with achievement); but they severally oppose one another in many relationships. For instance, the trade association secretary may counsel direct selling — for example, from factory to retailer — but the management adviser may argue against alienation of the traditional agents of distribution.

Insofar as elements of the whole culture may be involved, general social perspectives, what Professor Cochran called "cultural themes," there is even greater latitude of action permissible to entrepreneurial actors. For one thing, cultural themes are not always concurrent in their admonitions. For instance, one strand of social thought may encourage entrepreneurs to be bold, to crash ahead and do new things, but another strand may lay upon his shoulders at least decent care for his work, for people, and for the community in which he is, or has been, located. Again, many elements of social thought are but floating ideas — honorable conduct, respect for the dignity of others, the insurance of real freedom — many of them inheritances from the past. Even fewer of these cultural themes form the basis of social institutions by force of which they may be propagated and their values be continuously driven home. Those stemming from the Christian faith do enjoy the support of the churches, but the latter do not in fact speak with wholly uniform admonitions. And the precepts supported by schools and brotherhoods, Better Business Bureaus, and the editorials of the *New York Times* are by no means always uniform, and, for the most part, given to the expression of pious hopes. In such circumstances, entrepreneurs have considerable freedom in the shaping of their roles. There is much opportunity for change.

Parenthetically, it may be observed that the element of time makes itself noteworthy at various points. We are indeed concerned here with a set of flows also. I have spoken of the cultural themes as often being inheritances from the past. In fact such themes have sometimes varied in force from era to era and place to place. For example, an inventor of a textile spinning machine or apparatus was drowned in Danzig harbor in the seventeenth century, but another somewhat equivalent person was knighted in England in the eighteenth century. In the United States, "tied" houses for the distribution of malt liquors (saloons owned or financially aided by brewing companies in return for agreement to dispense only the products of the particular supporting brewer) threatened to become a common phenomenon in the nineteenth century. The practice aroused public disapproval, largely in consequence of the whole prohibition campaign, and now the local bar or tavern is free, both in the sense of being under no financial obligation to suppliers and in being able to dispense more than one brand of beverage, and of course to switch from one supplier to another. In England, on the other hand, "tied" houses arose in the early nineteenth century, and still flourish. The "free" house is the exception.

Time is involved also through the circumstance that entrepreneurial practices, like other human actions, tend to harden into conventions or thought-patterns that possess force in part because "the memory of man runneth not to the contrary," as was said in English manorial courts. The French local baker produces fresh loaves several times a day, and the French housewife goes to his shop as often in a day as she runs out of bread. The reception clerks in an English automobile-repair shop appear in cutaway coats and striped trousers — as have those in English retail stores since time immemorial. American banks must always be housed in edifices that look substantial. Correspondingly, an old enterprise, industry, or industrialized country possesses less flexibility than its younger equivalents, in entrepreneurial attitudes as in other features, such as the more familiar industrial technology.

A dynamic or growth element is provided within the individual enterprise by what may be called trading on experience — or trading upon history, if you will — provided an active entrepreneurial system exists in the society. W. Hastings Lyon gave an illustration of this factor forty years ago in his "trading on equity" in the financial aspect of corporate life. Lyon's illustrative or ideal case is that of a company that gets started on the capital secured through the issuance of common stock; when the concern has established earning power of adequate proportions and stability, it may secure added capital by issuing preferred stock; that is, trading on its relatively assured income; and then, later still, it could, as it were, give away more of its security in return for capital acquired through the issuance of bonds, capital that would not have been attracted into the enterprise until the concern had demonstrated a substantial and steady "equity" and become willing to "trade" upon the latter.

The same notion can be extended, even in the financial area. Proven stability of net earnings encourages commercial and investment bankers to take a friendlier view of the enterprise; and the same set of circumstances will permit the professional managers of the company to attain a greater degree of freedom from stockholder inspection and "interference." Such managers are enabled to engage the concern in projects of longer incubation than stockholders might contemplate agreeably, at least if a goodly sized regular dividend were not quite reasonably assured.

Processes of similar character are visible in other segments of company operations. In employee relations, for example, it seems clear that good relationships proceed step by step, each favorable move being prepared by the favorable acceptance of the previous action. The same is true in the extension of the line of goods that a concern produces or sells. The "equity" or good repute gained by Hotpoint stoves led the General Electric Company to add Hotpoint refrigerators, despite the incongruity of name; the American Telephone and Telegraph Company is engrossed in a number of electrical activities that have nothing to do with either "telegraph" or "telephone"; and so it goes with many other enterprises.

239

At one time American corporations used frequently to exhibit an appreciation of the foregoing conditions, at least in a vague sort of way, by carrying a substantial sum on the asset side of their balance sheets under the rubric of "good will." Accounting houses, typically conservative in outlook and apperceptive particularly of the short-run phenomena of the business cycle, have persuaded most concerns to eliminate this item or to carry it at a nominal figure. However, what may be good accounting practice may be inadequate long-term business theory. The good repute of a company and its products (or the quality of its services), its demonstrated earning power in various sets of circumstances, its apparent capacity for survival cannot be shrugged aside as valueless, especially when assessing the potentialities of growth of the institution. In the simpler, slower-moving conditions of eighteenth-century foreign mercantile operations, it seems evident that not a few houses expanded, as well as survived, on a modest supply of ability but a large quantity of integrity. Such intangible elements have not ceased to be of importance in company growth in later times. And the important socio-economic point is that here, "built into" the individual unit of a properly oriented business system, is a propensity, as it were, to lift one's self by one's bootstraps, and a method for accomplishing that feat. A somewhat similar condition will shortly be shown to exist for the business system as a whole.

The introduction of a new feature in entrepreneurial practice in a given area or industry — the inauguration of a public-relations department, the initiation of an executive training program, or the determination to take a firmer attitude vis-à-vis labor unions — is the act of an individual (or group of individuals) taken, in most cases, on behalf of the business enterprise with which they chance to be associated. The basic psychological impulse may be self-aggrandizement, the need for achievement, but the form is usually betterment of the individual's enterprise.

Entrepreneurial actors, like college presidents or managers of baseball teams, are all individual in the sense that for each the physical inheritance, the nurture, and the experiences in early life have been variant, even though the young men of a given "generation" may share many sentiments.[15]

Robert Owen had the misfortune in his youth to burn his stomach severely with hot porridge; and ever after he grew to think of himself as different from other men; Charlemagne Tower chanced to be christened with a name that never ceased to stir his ambitions; and Erastus B. Bigelow happened to be born with an unusual instinct for contrivance. Each business situation, a brief conjuncture, as it were, in a time-bound flow, is also individual, for each enterprise has its own evolved past. Accordingly, a man of perhaps peculiar acquired characteristics, confronted with a hitherto-unknown situation, may well exhibit what Professor Schumpeter called the "creative response."[16] An innovation in entrepreneurial behavior is born. What could not be anticipated from the precedent material conditions does in fact occur. Thus, Jay Cooke in the 1860's and J. P. Morgan in the early 1890's rendered valuable support to the federal treasury, and gave new stature to investment banking in this country; John Murray Forbes imparted a fresh impetus toward higher business ethics among top executives, a step toward the idea of trusteeship, when he refused to allow his railroad officers to participate in railroad construction companies concerned with their own railroad enterprises; and Frank W. Abrams appears possibly to have added almost a whole new facet to American entrepreneurial responsibilities when he advocated, and subsequently helped to implement, corporate aid to education.

However, many innovations in enterpreneurial behavior

241

are, in a sense, successful orphans. So many people, within enterprises, in service organizations, or elsewhere, have participated in the evolution of the idea that no one deserves the title of parent. Surely there is in each instance a first exponent of a new attitude, the first user of a new practice, but the last step in the process of change may be a small one and frequently — indeed in entrepreneurial history one can say "usually" — this true innovator passed unnoticed. An illustrative case is that related to the proper preservation of company records. One can trace the original impulse back at least to the practices of English and German scholars to uncover various phases of medieval and early modern history by the examination of municipal, guild, manorial, and other primary manuscript records. The first two deans of the Harvard Business School, Gay and Donham, were instrumental in the promotion of business history in the United States on a basis comparable with this European practice. Dr. Joseph H. Willits of the Rockefeller Foundation was interested in promoting historical research in this country. Finally, Emmet J. Leahy had had experience during World War II in the handling of U. S. Navy records. Out of this convergence arose the National Records Management Council, and out of the Council stemmed the modern professionalized treatment of corporate archives. And if it had not chanced that Professor Cochran, Professor Shepard B. Clough, and I had not been mixed up in the whole development, this significant evolution in entrepreneurial practice would probably never have been recorded.

As will have appeared already, at least by implication, many, if not most, innovations in entrepreneurial behavior are evolutionary in character, whether they be instrumental or affective in nature. I mean that they are constituted chiefly of carrying somewhat further some idea or aspiration already entertained in enterpreneurial life. Thus, Filene's "bargain basement" was in large measure merely a development from well-known bargain sales; and the commuter's ticket was the old railroad "pass" with places for the conductor to punch. The path of progress, however, is not always as smooth as the foregoing would tend to indicate. Human beings are variable; indeed, there appears even to be a small group that revels in being contrary or rebellious. I know an academic man who admitted that he had unwittingly picked up the mental habit of challenging any generalization: that Sundays in London were dull; that country-bred men were healthier than city-bred ones; and so on. Some businessmen are reportedly of similar character. An episode will illustrate what I mean. Mr. Richard Lenihan, the manager of a Toledo department store, and an old friend of mine, found his fur sales slumping during the war and early postwar years. As everywhere else, fur coats there were sold in "salons" with the help of "models," of course, but the people with the newly-expanded purses were not used to sitting in salons and looking at models; at most their daughters might *aspire* to becoming models. So Dick broke with tradition, put his mink and other coats on racks on the ground floor of his establishment where the women could handle the "goods," and found that the garments sold "like hotcakes."

Once a new practice or attitude has been initiated — by the action of an individual entrepreneur, by a writer in *Fortune*, or the counsel of a management consultant — the novelty is bound to be copied, if it is of the instrumental variety. The innovating enterprise, through the introduction of the new process or product, has gained a differential advantage; and its competitors are moved by the desire for profits, if not for survival, to recapture a position of equivalence. Even in the case of "affective" innovations, there may be competitive pressure promotive of imitation: public approval of such measures as a complaint section in a depart-

243

ment store, a helpful housing program for employees, or a real effort to install a nondiscriminatory labor policy, so that institutions comparably situated have to follow suit.

But the speed of imitation may vary widely. The rapidity of spread, and, therefore, the degree and speed of its general impact would seem, indeed, to depend on a number of variables. One is the quality of the entrepreneurial talent in the economy in question. The higher the percentage of top-caliber men, in the Danhof or any similar classification, and the smaller proportion of "Fabians" and "drones," the more rapid and enthusiastic is likely to be the reception of the new notion or technique.

Innovation, however, occurs in the whole system as well as within the individual enterprise. Stimulated by progress in the "arts," the advent of a new intellectual concept, even the prior expansion of the economy itself, entrepreneurs will find it alluring to attempt to establish a new ancillary or service institution — a credit-reporting agency, a counseling bureau in public relations, or just a means of preserving outgoing correspondence simpler than copying the messages into a letter-book. And, of course, here also there is imitation — Dun was followed by Bradstreet, Bernays by a host of others — while improvement in the conduct of such institutions over time, partly the consequence of competition between the first and the later arrivals, will have its own effect: the net contribution of the whole system to economic productiveness will be enhanced.

Another factor is the presence, perhaps the proportion, of new industries, with more flexible entrepreneurs. Erik Dahmen seems to have found a difference in the response of the entrepreneurs in old and in new industries to the pressures of the interwar period in Sweden.[17] In the United States the leaders in the electrical and chemical industries have manifested the quickest appreciation of scientific research. Again, it was the airplane and petroleum companies that responded first to the opportunity for better records management.

Surely a third factor could be the quality of the communication media. In an economically immature area, old or modern, efforts at secrecy of operations and paucity of public vehicles of communication are usual conditions. The gossip of the Rialto, the marketplace, or the coffeehouse had to suffice the early merchants. Early industrial entrepreneurs lived in even greater isolation. In the United States only the rise of first the commercial and then the industrial press gave motion to new ideas. More recently, professional associations, advisory organizations, teaching in schools of business, services of business libraries, and so forth, have speeded the course of new ideas.

Finally, there is the circumstance which might be called sympathetic alignment of institutions. (Here again the basic idea has been contributed by Professor Cochran, while I have obviously also borrowed a notion from Professor Cyert.) My idea is that maximum spread and maximum speed in entrepreneurial change will be found to come, and to have come in the past, where the various elements in the concentric circles of our imagined entrepreneurial world are all, as it were, pointing in the same direction, or charged with the same brand of electricity. A crop of unusually able leaders, business institutions flexible enough to respond to new developments, ancillary and service organizations tuned to encourage novelty and transmit knowledge of them, and an outside society friendly, if not forthrightly beneficent. Under such conditions, the "need for achievement" or "need of recognition" will bloom and thrive; improvement in entrepreneurial quality and resources will be stimulated; and the fruits of such striving will be given recognition of a wide character. An able young entrepreneur's program of cost reduction will "die aborning" if his board of directors and the association of his fellow industrialists frown on any exploitation of the notions which would drive marginal producers out of business. At times in the past the difficulties of New England manufacturers have been laid at the doors of unsympathetic bankers, uncooperative labor unions, overzealous tax authorities, and surely the endeavors, of innovation-riding entrepreneurs would not have much effect if the consumers of the relevant economy were habit-bound. The appeal of "streamlined" refrigerators or "1959 model" beds would hardly overreach the threshold of consciousness in a consuming public where cold cellars and durable consumers' goods were expected to serve generation after generation. At all events, there have been occasions in American experience, and there seem to have been rather more frequent occasions in foreign economies, where one or more of the elements was "out of line," as it were, or negative when it might better (for this purpose) to have been positive; — a family content with high current income, whatever the future; a society that did (or does not) give adequate recognition to entrepreneurial achievement; or a political system that thrives on the baiting of businessmen.

Entrepreneurial change is rather obviously an important phenomenon. The higher the quality of entrepreneurial talent, the greater the zeal of that talent for achievement, the more developed the ancillary and service institutions, and the more parallel the outlook of the whole entrepreneurial world, the greater will be the likelihood of higher productivity in the economy, and a higher national income, provided, of course, that the easy course of monopolistic control is effectively blocked, and provided the corruption of a cult of wealth can be moderated, if not replaced, by the valuation of other indicia of achievement.

The course of entrepreneurial change, however, is a complicated matter. Obviously it is a social phenomenon, and social in various ways: the innovating entrepreneur is in part a product of his society; he operates through and is operated upon by social organizations; and he and the personnel of these social bodies are influenced by waves of social thought, past and current.

Social change is also a phenomenon of communication. Specific individual changes are rarely of importance, each by itself; the economic or social value comes through imitation, and often also through a continuance of the trend which the specific change signalizes.

The change is usually a deviation from the pre-existing role, and entrepreneurial roles are "prescription-slack" in a degree adequate to permit, if not to encourage, deviation. Such deviation is likely to be progressive, in the sense of continuing a trend already begun and proved acceptable to at least some important censors. However, there are also occasional deviations that seem to run counter to pre-existent and prevailing thought.

The propagation of an entrepreneurial change will be promoted if it takes place in an entrepreneurial world wherein all the elements are beneficent: alert potential imitators; sclerosis-free industries and geographical areas that are not tradition-bound but are sophisticated and alert enough to make effective use of appropriate institutions available in the entrepreneurial stream; and a climate of cultural themes that is beneficent, tolerating, if not encouraging, changes that promise increased entrepreneurial effectiveness.

Obviously, as far as this exposition of entrepreneurial change is concerned, there is point in taking seriously Professor Rostow's reference to the biological antecedents of present-day economics. Long-term economics — which, it seems, can hardly overlook entrepreneurship, social institutions, and cultural themes — appears likely to resemble botany, perhaps, indeed, the "trees of the forest" to which Marshall referred more than a half-century ago.

WORKS CITED

NOTES

INDEX

WORKS CITED

Abbott, Charles C. "Broad View of Administration," University of Virginia *Alumni News.* October, 1956.

Abramovitz, Moses. *Resource and Output Trends in the United States since 1870.* New York, 1956. 23 pp.

Abrams, Frank W. "Management's Responsibilities in a Complex World," in *Harvard Business Review,* 29: 29–34 (1951).

Aitken, Hugh G. J. "Entrepreneurial Biography: A Symposium, Part III," in *Explorations in Entrepreneurial History,* 2: 230–232 (1949–50).

—— *The Welland Canal Company: A Study in Canadian Enterprise.* Cambridge, Mass., 1954. 178 pp.

The Art of Growing Rich. London, 1796. 31 pp.

L'Artisan de la fortune, ou les moyens de s'avancer dans le monde. Toulouse, 1691. 188 pp.

Ashton, Thomas S. *Economic History of England: The Eighteenth Century.* London, 1955. 257 pp.

Aubrey, Henry G. "Investment Decisions in Underdeveloped Countries," in *Capital Formation and Economic Growth,* Princeton, 1955, pp. 397–440.

Bailyn, Bernard. *The New England Merchants in the Seventeenth Century.* Cambridge, Mass., 1955. 249 pp.

—— "The *Apologia* of Robert Keayne," in *William and Mary Quarterly,* 3d ser., 7: 568–587 (1950).

Baldwin, George B. "The Invention of the Modern Safety Razor," in *Explorations in Entrepreneurial History,* 4: 73–102 (1950–51).

Bamford, Paul W. "Entrepreneurship in Seventeenth and Eighteenth Century France: Some General Conditions and a Case Study," in *Explorations in Entrepreneurial History,* 9: 204–213 (1956–57).

Belshaw, Cyril S. "The Cultural Milieu of the Entrepreneur: A Critical Essay," in *Explorations in Entrepreneurial History,* 7: 146–163 (1954–55).

Bendix, Reinhard. *Work and Authority in Industry: Ideologies of*

251

Management in the Course of Industrialization. New York, 1956. 466 pp.

Benson, Lee. *Merchants, Farmers & Railroads: Railroad Regulation and New York Politics*. Cambridge, Mass., 1955. 310 pp.

Berle, Adolf A., Jr. *The 20th Century Capitalist Revolution*. New York, 1954. 192 pp.

Bernstein, Peter L. "Profit Theory — Where do We Go from Here?" in *Quarterly Journal of Economics*, 67: 407–422 (1953).

Boulding, Kenneth E. *The Organizational Revolution. A Study in the Ethics of Economic Organization*. New York, 1953. 286 pp.

—— "Religious Foundations of Economic Progress," in *Harvard Business Review*, 30: 33–40 (1952).

Bowen, Howard R. *Social Responsibilities of the Businessman*. New York, 1953. 276 pp.

Bridges, Hal. *Iron Millionaire: Life of Charlemagne Tower*. Philadelphia, 1952. 322 pp.

Bruchey, Stuart W. *Robert Oliver, Merchant of Baltimore, 1783–1819*. Baltimore, 1956. 411 pp.

Buchanan, Norman S., and Howard S. Ellis. *Approaches to Economic Development*. New York, 1955. 494 pp.

Burnham, James. *Management Revolution: What is Happening in the World*. New York, 1941. 285 pp.

Butel-Dumont, Georges Marie. *Histoire et commerce des colonies angloises* . . . La Haye, 1755.

Butlin, Noel G. "Borderlands or Badlands," in *Explorations in Entrepreneurial History*, 3: 44–50 (1950–51).

Butters, J. Keith, and John Lintner. *Effect of Federal Taxes on Growing Enterprises*. Boston, 1945. 226 pp.

Chandler, Alfred D., Jr. "Management Decentralization: An Historical Analysis," in *Business History Review*, 30: 111–174 (1956–57).

Change and the Entrepreneur. Cambridge, Mass., 1949. 200 pp.

Choi, Kee Il. "Tokugawa Feudalism and the Emergence of the New Leaders of Early Modern Japan," in *Explorations in Entrepreneurial History*, 9: 72–90 (1956–57).

Clark, Samuel D. *The Social Development of Canada*. Toronto, 1942. 484 pp.

Cochran, Thomas C. *The American Business System: A Historical Perspective, 1900–1955*. Cambridge, Mass., 1957. 227 pp.

—— "The Organization Man in Historical Perspective," in *Pennsylvania History*, 25: 9–24 (1958).

—— *Railroad Leaders, 1845–1890: The Business Mind in Action*. Cambridge, Mass., 1953. 564 pp.

Cochran, Thomas C., and William Miller. *The Age of Enterprise: A Social History of Industrial America*. New York, 1942. 394 pp.

WORKS CITED

Cole, Arthur H. "Agricultural Crazes: A Neglected Chapter in American Economic History," in *American Economic Review*, 16: 622–639 (1926).

—— *The American Wool Manufacture.* Cambridge, Mass., 1926. 2 vols.

—— "An Appraisal of Economic Change; Twentieth-Century Entrepreneurship in the United States and Economic Growth," in *American Economic Review*, 40: No. 2: 35–50 (1954).

—— "An Approach to the Study of Entrepreneurship," in *Journal of Economic History*, 6, Suppl.: 1–15 (1946).

—— "Conspectus for a History of Economic and Business Literature," in *Journal of Economic History*, 17: 333–388 (1957).

—— "Entrepreneurship and Entrepreneurial History: The Institutional Setting," in *Change and the Entrepreneur* (1949), pp. 85–107.

—— "A New Set of Stages," in *Explorations in Entrepreneurial History*, 8: 99–107 (1955–56).

Cooper, William W. "A Proposal for Extending the Theory of the Firm," in *Quarterly Journal of Economics*, 65: 87–109 (1951).

—— "Theory of the Firm: Some Suggestions for Revision," in *American Economic Review*, 39: 1204–1222 (1949).

Cyert, Richard M., and J. G. March. "Organizational Factors in the Theory of Oligopoly," in *Quarterly Journal of Economics*, 70: 44–64 (1956).

—— "Organizational Structure and Pricing Behavior in an Oligopolistic Market," in *American Economic Review*, 45: 129–139 (1955).

Dahmen, Erik. *Svensk industriell företagarverksamhet: Kausalanalys av den industriella utvecklingen 1919–1939* (with an English summary). Stockholm, 1950. 2 vols.

Danhof, Clarence H. "Economic Values in Cultural Perspective," in *Goals of Economic Life*, A. Dudley Ward, ed., pp. 84–117. New York, 1953.

Davis, Ralph. "Merchant Shipping in the Economy of the Late Seventeenth Century," in *Economic History Review*, 2d. ser., 9: 59–73 (1956).

Dean, Joel. *Managerial Economics.* New York, 1951. 621 pp.

Diamond, Sigmund. "From Organization to Society: Virginia in the Seventeenth Century," in *American Journal of Sociology*, 63: 457–475 (1957–58).

—— *The Reputation of the American Businessman.* Cambridge, Mass., 1955. 209 pp.

Dimock, Marshall E. *The Executive in Action.* New York, 1945. 276 pp.

Donaldson, James. *The Undoubted Art of Thriving.* Edinburgh, 1700. 135 pp.

WORKS CITED

Drucker, Peter F. *The Practice of Management.* New York, 1954. 404 pp.

Duesenberry, James S. "Some Aspects of the Theory of Economic Development," in *Explorations in Entrepreneurial History,* 3: 63–102 (1950–51).

Easterbrook, William T. "The Climate of Enterprise," in *American Economic Review,* 39: 322–335 (1949) Suppl.

Follett, Mary Parker. *Dynamic Administration: The Collected Papers* . . . , edited by Henry C. Metcalf and L. Urwick. New York, 1943. 320 pp.

Foster, Charles A. "Honoring Commerce and Industry in 18th Century France." Unpublished Ph.D. thesis, Harvard University, 1950.

Fusfeld, Daniel R. "Heterogony of Entrepreneurial Goals," in *Explorations in Entrepreneurial History,* 9: 8–18 (1956–57).

Gay, Edwin F. "The Rhythm of History," in *Harvard Graduates' Magazine,* 32: 1–16 (1923–24).

General Motors Builds its First Fifty Million Cars. Pamphlet issued by the company, 1954.

Goodrich, Carter, "Local Planning of Internal Improvements," in *Political Science Quarterly,* 66: 411–445 (1951).

—— "National Planning of Internal Improvements," in *Political Science Quarterly,* 63: 16–44 (1948).

—— "Public Spirit and American Improvements," in *Proceedings of the American Philosophical Society,* 92: 305–309 (1948).

—— "The Revulsion against Internal Improvements," in *Journal of Economic History,* 10: 145–169 (1950).

—— "The Virginia System of Mixed Enterprise. A Study of State Planning of Internal Improvements," in *Political Science Quarterly,* 64: 355–387 (1949).

Goodrich, Carter, and Harvey H. Segal. "Baltimore's Aid to Railroads. A Study in the Municipal Planning of Internal Improvements," in *Journal of Economic History,* 13: 2–35 (1953).

Gordon, Robert A. *Business Leadership in the Large Corporation.* Washington, D.C., 1945. 369 pp.

Habakkuk, H. J. "Economic Functions of English Landowners in the Seventeenth and Eighteenth Centuries," in *Explorations in Entrepreneurial History,* 6: 92–102 (1953–54).

Handlin, Oscar, and Mary F. Handlin. *Commonwealth: A Study of the Role of Government in the American Economy. Massachusetts, 1774–1861.* New York, 1947. 364 pp.

—— "Ethnic Factors in Social Mobility," in *Explorations in Entrepreneurial History,* 9: 1–7 (1956–57).

Hartz, Louis. *Economic Policy and Democratic Thought: Pennsylvania, 1776–1860.* Cambridge, Mass., 1948. 366 pp.

254

WORKS CITED

Heath, Milton S. *Constructive Liberalism: The Role of the State in Economic Development in Georgia to 1860*. Cambridge, Mass., 1954. 448 pp.

Heaton, Herbert. "An Economic Historian's View of Enterprise." A Summary of Lectures. Claremont Men's College, Institute on Freedom and Competitive Enterprise, June, 1956. Mimeographed. 20 pp.

Heckscher, Eli F. *An Economic History of Sweden*. Trans. by Göran Ohlin. Cambridge, Mass., 1954. 308 pp.

Hedges, James B. *The Browns of Providence Plantations. Colonial Years*. Cambridge, Mass., 1952. 379 pp.

Helleiner, Karl F. "The Vital Revolution Reconsidered," in *Canadian Journal of Economics and Political Science*, 23: 1–9 (1957).

Hoover, Calvin B. "Institutional and Theoretical Implications of Economic Change," in *American Economic Review*, 44: 1–14 (1954).

Hoselitz, Bert F. "The Early History of Entrepreneurial Theory," in *Explorations in Entrepreneurial History*, 3: 193–220 (1950–51).

Jenks, Leland H. "The Role Structure of Entrepreneurial Personality," in *Change and the Entrepreneur* (1949), pp. 108–152.

Keirstead, Burton S. *An Essay in the Theory of Profits and Income Distribution*. Oxford, 1953. 110 pp.

Kellenbenz, Hermann. "German Aristocratic Entrepreneurship: Economic Activities of the Holstein Nobility in the Sixteenth and Seventeenth Centuries," in *Explorations in Entrepreneurial History*, 6: 103–114 (1953–54).

King, Doris E. "Early Hotel Entrepreneurs and Promoters, 1793–1860," in *Explorations in Entrepreneurial History*, 8: 148–160 (1955–56).

Kirkland, Edward C. *Dream and Thought in the Business Community, 1800–1900*. Ithaca, N.Y., 1956. 175 pp.

Knauth, Oswald. *Business Practices, Trade Position, and Competition*. New York, 1956. 181 pp.

—— *Managerial Enterprise, its Growth and Methods of Operation*. New York, 1948. 224 pp.

Konetzke, Richard. "Entrepreneurial Activities of Spanish and Portuguese Noblemen in Medieval Times," in *Explorations in Entrepreneurial History*, 6: 115–120 (1953–54).

Lamb, Helen B. "Business Organization and Leadership in India Today," prepared for the Seminar on Leadership and Political Institutions in India, University of California, Berkeley, August, 1956. Mimeographed.

—— "Development of Modern Business Communities in India," in *Labor Management and Economic Growth*, in *Proceedings of a*

WORKS CITED

Conference on Human Resources and Labor Relations in Under-developed Countries. Ithaca, N.Y., 1954.
—— "The Indian Business Communities and the Evolution of an Industrial Class," in *Pacific Affairs,* 28: 101–116 (1955).
Lamb, Robert K. "The Development of Entrepreneurship in Fall River, Massachusetts, 1813–1859." Unpublished Ph.D. thesis, Harvard University, 1935.
—— "The Entrepreneur and the Community," in *Men in Business* (1952), pp. 91–119.
—— "Entrepreneurship in the Community," in *Explorations in Entrepreneurial History,* 2: 114–127 (1949–50).
Landes, David S. "Business and the Businessman in France," in *Modern France: Problems of the Third and Fourth Republics,* Edward Meade Earle, ed., pp. 334–353. Princeton, 1951.
—— "French Entrepreneurship and Industrial Growth in the Nineteenth Century," in *Journal of Economic History,* 9: 45–61 (1949).
—— "Observations on France: Economy, Society, and Polity," in *World Politics,* 9: 329–349 (1956–57).
Lane, Frederic C. *Andrea Barbarigo, Merchant of Venice, 1418–1449.* Baltimore, 1944. 224 pp.
Larson, Agnes M. *History of the White-pine Industry in Minnesota.* Minneapolis, 1949. 432 pp.
Layer, Robert G. *Earnings of Cotton Mill Operatives, 1825–1914.* Cambridge, Mass., 1955. 71 pp.
Lincoln, Jonathan Thayer. "Material for a History of American Textile Machinery: The Kilburn-Lincoln Papers," in *Journal of Economic and Business History,* 4: 259–280 (1931–32).
Littleton, A. C. *Accounting Evolution to 1900.* New York, 1933. 373 pp.
Lively, Robert A. "The American System," in *Business History Review,* 29: 81–96 (1955).
McClelland, David C. "The Psychology of Mental Content Reconsidered," in *Psychological Review,* 62: 297–303 (1955).
—— "Some Social Consequences of Achievement Motivation," in *Nebraska Symposium on Motivation III,* Lincoln, Nebraska, 1955.
—— *Studies in Motivation.* New York, 1955. 552 pp.
McClelland, David C., and others. *The Achievement Motive.* New York, 1953. 384 pp.
McLaughlin, Charles C. "The Stanley Steamer: A Study in Unsuccessful Innovation," in *Explorations in Entrepreneurial History,* 7: 37–47 (1954–55).
Maclaurin, W. Rupert. *Invention & Innovation in the Radio Industry.* New York, 1949. 304 pp.

WORKS CITED

Manuel, Frank E. *The New World of Henri Saint-Simon.* Cambridge, Mass., 1956. 433 pp.

Marquette, Clare L. "The Business Activities of C. C. Washburn." Unpublished Ph.D. thesis, University of Wisconsin, 1940.

Marshall, Alfred. *Principles of Economics.* 6th ed. London, 1910. 871 pp.

Meany, Edmond S. "History of the Lumber Industry in the Pacific Northwest to 1917." Unpublished Ph.D. thesis, Harvard University, 1935.

Meier, Gerald M., and Robert E. Baldwin. *Economic Development: Theory, History, Policy.* New York, 1957. 588 pp.

Merton, Robert K. "The Role-Set: Problems in Sociological Theory," in *British Journal of Sociology,* 8: 106–120 (1957).

Mill, John Stuart. *Principles of Political Economy.* Boston, 1848. 2 vols.

Miller, William. "The Business Elite in Business Bureaucracies," in *Men in Business* (1952), pp. 286–305.

Moulton, Charles W. *The Library of Literary Criticism.* Vol I. Buffalo, N.Y., 1901.

Muir, Valerie. "The Emergence of State Enterprise in New Zealand in the Nineteenth Century," in *Explorations in Entrepreneurial History,* 5: 186–192 (1952–53).

Navin, Thomas R. *The Whitin Machine Works since 1831.* Cambridge, Mass., 1950. 654 pp.

Nestor, Oscar W. "History of Personnel Administration, 1890–1910." Unpublished Ph.D. thesis, University of Pennsylvania, 1954.

Neu, Irene D. "A Business Biography of Erastus Corning." Unpublished Ph.D. thesis, Cornell University, 1950.

Orcutt, Guy H. "A New Type of Socio-Economic System," in *Review of Economics and Statistics,* 39: 116–123 (1957).

Parker, William N. "Coal and Steel Output Movements in Western Europe, 1880–1956," in *Explorations in Entrepreneurial History,* 9: 214–230 (1956–57).

——— "Entrepreneurial Opportunities and Response in the German Economy," in *Explorations in Entrepreneurial History,* 7: 26–36 (1954–55).

Parsons, Talcott, and Neil J. Smelser. "A Sociological Model for Economic Development," in *Explorations in Entrepreneurial History,* 8: 181–204 (1955–56).

Passer, Harold C. "E. H. Goff: An Entrepreneur Who Failed," in *Explorations in Entrepreneurial History,* 1, No. 5: 17–25 (1949).

——— *The Electrical Manufacturers, 1875–1900. A Study in Competition, Entrepreneurship, Technical Change, and Economic Growth.* Cambridge. Mass., 1953. 412 pp.

WORKS CITED

Pelzel, John. "The Small Industrialist in Japan," in *Explorations in Entrepreneurial History*, 7: 79–93 (1954–55).

Porter, Kenneth W. *The Jacksons and the Lees. Two Generations of Massachusetts Merchants, 1765–1844.* Cambridge, Mass., 1937. 2 vols.

Potter, Dalton. "The Bazaar Merchant," in *Social Forces in the Middle East*, ed. by Sydney N. Fisher. Ithaca, N.Y., 1955, pp. 99–115.

Powell, Thomas. *Tom, of All Trades.* London, 1631. 49 pp.

Primm, James N. *Economic Policy in the Development of a Western State. Missouri, 1820–1860.* Cambridge, Mass., 1954. 174 pp.

Quandt, Richard E. "Review of *Capital Formation and Economic Growth*," in *Review of Economics and Statistics*, 39: 480–481 (1957).

Rae, John B. "The Engineer as Business Man in American Industry," in *Explorations in Entrepreneurial History*, 7: 94–104 (1954–55).

Ranis, Gustav. "The Community-Centered Entrepreneur in Japanese Development," in *Explorations in Entrepreneurial History*, 8: 80–98 (1955–56).

Redlich, Fritz L. "European Aristocracy and Economic Development," in *Explorations in Entrepreneurial History*, 6: 78–91 (1953–54).

—— "Der fürstliche Unternehmer: eine typische Erschunung des 16. Jahrhunderts," in *Tradition*, 3: 17–34, 98–112 (1958).

—— *History of American Business Leaders.* Vol. I. Ann Arbor, 1940. 185 pp.

—— "The Leaders of the German Steam-Engine Industry during the First Hundred Years," in *Journal of Economic History*, 4: 121–148 (1944).

—— "The Origin of the Concepts of 'Entrepreneur' and 'Creative Entrepreneur,' " in *Explorations in Entrepreneurial History*, 1, No. 2: 1–7 (1949).

Riemersma, Jelle C. "The Role of Religion in Economic Development," in *Explorations in Entrepreneurial History*, 2: 297–303 (1949–50).

Ripley, William Z. *Main Street to Wall Street.* Boston, 1927. 359 pp.

Rosovsky, Henry. "The Serf Entrepreneur in Russia," in *Explorations in Entrepreneurial History*, 6: 207–233 (1953–54).

Rostow, Walt W. "The Interrelation of Theory and Economic History," in *Journal of Economic History*, 17: 509–523 (1957).

Rottenberg, Simon. "Entrepreneurship and Economic Progress in Jamaica," in *Inter-American Economic Affairs*, 7: 74–79 (1953–54).

Sawyer, John E. "The Entrepreneur and the Social Order: France and the United States," in *Men in Business* (1952), pp. 7–22.

—— "Entrepreneurial Error and Economic Growth," in *Explorations in Entrepreneurial History*, 4: 199–204 (1951–52).

——"Entrepreneurship in Periods of Rapid Growth: The United

WORKS CITED

States in the 19th Century." A paper presented at a conference on Entrepreneurship and Economic Growth in Cambridge, Massachusetts, November 12 and 13, 1954, Part C. 7 pp.

—— "Strains in the Social Structure of Modern France," in *Modern France: Problems of the Third and Fourth Republics*, Edward Meade Earle, ed., pp. 293–312. Princeton, 1951.

Schumpeter, Joseph A. "The Creative Response in Economic History," in *Journal of Economic History*, 7: 149–159 (1947).

—— *History of Economic Analysis*. New York, 1954. 1260 pp.

Scitovszky, Tibor de. "On the Decline of Competition," in *Social Change*, 3: 28–36 (1941).

Scoville, Warren C. *Revolution in Glassmaking: Entrepreneurship and Technological Change in the American Industry, 1880–1920*. Cambridge, Mass., 1948. 398 pp.

Smith, Roderick H. *The Science of Business*. New York & London, 1885.

Solomons, David, ed. *Studies in Costing*. London, 1952. 643 pp.

Stein, Stanley J. *The Brazilian Cotton Manufacture. Textile Enterprise in an Underdeveloped Area, 1850–1950*. Cambridge, Mass., 1957. 273 pp.

Thrupp, Sylvia L. "Entrepreneurial Theory and the Middle Ages," in *Explorations in Entrepreneurial History*, 2: 160–165 (1949–50).

Tosdal, Harry R. *Selling in Our Economy: An Economic and Social Analysis of Selling and Advertising*. Chicago, 1957. 333 pp.

United Nations Economic and Social Council. Economic Commission for Latin America. Economic Development of Latin America and Its Principal Problems. 1950. (UN. E/CN.12/89/Rev. 1). 49 pp.

Usher, Abbott P. *History of Mechanical Inventions*. Rev. ed. Cambridge, Mass., 1954. 450 pp.

Veblen, Thorstein. *The Engineer and the Price System*. New York, 1921. 169 pp.

Wellington, Raynor G. *The Political and Sectional Influence of the Public Lands, 1828–1842*. N.p., 1914. 131 pp.

Westebbe, Richard M. "State Entrepreneurship: King Willem I, John Cockerill, and the Seraing Engineering Works, 1815–1840," in *Explorations in Entrepreneurial History*, 8: 205–232 (1955–56).

Wiles, P. "Growth versus Choice," in *Economic Journal*, 66: 244–255 (1956).

Wilson, Charles. "The Entrepreneur in the Industrial Revolution in Britain." A paper presented at a conference on Entrepreneurship and Economic Growth in Cambridge, Massachusetts, November 12 and 13, 1954, Part A. 17 pp.

—— *The History of Unilever: A Study in Economic Growth and Social Change*. London, 1954. 2 vols.

WORKS CITED

Wohl, R. Richard. "An Historical Context for Entrepreneurship," in *Explorations in Entrepreneurial History*, 1, No. 2: 8–16 (1949).

—— "Henry Noble Day, the Development of an Entrepreneurial Role." Unpublished Ph.D. thesis, Harvard University, 1951.

—— "Henry Noble Day. A Study in Good Works, 1808–1890," in *Men in Business* (1952), pp. 153–192.

—— "The 'Rags to Riches Story': An Episode of Secular Idealism," in *Class, Status, and Power*, ed. by Reinhard Bendix and Seymour M. Lipsit. Glencoe, Ill., 1953, pp. 388–395.

—— "Three Generations of Business Enterprise in a Midwestern City: the McGees of Kansas City," in *Journal of Economic History*, 16: 514–528 (1956).

Wood, Richard G. *History of Lumbering in Maine, 1820–61*. Orono, Me., 1935. 267 pp.

Wyllie, Irvin G. *The Self-made Man in America: The Myth of Rags to Riches*. New Brunswick, N.J., 1954. 210 pp.

Young, Allyn A. "Increasing Returns and Economic Progress," in *Economic Journal*, 38: 527–542 (1928).

NOTES

CHAPTER I
The Nature of Entrepreneurship

1. Professor Innis served with me for more than a decade on the Committee on Research in Economic History. His concern with time is reflected in the title of one of his last books, *Changing Concepts of Time*.

2. T. S. Ashton, *Economic History of England: The Eighteenth Century* (1955), p. 22.

3. N. S. Buchanan and H. S. Ellis, *Approaches to Economic Development* (1955), pp. 74, 87. No more economistic statement could be found. It seems to envisage a one-punch set of "cultural changes," and it surely suggests that a dosage of capital is, to some extent, required in all alterations of social thought and practices.

4. See B. F. Hoselitz, "The Early History of Entrepreneurial Theory," *Explorations in Entrepreneurial History*, 3: 193–220 (1950–51), and F. L. Redlich, "The Origin of the Concepts of 'Entrepreneur' and 'Creative Entrepreneur,'" *Explorations*, 1 (no. 2): 1–7 (1949). This publication of the Center will be referred to hereafter as *Explorations*.

5. "Entrepreneur" in *Shorter Oxford Dictionary on Historical Principles* (1955).

6. J. S. Mill, *Principles of Political Economy* (1848), I, 485.

7. D. Potter, in *Social Forces in the Middle East* (1955), p. 112.

8. A. H. Cole, in *Change and the Entrepreneur* (1949), p. 88.

9. See an essay by Mrs. Valerie Muir on Julius Vogel, entitled "The Emergence of State Enterprise in New Zealand in the Nineteenth Century," *Explorations*, 5: 186–197 (1952–53).

10. There is also an important difference in the value in exposition of the two sets of terms; "entrepreneurship" and "entrepreneur," on the one hand, and "business" and "businessman" on the other. One phase of this matter is pure linguistics. "Business," as a word, does not lend itself to the permutation that "entrepreneur" does in the adjectival form "entrepreneurial." More importantly, the latter group of terms carries a smaller load of connotation. The terms "business"

and "businessman" signify mere money-making to most people; the phrase "social responsibility of business," for example, seems an internal contradiction. The other set of terms conveys fewer "sentiments," and so may be employed with greater hope of scientific precision. For somewhat similar reasons, I have, on the whole, chosen to avoid the terms "enterpriser" and "enterprise." There is no satisfactory adjectival form, and surely an enterpriser would be conceived to be, by nature, enterprising. I do frequently use the term "enterprise" to mean business unit.

I call "entrepreneur" only such businessmen who make decisions within a formal organization called a business enterprise, which is itself a unit in a group of social institutions. My friend Mr. LaFrance, who has operated a stationery store in Brattle Square, Cambridge, for many years all by himself, or Mr. William Harnden, who started the express business in this country by carrying valuable papers from New York to Boston in a half-bushel carpetbag, or the proprietors of thousands of boutiques scattered over the world, have made or do make decisions and they have had (or have) some sorts of social relations. But I choose not to become involved in psychology in thought processes and emotions and perhaps Freudian "compensations." Someone may want to cover this area, which might be looked upon as primitive entrepreneurship, and try to draw a logical line among individuals more or less involved in pecuniary pursuits, from the itinerant peddler down through the widow who invests her funds to provide her with the maximum income.

11. Professor Rostow made an address before the Economic History Association in September, 1957. His paper appeared in the *Journal of Economic History,* 17: 509–23 (1957), entitled "The Interrelation of Theory and Economic History."

12. A recent effort to deal with the problems of invention, innovation, and the like is to be found in the early chapters of A. P. Usher's second edition of his *History of Mechanical Inventions* (1954).

13. Obviously, the foregoing is, in part, restatement of what is to be found in Professor Schumpeter's "novel" and "innovating" ideas; in part revision and in part criticism. And there is this much more to be added, although it is tangential to my argument. The essential element in the tactics of entrepreneurship is the attainment of a differential cost or profit position; the effort to gain such a position is not necessarily coincident with the promotion of economic growth, as, for example, in a case where a manufacturer imitates his neighbors as far as the adoption of the steam engine is concerned, but goes ahead with what is at the moment *more* important to him, the use of a particular dyestuff or the signing up of a particular sales agency. As a result, the "economic development" in which Schumpeter (and

we) are interested must be viewed as a mere incident in entrepreneurial life—a sort of "built-in" feature—with the real entrepreneurial
action pointed in another direction, especially the maintenance and
aggrandizement of the relevant profit-oriented enterprise.

14. I am reminded of the agriculturalist connected with the Bureau
of Agricultural Economics who complained to me many years ago
that the economic theorists were all wrong: shifting of process or
product did not take place at the margin of cultivation; only infra-
marginal farmers could afford to shift into new methods or the production of new crops.

15. R. A. Gordon, *Business Leadership in the Large Corporation*
(1945); M. E. Dimock, *The Executive in Action* (1945); O. Knauth,
Managerial Enterprise, Its Growth and Methods of Operation (1948);
T. C. Cochran, *The American Business System: A Historical Perspec-
tive, 1900–1955* (1957); H. R. Bowen, *Social Responsibilities of the
Businessman* (1953), etc.

16. Dimock, *The Executive in Action.*

17. C. H. Danhof, "Economic Values in Cultural Perspective," in
Goals of Economic Life (1953).

18. F. C. Lane, *Andrea Barbarigo* (1944).

19. Relative to changes in the United States over recent decades,
see the path-breaking essay by Alfred D. Chandler, Jr., "Management
Decentralization," *Business History Review*, 30: 111–174 (1956–57).

20. J. K. Butters and J. Lintner, *Effects of Federal Taxes on Growing Enterprises* (1946).

21. W. T. Easterbrook, "The Climate of Enterprise," *American
Economic Review*, 39: 322–335 (1949), Supp. Another form in past
centuries was a specially chartered company, usually with monopoly
privileges which contributed a variant sort of "security."

22. B. Bailyn, *The New England Merchants in the Seventeenth
Century* (1955).

23. A. Gerschenkron, quoted by H. Rosovsky in *Explorations*, 6:
208 (1953–54).

24. J. E. Sawyer, "Strains in the Social Structure of Modern France,"
in *Modern France: Problems of the Third and Fourth Republics*
(1951), pp. 293–312; D. S. Landes, "Business and the Businessman
in France," *ibid.*, pp. 334–353.

25. T. C. Cochran and W. Miller, *The Age of Enterprise* (1942);
A. H. Cole, "An Appraisal of Economic Change," *American Economic
Review*, 44 (No. 2): 35–50 (1954).

26. In view of the purposes of the present volume as indicated in
the Preface, I believe it inappropriate that I should take up space in
an effort to compare the foregoing ideas with all those respecting the
essential characteristics of entrepreneurs and entrepreneurship that

writers of all nations, living and dead, have put on paper at one time or another. The catalogue of such concepts is a long one, as can be gained from the excellent surveys and special studies of Messrs. Hoselitz and Redlich, cited above, n. 4. However, a few brief comments may be in order. For example, for purposes of empirical research I found rather futile the concept, with which the name of Professor Frank H. Knight is usually associated, of the entrepreneur as the bearer of risks. The bearing of risks or uncertainties is a negative element and does not tell one what the actor contributes. A definition in terms of function is more useful.

A somewhat similar objection can be made to the ideas of Professor Schumpeter. One could not study paintings by looking only for indications of genius; and, in the case of innovations, the practical research worker is confronted, as already indicated above (p. 14) with the difficulty of defining the phenomenon in real life, of pinning it down so that he can separate innovations from noninnovations. He finds a myriad of innovations from the railroad and the electric motor down to a machine for laying new rails on old railroads, and to plastic handles for electric switches, and many applications of new gadgets and new business methods. The best that one can do is to recognize that the search for novelties has always been a feature of business life, that this element has become increasingly prominent as the tempo of business has changed, and that the installation of novelties of equipment or mode of operation constitutes one means of the preservation of business enterprises in the face of competition.

In the third place, I would protest against the dichotomy between "entrepreneur" and "manager," which is found often in economic and sociological literature. (See, for example, R. Bendix's valuable study, Work and Authority in Industry [1956].) The dichotomy is just unrealistic and inoperable in research. One cannot study women by first setting up the categories of beautiful and homely. All businessmen have some elements of both characteristics or qualities. They are imaginative, innovating, vigorous, etc., sometimes and to some degree; and they are unimaginative, traditionally minded, lazy, etc., also sometimes and in some degree. And most of the discussions overlook what Professor Schumpeter once stressed. At a luncheon at the Harvard Business School Dean Wallace B. Donham asked him what he thought to be the most important element in business success, and Professor Schumpeter replied, without a moment's hesitation, "Why, to be sure, good health!"

27. A. H. Cole, "An Approach to the Study of Entrepreneurship," Journal of Economic History, 6, Suppl.: 8 (1946).

CHAPTER II
The Need of a Positive View

1. Actually, in the theory of monopolistic competition, the entrepreneur can hardly be distinguished from the enterprise. The assumption of profit-maximization as the sole rule of action in the formation of business policy made further thought on these matters seem unnecessary, as will be suggested in a moment.

2. J. Dean, *Managerial Economics* (1951), p. 28.

3. C. B. Hoover, "Institutional and Theoretical Implications of Economic Change," *American Economic Review*, 44: 11, 12 (1954).

4. One can add testimony of other writers. Mr. Peter L. Bernstein, himself associated with business, asserts that because "a very large proportion of business capital" today is economically or institutionally immobile, the tendency of profits to be equalized in the economy would be appropriate only to "long period analysis," when the period was conceived to be "very, very long indeed." See Bernstein's article, "Profit Theory—Where Do We Go From Here?" *Quarterly Journal of Economics*, 67: 419 (1953). With an even somewhat broader sweep A. A. Berle, Jr., writes, "It is indefensibly disingenuous to assert that these operations [those of modern large-scale corporations] are primarily following economic laws more or less accurately outlined by the classic economists a century ago when the fact appears to be that they are following a slowly emerging pattern of sociological and political laws, relevant to the rather different community demands of our time." *The 20th Century Capitalist Revolution* (1954), p. 12.

5. H. G. J. Aitken, "Entrepreneurial Biography: A Symposium," Part III, *Explorations*, 2: 231 (1949–50).

6. W. W. Cooper, "A Proposal for Extending the Theory of the Firm," *Quarterly Journal of Economics*, 65: 90 (1951).

7. W. W. Cooper, "Theory of the Firm," *American Economic Review*, 39: 1207 (1949).

8. Cooper, "A Proposal . . . ," p. 92.

9. *Ibid.*, p. 92.

10. *Ibid.*, p. 91.

11. R. M. Cyert and J. G. March, "Organizational Structure and Pricing Behavior in an Oligopolistic Market," *American Economic Review*, 45: 129–139 (1955) and "Organizational Factors in the Theory of Oligopoly," *Quarterly Journal of Economics*, 70: 44–64 (1956).

12. B. S. Keirstead, *An Essay in the Theory of Profits and Income Distribution* (1953), p. 44.

13. *Ibid.*, p. 28.

14. *Ibid.*, p. 29.

15. Unhappily, the term "dynamic" has been purloined to the labeling of a form of analysis which is dynamic only in a very limited degree: the shift from one equilibrium to another. Obviously, this is not the place to argue the propriety of names, or even the utility or disutility of the notion of an equilibrium; but perhaps one may properly note that to the economic historian "dynamic" connotes something more extensive than short-run or medium-run adjustment, and that to him the appearance of an equilibrium in the historical record is, indeed, a very rare occurrence. Given a tempo or metronome appropriate to economic or social change, everything is in process of flux. It is clear that the foregoing is in strong disagreement with Professor Parsons and Mr. Neil Smelser, who in a recent essay stated categorically, "Like any system, a going economy tends to equilibrium." *Explorations*, 8: 193 (1955–56). Historically, it seems more accurate to assert that for the Western world since the twelfth century no appreciable periods of equilibrium have been observable in any "going economy."

16. G. H. Orcutt, "A New Type of Socio-economic System," *Review of Economics and Statistics*, 39: 116–123 (1957).

17. P. Wiles, "Growth versus Choice," *Economic Journal*, 66: 244 (1956).

18. N. G. Butlin, "Borderlands or Badlands?" *Explorations*, 3: 50 (1950–51).

19. F. E. Manuel, *The New World of Henri Saint-Simon* (1956), p. 137.

20. G. M. Meier and R. E. Baldwin, *Economic Development* (1957).

21. *Ibid.*, p. 120.

22. *Ibid.*, p. 121.

23. *Ibid.*, p. 123. I should like to call attention to a recent independent appraisal of the situation: "One finds it difficult to relate them [the factors of income distribution, the propensity to save, the role of capital intensity, the significance of channels of finance, etc.] to each other because no theoretical framework exists within which these factors could find a comfortable niche. This is not to say that there exists no theory at all: Ricardo or Weber or Schumpeter or Harrod-Domar represent some possible approaches. But none of these really fulfils the need. Information about particular countries, particular eras, particular factors accumulates rapidly but no strides seem to be made toward establishing relationships between the various factors." R. E. Quandt's review of *Capital Formation and Economic Growth* (1955) in *The Review of Economics and Statistics*, 39: 480–481 (1957).

24. See above, p. 28.
25. A. Marshall, *Principles of Economics* (1910), pp. 138–139.
26. S. W. Bruchey, *Robert Oliver* (1956), p. 370.
27. Chandler, "Management Decentralization."
28. When I knew one of the brothers in his later years, he was interested in the construction of fine violins fabricated in a shop attached to his house in Newton, Mass.
29. C. C. McLaughlin, "The Stanley Steamer," *Explorations*, 7: 46 (1954–55).
30. D. E. King, "Early Hotel Entrepreneurs and Promoters, 1793–1860," *Explorations*, 8: 156 (1955–56).
31. Professor Sawyer's comments are contained in a research note entitled, "Entrepreneurial Error and Economic Growth," *Explorations*, 4: 199–204 (1951–52) and in a paper, "Entrepreneurship in Periods of Rapid Growth: The United States in the 19th Century," presented at a conference on Entrepreneurship and Economic Growth in Cambridge, Mass., November 12 and 13, Part C, p. 3 (1954).
32. Sawyer, "Entrepreneurship in Periods of Rapid Growth," p. 3.
33. *Ibid.*, pp. 5–6.
34. *Ibid.*, p. 6.
35. C. Wilson, "The Entrepreneur in the Industrial Revolution in Britain," a paper presented at the conference (1954) just mentioned (see n. 31), Part A, pp. 5, 11, 17; and *The History of Unilever* (1954).
36. M. Abramovitz, *Resource and Output Trends in the United States since 1870* (1956).
37. *Ibid.*, p. 13.
38. K. E. Boulding, "Religious Foundations of Economic Progress," *Harvard Business Review*, 30: 33 (1952).

CHAPTER III

The Elements in a Positive View:
The Entrepreneur and His Organization

1. Economists familiar with the ideas of John R. Commons as expressed in his later works, and especially in his *Economics of Collective Action* (1950), will note some parallelism of thought with parts of what follows. I regret to have to admit that I was not familiar with this line of thought in any useful way until the present book was nearly completed. At that time my attention was called to group organizations, "going concerns," and the like by my friends Professor Benjamin M. Selekman and his wife, who had reviewed Commons' last book in the *Harvard Business Review* for November, 1951 (vol. 29, pp. 112–128).

2. See p. 10 above.

3. M. P. Follett, *Dynamic Administration* (1941).

4. Here there may seem at first blush to be an inconsistency or at least a confusion of thought as to where in business units the entrepreneurial function is located, just who is "the entrepreneur." More specifically, it can well be asked, "If there is an ultimate authority, why should he not be identified as bearer of the function and appropriate bearer of the title? Why not take the possessor of this ultimate authority as *the* entrepreneur for purposes other than the current analysis?"

The answer is at least twofold. The traditional identification in economic literature of a single-person entrepreneur with the entrepreneurial function is untrue to the facts, at any rate in modern business life; and second, the possessor of final authority in a given action-situation is not necessarily the only person participating cooperatively and with some authority in that action.

An analogy with governmental conditions may serve quickly to elucidate the relationship. There is no doubt that the President carries the final responsibility for decisions in the executive branch of the federal government administration; but the executive function is also clearly dispersed among many officers in the administration. And one may properly consider the relations of "the President and his organization" as a means of understanding better the manifestations of the executive function in the federal government.

5. The degree to which the top executives are "policy-clinching" would depend much upon the constitution of that executive or its relations to a board of directors.

6. I made an effort to suggest some important lines of literary evolution in an essay entitled, "Conspectus for A History of Economic and Business Literature," which appeared in the *Journal of Economic History*, 17: 333–388 (1957). This essay was reprinted under a slightly different title as Brochure No. 12 of the Kress Library, Harvard University Graduate School of Business Administration.

7. See in particular the essay, "The Role Structure of Entrepreneurial Personality," by L. H. Jenks in *Change and the Entrepreneur* (1949), pp. 108–152. No effort will be made here to reproduce the elaboration of a sociological schema especially pertinent to entrepreneurship that Professor Jenks presents there. No one at the Center has added significantly to the system devised in 1948 by him.

8. R. R. Wohl, "An Historical Context for Entrepreneurship," *Explorations*, 1 (No. 2): 12 (1949).

9. My attention has recently been called to an article by Professor Robert K. Merton entitled "The Role-Set: Problems in Sociological Theory," which appeared in the *British Journal of Sociology*, 8: 106–

120 (June, 1957). Professor Merton draws the very useful distinction between "role-set" and "status-set" anent the occupier of any social status; e.g., teacher, doctor, etc. In relation to the entrepreneur, the distinction would be this: the entrepreneur as such is, as it were, the focus of several interests, those of stockholders, staff, customers, employees, in the sense that each such group expects something individual and distinctive as far as its interests are concerned. On the other hand, the individuals carrying the entrepreneurial roles, or occupying that status, are simultaneously in their own persons occupying other statuses, as, for example, fathers, church members, perhaps members of school committees or political parties.

In the ensuing analysis, the concept of role-set will appear most appropriate and important, although I am inclined myself to feel that the term "role-set" is hardly strong enough to carry the complex of entrepreneurial relationships that I am disposed to think significant. The term "role-galaxy" might be more suitable. As to status-set, however, one will observe its utility when the discussion touches upon the relation of the entrepreneurial actors to their families, to their professional associations, etc. Both the terms—and the concepts—are worth keeping in mind.

10. Bendix, *Work and Authority in Industry.*
11. Wilson, *History of Unilever,* vol. II, *passim.*
12. T. R. Navin, *The Whitin Machine Works* (1950), *passim.*
13. The partnership agreement will be rewritten on the death of a partner, but the new group may be a mere reorganization of the earlier one.
14. K. E. Boulding, *The Organizational Revolution* (1953); W. Z. Ripley, *Main Street to Wall Street* (1927); Gordon, *Business Leadership in the Large Corporations;* J. Burnham, *Management Revolution* (1941); O. Knauth, *Managerial Enterprise* (1948).
15. See below, pp. 238 ff.
16. *General Motors Builds Its First Fifty Million Cars* (1954).
17. See below, Chap. IV, *passim.*
18. O. W. Nestor, "History of Personnel Administration, 1890–1910" (1954).
19. Here I refer again to the recent article by Professor Merton (see above, n. 9) in which he elaborates the notion of role-set." Obviously, the several "interests" expect different actions of the entrepreneur, and they are in some measure willing to exert sanctions to get their respective ways. The entrepreneur is the bearer of a role viewed divergently by the several parties in his organization.

As Mr. Frank W. Abrams, erstwhile of the Standard Oil Company of New Jersey, once wrote, "The job of professional management, as I see it, is to conduct the affairs of the enterprise in its charge in such a way as to maintain an equitable and workable balance among the claims of the various directly interested groups. Business firms are man-made instruments of society. They can be made to achieve their greatest social usefulness—and thus their future can be best assured —when management succeeds in finding a harmonious balance among the claims of the various interested groups: the stockholders, employees, customers, and the public at large." F. W. Abrams, "Management's Responsibilities in a Complex World," *Harvard Business Review*, 29: 29–30 (1951).

20. R. G. Layer, *Earnings of Cotton Mill Operatives, 1825–1914* (1955).

21. The movement of prices, especially after the mid-1890's, adds confusion.

22. See above, p. 53.

23. See above, p. 10 f.

24. Regarding Mr. Abrams, see below, pp. 201 ff.

25. C. C. Abbott, "Broad View of Administration," University of Virginia *Alumni News*, October, 1956.

26. Quoted by T. C. Cochran, "The Organization Man in Historical Perspective," *Pennsylvania History*, 25: 18 (1958).

27. Berle, p. 70.

28. *Ibid.*, pp. 51–52.

29. T. C. Cochran, "The Organization Man . . . ," p. 22.

30. *Ibid.*, p. 18.

CHAPTER IV

The Elements in a Positive View: The Entrepreneurial Stream

1. See below, p. 107.

2. The nature of the interrelations of producing institutions, advertising organizations, marketing units, and the consuming public is exhibited by H. R. Tosdal in his new study, *Selling in Our Economy: An Economic and Social Analysis of Selling and Advertising* (1957).

3. A. A. Young, "Increasing Returns and Economic Progress," *Economic Journal*, 38: 539 (1928).

4. See above, Chapter III, n. 5.

5. A representative case of intellectual immaturity is provided by Roderick H. Smith's *Science of Business* (New York, 1885). After two preliminary chapters entitled "The Direction of Motion" and "The Rhythm of Motion" he presents a sequence of specific chapters as follows:

"Part Second; I. General Business, II. Iron, III. Railroad Building and Consumption of Rails, IV. Immigration, V. Stocks, VI. Exchange,

VII. Foreign Trade, VIII. Grain, IX. The Balancing of Prices or Equilibration, X. Summary and Conclusion."

6. E. C. Kirkland, *Dream and Thought in the Business Community, 1800–1900* (1956), p. 13.

7. T. C. Cochran, *Railroad Leaders, 1845–1890* (1953), p. 82.

8. I have in mind the varied activities of seeking tariff protection, promoting banks and railroads, etc.

9. L. Benson, *Merchants, Farmers, & Railroads* (1955), pp. 208–209.

CHAPTER V

The Elements in a Positive View: The Social Conditioning
of Entrepreneurship

1. C. S. Belshaw, "The Cultural Milieu of the Entrepreneur," *Explorations*, 7: 151 (1954–55).

2. S. L. Thrupp, "Entrepreneurial Theory and the Middle Ages," *Explorations*, 2: 161 (1949–50).

3. B. Bailyn, "The *Apologia* of Robert Keayne," *William and Mary Quarterly*, 3d ser., 7: 568–571 (1950).

4. A. Gerschenkron, quoted by H. Rosovsky, *Explorations*, 6: 208 (1953–54).

5. J. S. Duesenberry, "Some Aspects of the Theory of Economic Development," *Explorations*, 3: 73 (1950–51).

6. J. C. Riemersma, "The Role of Religion in Economic Development," *Explorations*, 2: 302 (1949–50).

7. H. Bridges, *Iron Millionaire* (1952), *passim*.

8. See the unpublished dissertation (1950) by C. A. Foster, "Honoring Commerce and Industry in 18th Century France."

9. H. Rosovsky, "The Serf Entrepreneur in Russia," *Explorations*, 6: 207–253 (1953–54).

10. S. Rottenberg, "Entrepreneurship and Economic Progress in Jamaica," *Inter-American Economic Affairs*, 7: 74–99 (1953–54).

11. Lane, pp. 45–53.

12. Perhaps a classification comparable to that of Danhof's might be devised, this one on degrees of boldness!

13. I do not mean to posit a "spirit of enterprise" or its equivalent. Entrepreneurship calls for the display of varied qualities of mental ability and conditioned valuations. All that I mean to imply above is that the threshold of entry is not a straight horizontality. To some men the role of entrepreneurship is more congenial than to others.

14. E. F. Heckscher, *An Economic History of Sweden* (1954), p. 98.

15. Danhof, *passim.*

16. Duesenberry, pp. 72, 73. Based upon Talcott Parson's "Economic Motivation," contained in his *Essays in Sociological Theory and Its Applications* (1949).

17. Riemersma, p. 302.

18. T. de Scitovszky, "On the Decline of Competition," *Social Change,* 3: 31 (1941).

19. Sawyer, "Strains . . ."; Landes, "Business . . ."; W. N. Parker, "Entrepreneurial Opportunities and Response in the German Economy," *Explorations,* 7: 26–36 (1954–55). A new, improved analysis of the situation, giving some of the influences of past experiences upon present-day conditions, is contained in Landes' article in *World Politics,* 9: 329–349, entitled "Observations on France: Economy, Society, and Polity."

20. de Scitovszky, p. 32.

21. Parker, p. 32.

22. See also *L'Artisan de la fortune, ou les moyens de s'avancer dans le monde* (1691); but on the whole, I have found less attention to the theme in Continental literature.

23. R. R. Wohl, "The 'Rags to Riches Story'" in *Class, Status and Power* (1953), pp. 388–395.

24. *Change and the Entrepreneur* (1949), pp. 23–24.

25. It also seems true that the young man who took the older woman to acquire the attached privileges of printing also took the opportunity later to annex a young woman as a second wife — who, in turn, acquired a younger husband. Whether this system could be defended on grounds other than the control of industry may well be doubted.

26. H. G. J. Aitken, *The Welland Canal Company* (1954), *passim.*

27. J. B. Hedges, *The Browns of Providence Plantations* (1952).

28. R. K. Lamb, "The Development of Entrepreneurship in Fall River, Massachusetts, 1813–1859" (1935).

29. S. D. Clark, *The Social Development of Canada* (1942).

30. On the frontier entrepreneur see pp. 161 ff. below.

31. For the ensuing data on innovations and on cooperation, I am indebted to Professor Clarence H. Danhof, whose findings I had hoped sometime since to have published as agent of the Committee on Research in Economic History.

32. A. H. Cole, "Agricultural Crazes," *American Economic Review,* 16: 622–639 (1926).

33. See below, pp. 143 ff.

34. Benson, p. 228.

35. See below, pp. 171 ff.

36. See below, pp. 175 ff.

37. See below, pp. 193 ff.

38. The engineer as entrepreneur is a subject that has engaged the attention of Professor John B. Rae of the Massachusetts Institute of Technology. See his article, "The Engineer as Business Man in American Industry," *Explorations*, 7: 94–104 (1954–55).

39. G. B. Baldwin, "The Invention of the Modern Safety Razor," *Explorations*, 4: 73–102 (1951–52).

40. T. Veblen, *The Engineers and the Price System* (1921). In this section I am concerned only with the movement of entrepreneurs, not handicraftsmen or workmen.

42. O. Handlin and M. F. Handlin, "Ethnic Factors in Social Mobility," *Explorations*, 9: 1–7 (1956–57).

43. See for example, G. Ranis, "The Community-centered Entrepreneur in Japanese Development," *Explorations*, 8: 80–98 (1955–56); K. I. Choi, "Tokugawa Feudalism and the Emergence of the New Leaders of Early Modern Japan," *Explorations*, 9: 72–90 (1956–57); and J. Pelzel, "The Small Industrialist in Japan," *Explorations*, 7: 79–93 (1955–56).

44. H. B. Lamb, "The Indian Business Communities and the Evolution of an Industrial Class," *Pacific Affairs*, 28: 101–116 (1955).

45. See above, Chap. II. *passim*.

46. A. H. Cole, "An Approach . . . ," *Journal of Economic History*, 6: 10–11 (1946).

47. A. H. Cole, "A New Set of Stages," *Explorations*, 8: 99–107 (1955–56).

48. Professor F. C. Lane tells me of the day-long buzzing among merchants that appears to have gone on on the Rialto; and Dr. Redlich reminds me of the importance that commercial exchanges and coffee-houses seem to have played in commercial life in various mercantile centers, not excluding the American seaboard cities.

49. W. R. Maclaurin, *Invention & Innovation in the Radio Industry* (1949), p. xv.

50. S. Diamond, *The Reputation of the American Businessman* (1955).

51. See above, pp. 58 f.

52. See above, p. 81.

PART TWO

Entrepreneurial Realities

1. Those familiar with German material would also recall the work of Wiedenfeld and Eulenburg.

2. F. L. Redlich, "European Aristocracy and Economic Development," *Explorations*, 6: 78–91 (1953–54).

3. Foster, "Honoring Commerce and Industry . . . ." I should in all honesty add that Dr. Redlich, on reading this section of my manuscript, has expressed a disagreement with my interpretation of Dr. Foster's materials. I hope that before long the latter will publish his own summary — or better, an extension of his thesis.

4. See, however, Redlich's very recent essay entitled "Der fürstliche Unternehmer: eine typische Erschunung des 16. Jahrhunderts," which appeared in *Tradition*, 3: 17–34, 98–112 (1958).

5. See H. J. Habakkuk, "Economic Functions of English Landowners in the Seventeenth and Eighteenth Centuries"; H. Kellenbenz, "German Aristocratic Entrepreneurship: Economic Activities of the Holstein Nobility in the Sixteenth and Seventeenth Centuries"; R. Konetzke, "Entrepreneurial Activities of Spanish and Portuguese Noblemen in Medieval Times." These articles all appeared in *Explorations*, 6: 92–120 (1953–54).

6. Foster, p. 308.

7. Professor D. S. Landes wrote about the French businessman in 1949. Professor Sawyer presented a broader view somewhat later.

8. J. E. Sawyer, "The Entrepreneur and the Social Order: France and the United States," in *Men in Business* (1952), p. 9.

9. See their essays in larger or narrower frames: D. S. Landes, "French Entrepreneurship and Industrial Growth in the Nineteenth Century," *Journal of Economic History*, 9: 45–61 (1949); J. E. Sawyer, "Strains . . . ," and D. S. Landes, "Business . . . ," in *Modern France: Problems of the Third and Fourth Republics* (1951), pp. 293–312 and 334–353, respectively; and J. E. Sawyer, "The Entrepreneur . . . ," pp. 7–22.

10. Sawyer, "Strains . . . ," p. 299.

11. Landes, "Business . . . ," p. 336.

12. Sawyer, "Strains . . . ," p. 303, and Landes, "Business . . . ," pp. 341–343, 348–349.

13. Parker, "Entrepreneurial Opportunities"; H. B. Lamb, "Business Organization and Leadership in India Today"; H. B. Lamb, "Development of Modern Business Communities in India"; Choi, "Tokugawa Feudalism . . ."; Rottenberg, "Entrepreneurship and Economic Progress . . ."

14. See above, p. 105 f.

15. Danhof, "Economic Values in Cultural Perspective."

16. Rosovsky, "The Serf Entrepreneur in Russia."

17. Easterbrook, "The Climate of Enterprise."

18. Of course, this latter case could be interpreted as the entrepreneurial units providing their own security and not really being deterred by the existing uncertainties.

19. Hedges, *The Browns* . . .

20. Here I draw on the unpublished Ph.D. dissertation (Cornell, 1950) of Miss I. D. Neu, entitled "A Business Biography of Erastus Corning."

21. Professor C. L. Marquette of the University of Mississippi investigated the life of Washburn for his doctoral dissertation at Wisconsin. He presented it in 1940 under the title, "The Business Activities of C. C. Washburn."

22. Some years ago Professor Frederick Merk of Harvard inspired a series of doctoral dissertations on the lumbering industry as it progressed across the country. They are not well known and are worth citing here for the data that they contain on entrepreneurship in pioneer areas, particularly, of course, in connection with lumbering companies: R. G. Wood, *History of Lumbering in Maine, 1820–61* (1935); A. M. Larson, *History of the White-pine Industry in Minnesota* (1949); E. S. Meany, Jr., "History of the Lumber Industry in the Pacific Northwest to 1917" (1935).

23. R. R. Wohl, "Three Generations of Business Enterprise in a Mid-western City," *Journal of Economic History*, 16: 514–528 (1956).

24. R. K. Lamb, "The Development of Entrepreneurship . . ."; "Entrepreneurship in the Community," *Explorations*, 2: 114–27 (1949–50); "The Entrepreneur and the Community," *Men in Business* (1952), pp. 91–119.

25. See above, p. 124.

26. See above, p. 45.

27. Butters and Lintner, p. 14.

28. I have taken the ensuing data mainly from R. R. Wohl's unpublished Ph.D. thesis entitled, "Henry Noble Day, the Development of an Entrepreneurial Role." He contributed a preliminary sketch to *Men in Business* (1952) entitled, "Henry Noble Day, A Study in Good Works, 1808–1890," pp. 153–192.

29. Wohl, "Henry Noble Day, A Study . . . ," p. 158.

30. Day sampled teaching and the law before turning to the ministry.

31. Wohl, "Henry Noble Day, A Study . . . ," p. 167.

32. *Ibid.*, pp. 172–173.

33. A. H. Cole, *The American Wool Manufacture* (1926), I, 91–93.

34. J. T. Lincoln, "Material for a History of American Textile Machinery," *Journal of Economic and Business History*, 4: 263 (1931–32).

35. F. L. Redlich, "The Leaders of the German Steam-Engine Industry during the First Hundred Years," *Journal of Economic History*, 4: 121–148 (1944).

36. See above, p. 44.

37. The ensuing sketch is based upon W. C. Scoville's *Revolution in Glassmaking* (1948).

38. Cf. O. Knauth, *Business Practices, Trade Position, and Competition* (1956).

39. J. A. Schumpeter, *History of Economic Analysis* (1954), p. 897.

40. *Ibid.*, p. 895.

41. H. C. Passer, *The Electrical Manufacturers, 1875–1900* (1953), and "E. H. Goff: An Entrepreneur Who Failed," *Explorations*, 1: 17–25, No. 5 (1949).

42. Bruchey, pp. 370–73. The fact that the author had studied under Professor Frederic C. Lane, author of *Andrea Barbarigo*, and dedicated his book to the latter, makes the comparison doubly "nice." Both are excellent studies.

43. Bailyn, *The New England Merchants* . . . , pp. 88–90.

44. R. Davis, "Merchant Shipping in the Economy of the Late Seventeenth Century," *Economic History Review*, 2nd ser., 9: 67 (1956).

45. G. M. Butel-Dumont, *Histoire et commerce des colonies angloises* (1755), pp. 263–264.

46. Letter of Professor J. B. Hedges to the author, April 15, 1957.

47. K. W. Porter, *The Jacksons and the Lees* (1937), I, 99.

48. Bailyn, "The Apologia . . . ," also *The New England Merchants* . . . , *passim*.

49. *Ibid.*

50. Cochran, *Railroad Leaders*, p. 9.

51. *Ibid.*, p. 34.

52. *Ibid.*, p. 82.

53. *Ibid.*, p. 56.

54. See Sawyer, "Entrepreneurial Error . . . ," p. 200.

55. Wilson, *History of Unilever*, I, 165–175, 237–239.

56. W. R. Maclaurin, *Invention & Innovation in the Radio Industry* (1949).

57. W. Miller, "The Business Elite in Business Bureaucracies," *Men in Business*, pp. 286–305.

58. Abrams, pp. 29–34.

59. *Ibid.*, p. 32.

60. *Ibid.*, pp. 29–30.

61. Heckscher, Chap. III, *passim*.

62. P. W. Bamford, "Entrepreneurship in Seventeenth and Eighteenth Century France," *Explorations*, 9: 204–213 (1956–57); R. M. Westebbe, "State Entrepreneurship," *Explorations*, 8: 205–232 (1955–56). In connection with the entrepreneur and the state I should call attention to what, in a way of speaking, was an identification of entre-

preneurship and the state — the ruler acting as entrepreneur. See essay by Dr. Redlich noted in n. 4, above.

63. See above, pp. 171 ff.

64. The books sponsored by the Committee include: O. Handlin and M. F. Handlin, *Commonwealth: A Study of the Role of Government in the American Economy, Massachusetts, 1774–1861* (1947); L. Hartz, *Economic Policy and Democratic Thought: Pennsylvania, 1776–1860* (1948); M. S. Heath, *Constructive Liberalism: The Role of the State in Economic Development in Georgia to 1860* (1954); J. N. Primm, *Economic Policy in the Development of a Western State: Missouri, 1820–1860* (1954). An able survey of this series is contained in the *Business History Review*, 29: 81–96 (1955). The author is R. A. Lively.

Among Professor Goodrich's essays may be cited: "Public Spirit and American Improvements," *Proceedings of the American Philosophical Society*, 92: 305–309 (1948); "National Planning of Internal Improvements," *Political Science Quarterly*, 63: 16–44 (1948); "The Virginia System of Mixed Enterprise. A Study of State Planning of Internal Improvements," *Political Science Quarterly*, 64: 355–387 (1949); "Local Planning of Internal Improvements," *Political Science Quarterly*, 66: 411–445 (1951); "The Revulsion Against Internal Improvements," *Journal of Economic History*, 10: 145–169 (1950); and (with H. H. Segal) "Baltimore's Aid to Railroads. A Study in the Municipal Planning of Internal Improvements," *Journal of Economic History*, 13: 2–35 (1953).

65. The ensuing sketch is based upon H. G. J. Aitken's *The Welland Canal*. . . .

66. See above, p. 124.

67. See above, p. 45.

68. Aitken, *The Welland Canal* . . . , p. 31.

69. D. R. Fusfeld, "Heterogony of Entrepreneurial Goals," *Explorations*, 9: 8–18 (1956–57).

70. S. Diamond, "From Organization to Society: Virginia in the Seventeenth Century," *American Journal of Sociology*, 63: 457–475 (1957–58).

71. Charles W. Moulton, *The Library of Literary Criticism* (1901), I.

72. Aitken, *The Welland Canal* . . . , p. 12.

73. R. G. Wellington, *The Political and Sectional Influence of the Public Lands, 1828–1842* (1914), *passim*, especially Chap. 3.

74. Aitken, *The Welland Canal* . . . , pp. 116–118.

75. S. J. Stein, *The Brazilian Cotton Manufacture* (1957).

76. H. G. Aubrey, "Investment Decisions in Underdeveloped Countries," *Capital Formation and Economic Growth* (1955), p. 424.

NOTES TO PART TWO

77. United Nations Economic and Social Council, Economic Commission for Latin America, *Economic Development of Latin America and Its Principal Problems* (1950).

PART THREE

Postlude: Process of Entrepreneurial Change

1. As a partial result of the disregard of the duration of the spans of life of business units, we know more about the life expectancy of cows, probably of insects, than we do of corporations.

2. Marshall, p. 379.

3. K. F. Helleiner, "The Vital Revolution Reconsidered," *Canadian Journal of Economics and Political Science*, 23: 9 (1957).

4. A. H. Cole, "Conspectus . . ."

5. H. Heaton, "An Economic Historian's View of Enterprise" (1956); E. F. Gay, "The Rhythm of History," *Harvard Graduates' Magazine*, 32: 1–16 (1923–24).

6. W. N. Parker, "Coal and Steel Output Movements in Western Europe, 1880–1956," *Explorations*, 9: 229 n. (1956–57).

7. Heckscher, p. 4.

8. See my comment above, p. 39 f.

9. See especially Chaps. III, IV.

10. D. C. McClelland *et al.*, *The Achievement Motive* (1953); D. C. McClelland, "The Psychology of Mental Content Reconsidered," *Psychological Review*, 62: 297–303 (1955); D. C. McClelland, "Some Social Consequences of Achievement Motivation," *Nebraska Symposium on Motivation*, III (1955); *Studies in Motivation* (1955). Unfortunately, I became familiar with this literature too late to make proper use of it.

11. P. F. Drucker, *The Practice of Management* (1954), p. 175.

12. See above, p. 82.

13. I. G. Wyllie, *The Self-made Man in America* (1954).

14. Much of the "case" material used for instruction in schools of business is based on the assumption of such internal stresses.

15. See F. L. Redlich, *History of American Business Leaders* (1940), I, 22–30.

16. J. A. Schumpeter, "The Creative Response in Economic History," *Journal of Economic History*, 7: 149–159 (1947).

17. E. Dahmen, *Svensk industriell företagarverksamhet* (1950), I, 414.

INDEX

279